LEADING DIVERSE SCHOOLS

by

JAMES RYAN

The Ontario Institute for Studies in Education,
University of Toronto, Ontario, Canada

KLUWER ACADEMIC PUBLISHERS

DORDRECHT / BOSTON / LONDON

A C.I.P. Catalogue record for this book is available from the Library of Congress.

ISBN 1-4020-1243-8 (HB)
ISBN 1-4020-1253-5 (PB)

Published by Kluwer Academic Publishers,
P.O. Box 17, 3300 AA Dordrecht, The Netherlands.

Sold and distributed in North, Central and South America
by Kluwer Academic Publishers,
101 Philip Drive, Norwell, MA 02061, U.S.A.

In all other countries, sold and distributed
by Kluwer Academic Publishers,
P.O. Box 322, 3300 AH Dordrecht, The Netherlands.

Printed on acid-free paper

Printed in the Netherlands.

FOR KATHERINE AND KELLY

TABLE OF CONTENTS

ACKNOWLEDGEMENTS

This book became possible only through the efforts of many people. I am grateful for their help through the various stages of this enterprise -- the genesis, the research and the writing. I should first of all thank the Social Sciences and Humanities Council of Canada for its financial support of the empirical side of the research. Rouleen Wignall worked with me on the initial proposal for this funding, and Shawn Moore helped me conduct the interviews with principals. John Tucker assisted in the design of the survey, its circulation and collection, while the late Muriel Fung analyzed the quantitative data. Many other people helped in the writing stage, either providing feedback on portions of the text or discussing ideas with me. These include Steve May, Michelle Stack, Erin Kelly, John Tucker, Ken Leithwood, Reva Joshee, Malcolm Richmon, and of course, Don Richardo Townsendo. Malcolm Richmon also helped me with many of the more tedious details associated with putting the book together. Esther de Jong and Tamara Welschot at Kluwer have also been very helpful. I am also grateful for the ongoing support and inspiration I received during the course of the writing from Ken Leithwood, editor of this series, and the late David Corson.

CHAPTER 1

DIVERSITY, EDUCATIONAL LEADERSHIP AND INCLUSION

MONDAY MORNING, 6:10 A.M.

Kathaleen awoke with a start. Glancing over at the clock, she realized that she had overslept, again. Either Kathaleen had not heard the alarm or it was no longer working. She had no time to consider this problem right now, however. It was 6:10 and she was running late. Kathaleen jumped out of bed, grabbed some clothes and ran to the bathroom. After a two-minute shower, she dressed, brushed her hair, slapped on some make-up and stepped over the ever-present and quickly growing laundry pile into the hall. She tiptoed past her sons' bedrooms, smiling to herself as she did so. She knew that her two teenagers could sleep through a bomb blast at this time of the morning, so her stealth was really not needed. But old habits and motherly instincts die hard, and she could not help but try to be as quiet as possible. Kathaleen only hoped that the boys would rise in time to make it to school before the morning bell. She was becoming increasingly concerned with their tardiness of late. One or the other failed to make it to school on time on three occasions last week. She felt a twinge of guilt, and wished she could see them off to school every morning. But alas, this would never be. Her job precluded such things.

Kathaleen was principal of Althaven Secondary School and well into her second year in this position. She was no stranger to administration. Before this appointment she had been principal of another high school in the more northerly reaches of the board. In the years prior to this Kathaleen held a series of vice-principalships, all of them in secondary schools in this district. She had come into administration from teaching, as had all of her principal colleagues. Many lifetimes ago, or so it seemed to Kathaleen, she had been a Math teacher, one of a handful of women in this area in the entire board. She had never seriously considered a career in administration when she was teaching. Yet her second principal had seen promise in her, and he had gone out of his way to encourage Kathaleen to pursue an administrative path. He had pleaded with her to apply for the Math headship when it became available, and later to the vice-principal pool. Kathaleen was convinced that her mentor played a decisive role in her getting the headship and her first vice-principal position. After that, Kathaleen hadn't needed a champion to help her acquire subsequent positions. She worked hard and she was good at what she did. These days, however, there were times when she seriously questioned whether she was suited to this job.

She had no time for a sit-down breakfast – not that there ever was in the morning. Kathaleen threw on a coat, slipped into some shoes and opened the door to the

1

garage. She navigated her way around the heaps of bikes, skis, hoses, lawnmowers, shovels and just plain junk and hopped into her five-year old Toyota Corolla. It roared to life as it always did when she turned the key. At least there was one thing in her life she could be sure about these days, she thought. Her satisfaction was short-lived, however, as she glanced at the gas gauge and noticed that the indicator was pointing to empty. She howled in frustration as she remembered that Bob, her eldest, had borrowed the car last night for what he referred to as a late date. As usual, he had drained the gas tank. This was not all that was amiss, however. Out of the corner of her eye, Kathaleen spotted paraphernalia in the back seat that didn't belong. She didn't dare turn around, afraid of what she might find. She didn't need this extra complication right now. Her immediate concern was to get to a gas station before the car ran out of gas. This would cost her even more time, time that Kathaleen did not have right now.

Kathaleen pulled out of the garage and driveway, turned on her car lights, and pointed the car in the direction of the nearest gas station. She calculated that she would barely make it for her 7:00 a.m. meeting, that is if she could get gas at this station and the roads were driveable on this dark and foggy January morning. No time for Tim Horton's coffee and donuts today. As she approached the gas station and began thinking about the day that lay ahead of her, she came to the conclusion that her heightened anxiety was not due exclusively to being short on time and gas. She also realized that she was not looking forward to her first meeting, or for that matter, to some of the other issues that she knew she would have to deal with today. The 7:00 meeting, though, was her biggest concern right now. The private meeting was being held so early because the parents of the two Asians girls – Kathaleen wasn't sure whether they were from Pakistan or India – did not want anyone to know that they were meeting with the principal. She couldn't understand their desire for secrecy, but nevertheless went along with their request for an early meeting. Apparently, they were blaming the school for the anonymous calls they were receiving. Much to the parents' consternation, the callers were telling them that their teenage daughters were behaving in ways that were considered by the parents to be taboo. The situation itself aside, Kathaleen did not like the man to whom she initially spoke. She felt that he was arrogant and sensed that he treated her with disrespect because of her gender. She also disapproved of the way he was threatening her. This gentleman had told her that he would go to the Director of Education if Kathaleen couldn't solve his problem in short order. Right now she didn't have a strategy for resolving the situation, other than to listen, or at least try to listen, to what they had to say.

Kathaleen's blood pressure went up another notch when she pulled into the gas station. No one seemed to be around. Then it dawned on her that none of the gas stations in the area were likely to be open before 7:00. Kathaleen quickly sized up the situation. She had to make a decision and she had to do it quickly. If she waited for the station to open she would be at least forty minutes late for the meeting, and she anticipated that the parents would respond unsympathetically to her tardiness. On the other hand, Kathaleen had never run out of gas in her trusty Corolla, and her school was only twenty-five miles away. Besides, part of her route took her along uncongested country roads where she could make good time. She decided to go for it. She pulled out of the gas station, and put her foot to the floor. She had heard somewhere that drivers get the best gas mileage if they drive at moderate speeds. Kathaleen, however, didn't buy this theory. She was convinced that while the car might use more gas at higher speeds, it also covered more ground. Anyway, she was in a hurry and couldn't be bothered at staying within the posted speed limit – not that she ever did at the best of times. She smiled with satisfaction knowing that she had so far this year eluded the police speed traps in the area.

Kathaleen began to feel a little better as she watched the countryside fly by and the first rays of sunlight penetrate the fog and the retreating darkness. At this rate, she was actually going to be a little early. Once again her thoughts turned to her meeting and her school. The situation that gave rise to the parents' wish for a meeting was just one among an infinite number of new and different kinds of situations that Kathaleen grappled with since coming to Althaven last year. The source of many of the challenges that accompanied these situations, she believed, was the incredible diversity in the school and surrounding community. She had never seen so much diversity in one place. At last count, students identified sixty different countries as their places of birth. And this was even not counting those students born in this country whose parents had emigrated from distant lands. Before coming to Althaven, Kathaleen would never have thought that she would have encountered so many religions, languages, modes of dress, interactional styles, temperaments, dietary preferences, and values on countless issues in a single school community. Needless to say, all of this presented her with many new yet demanding challenges – challenges that she sometimes wondered whether or not she welcomed.

The problem for Kathaleen was not the diversity in and of itself. In fact, she found herself fascinated with the many differences that she encountered in her students and in the community. The problem, or at least part of it, revolved around her unfamiliarity with these differences, that is, with many of the student groups that populated her school. Not only did Kathaleen know little about these groups, she discovered that she was not able to understand many of the practices and values that students and parents did display. Like most administrators in the board, Kathaleen was of Anglo heritage. Her four grandparents were of Western or Northern European background, and three of them were born in Canada. She had grown up in a rural Ontario that was very White and European. In contrast, most of the students at Althaven were not of Western European heritage. Rather, they or their parents had emigrated from countries in Asia, the West Indies, Eastern Europe, and Africa. The problem for Kathaleen was that her life experiences and her seasoning as a teacher and administrator had not prepared her to understand and solve many of the diversity-related challenges that arose in her school. At the best of times, she found herself scrambling to learn more about the various groups and situations that she regularly encountered so she would be in a position to make appropriate decisions. But she did not always have the time to dedicate to this kind of research, and she was constantly plagued with doubts about the decisions that she did make. In some ways, Kathaleen longed for the kinds of problems she had been used to facing in her previous schools, problems where her expertise and background would be of use.

The countryside now flew by, and Kathaleen's confidence soared as she neared her destination. Her good spirits quickly vanished, however, as she glanced in the rear-view mirror to see the telltale flashing lights of the highway patrol. Realizing then that she was going well over the posted speed limit, she pulled over to side of the road, and immediately turned off the car to save on gas. At this point, she did not really care about the inevitable speeding ticket; she just wanted to get this over as soon as possible and be on her way. The police officer sauntered up to Kathaleen's window, and went through the perfunctory greetings and requests. Kathaleen said as little as possible, gave the man her license, ownership and insurance, and waited while he went back to his car. His distant and accusatory attitude bothered her a little; but then again, she had just broken the law, so she figured that perhaps she shouldn't be too upset about it. He reminded her of some of the police officers she had dealt with at Althaven. While some were confident in their dealings with the diverse community, others, like many of her teaching staff, were uncomfortable. She had personally witnessed incidents where she felt police officers handled situations poorly. Not that she could blame them; she realized that probably many times she had not acted appropriately in similar kinds of situations.

Five minutes later, the officer came back to Kathaleen's car, handed her the ticket and her license, and wished her a good day. Kathaleen did not respond. Instead she started her car and pulled back out onto the highway. No sooner had she lost sight of the patrol car than her trusty Corolla sputtered to a stop. Not ten minutes from the school, her car had finally run out of gas. She had anticipated this moment and reached for her cellular phone. The first place she called was the school. No answer. This wasn't unusual after all; it was not yet 7:00. Next she phoned her vice-principal's cellular phone. After the second ring, her phone died, and Kathaleen remembered that she had neglected to recharge it. What next? she thought. Well, the only thing left was to climb out of the car and hope that someone would pick her up. She tried not to think about the risks involved. Kathaleen couldn't afford to miss the meeting and was quite prepared to chance the risk. She then considered the best way to get someone to stop. She couldn't bring herself to stick out her thumb, nor did she have the guts to wave her arms. Instead she figured that she would just stand by her car and hope that someone she knew would come by, recognize her and offer a ride. She knew that some of her staff used this road, and hoped that a few would be out this early in the morning.

Kathaleen only had to wait about a minute for the first car to come into sight. Her hopes rose as she thought she recognized it. Much to her disappointment, the car failed to slow. Kathleen, however, did recognize the driver. She also felt quite sure that he had recognized her. It was one of her teachers, John Smith. She had had her share of conflicts with him over the past year, and was not too surprised that he had chosen to ignore her. Smith, she believed, was a out-and-out racist. She wouldn't have been too shocked to see him parading around with a white gown and pointed hat. She had irrefutable evidence that he treated non-White students and parents in unacceptable ways. Kathaleen also knew of inappropriate things that he had said and done in the classroom, the halls of the school, the staffroom and in public. According to Smith, the White culture was under siege from outsiders and that it was up to him and others in positions of influence to ensure the continuity of this sacred culture by whatever means they had at their disposal. Kathaleen found it hard to believe that someone like him was teaching at a school as diverse as

Althaven, let alone any school. She was grateful that she didn't have any more Smiths on her staff, although she suspected a couple of others, while not overtly advertising their positions, held similar beliefs. Over the past year, she had been forced to confront Smith, going so far as threatening to initiate dismissal procedures. In response, he had toned down his rhetoric and adjusted his behaviour. But in the interim, he had also found other more legitimate avenues through which he could advance his cause. For example, he had gotten himself nominated to the latest hiring committee, the first meeting which was to be held at 8:00, immediately after Kathaleen's 7:00 meeting. Kathaleen groaned as she visualized his position, and she knew it would be a struggle to follow through on her promise to diversify her almost all White staff at Althaven.

The next vehicle came over the hill approximately three minutes later. To Kathaleen's relief, it was her vice-principal's sleek sports car. She had a very good relationship with Robbie, so she knew that he would stop for her. But like Smith, he roared on by, waving at Kathaleen and grinning as he did so. She turned to watch in astonishment at the back of his red car, expecting him to stop and turn around. But he did not, and sped out of sight. Most times Kathaleen appreciated his sense of humour and his practical jokes. But this was not one of those times. While she regarded Robbie as a superb administrator, she had noticed from time to time that he was reluctant to take matters – any matters – very seriously. And this included issues that related to diversity. In some ways, he reacted like most of her well-meaning staff to student and parent charges of staff and school racism. While she felt that Robbie, like some of her staff, was too quick to dismiss outright some of these accusations, Kathaleen supported him in most instances, particularly when they had to field allegations against the school. She thought that the school itself was not a racist institution, but that a few staff, some students and certain parents did on occasion say and do things that could be interpreted as racist. Kathaleen also worried about some of Robbie's other tendencies, tendencies that she could see reflected in more than a few of her teachers. She had heard them on many occasions use what she believed were common racial stereotypes. Kathaleen had also seen staff members act towards individuals as if these stereotypes were true. She also wondered how many of these stereotypes she unwittingly adopted in her views and interactions with others, and about the kinds of effects these had on others. And she realized on more than one occasion that she needed to find ways to educate her staff about diversity. She believed that she and they needed to know more about the groups in their school community, about racism and about themselves and their taken-for-granted views and actions.

While crucial, Kathaleen nevertheless believed that her and her teachers' learning about diversity were merely a means to an even more important end. She felt that she was justified in her concern for her staff and herself in these matters. Indeed, if she and her teachers knew more about diversity issues, then they would probably have an easier time doing their jobs. But Kathaleen also was convinced that in the final analysis her job was to promote student learning, and in doing so, play her part in making the world a better place. So what troubled Kathaleen most was the ways in which many of her non-Anglo students struggled. While some of the more economically privileged of these students performed well academically, many more did not. She saw first-hand, moreover, that many of these students struggled with many other challenges that the Anglo teachers and students took for granted, like language, or racism. Kathaleen was disturbed by ways in which she saw these students and their parents excluded from, and intimidated by, the current and favored language, knowledge bases, interactional conventions, pedagogical styles, curricula, social groupings, and decision-making processes. She wanted to find ways to include them in these aspects of schooling, to make them feel that they were part of the school community, but she was unsure that she understood this process well enough to take action that would really help them.

Kathaleen came out of her reverie, and looked up as Robbie came roaring back from the direction of the school, did a U-turn, pulled in behind her disabled vehicle, and jumped out of his car. In predictable fashion, he proceeded to ask her if this was her latest ruse for trying to scare up a date. When Kathaleen didn't smile, he asked her what the trouble was. She went on to say that they had better get going pronto; she would take care of her car later. During the remaining ten-minute drive to the school, Robbie offered her an apple-fritter doughnut and talked about what he had been up to over the weekend. As they pulled into the school parking lot at one minute after 7:00, Kathaleen began to choke on her doughnut as she looked up to see the artwork that now adorned the outside of the school. Someone – probably the same individual that had been at work on previous occasions – had painted a huge black swastika on the side of the gymnasium. It had to have measured at least 30 feet by 30 feet. Looking over at Kathaleen and catching her surprise, Robbie told her that he assumed that she already knew about this. He then handed her the morning paper. On the front page was a picture of the offending artwork under the caption, "Racists at work at Althaven."

Kathaleen just shook her head, climbed out of Robbie's car and hurried into the school. She was not terribly surprised by the commotion she perceived when she entered the office area, despite the early hour. Five or six people were all speaking at the same time, trying to get the attention of her secretary, Grace. She recognized a couple of the people, one a teacher, the other a parent. Grace was doing an admirable job of fending them off, but looked relieved to see Kathaleen, who, assuming that they wanted to see her, told them to give her a minute while she conferred with her secretary. Grace quickly summed up the situation, telling her that two of the people were reporters and two were parents. Kathaleen recognized the reporters as two of the more aggressive in the region who would stop at nothing to scoop their fellows, particularly on the more sensational stories. So she was not really too surprised to see them there so early. She was more surprised to see the two parents. The four wanted to talk to Kathaleen about the recent "artwork." The other, a teacher and chronic complainer, was claiming that he had been assaulted by a student who he had been forced to confront that morning. Grace also told her that the Director had called and wanted Kathaleen to call her back as soon as possible. She then glanced into her office to see six somber faces staring out at her. To top things off, she saw Smith out of the corner of her eye talking in conspiratorial terms to a couple of other teachers. "Just another day," she thought, as she stepped into her office and to her first official crisis of the day.

BEING AN ADMINISTRATOR IN A DIVERSE SCHOOL

Kathaleen is not a real person; she does not exist. Nor does Althaven. I created them and the situations in which they are implicated as a way of introducing readers to a book that explores educational leadership and diversity. I figured that this narrative was the best way of providing readers with a sense of the challenges that administrators of diverse schools regularly face. Kathaleen's experiences, however, are not figments of my imagination. I put her story together after talking to many principals of diverse schools. At least one, and in some cases, many more, have gone through some of these experiences. Principals really do have to deal with these sorts of challenges. The narrative provided me with a means of making a number of key points. I wanted to emphasize the personal side of the job of administration, that cultural diversity is now a fact of life in many schools, and that as a result, the dynamics that administrators face are not always the same as they once were in the "good old days." I also wanted to illustrate that teachers and administrators are not always prepared for the challenges that accompany this diversity. They often know little about the people they regard as different and they also often fail to fully appreciate diversity or the issues that accompany it.

The most important point I wanted to make, however, is one that can easily get lost in talk of all the problems that educators face. While teachers and administrators certainly do face substantial challenges in their adjustments to increasing levels of diversity, their challenges pale in comparison to the challenges that non-Anglo students (and their parents) face. The more significant problem, then, revolves around the fact that many students from certain ethnic backgrounds encounter substantial difficulties in school (and elsewhere). Research consistently demonstrates that most "minority" students do less well academically than their majority culture counterparts (see, for example, Paquette, 1990; Ogbu, 1994; Darling-Hammond, 1995; Bennett, 2001). They are overrepresented in general and vocational tracks (Bennett, 2001; College Board, 1985; Kozol, 1991; Oakes, 1985; Orfield, 1999) and attend colleges and universities in proportionately fewer numbers than their Anglo brethren (Bennett, 2001; Orfield, 1988, 1999). While there are exceptions to this pattern (Paquette, 1990; Lee, 1996), those who do manage to excel academically still face significant barriers. These students have to learn a second and sometimes a third language, adjust to different pedagogical and interactional styles, understand a range of educational attitudes and protocols about which they know little, and attempt to come to terms with personal and systemic forms of racism (Alladin, 1996; Dei et. al. 1997; Gillborn, 1995; McCarthy & Critchlow, 1993; McLaren, 1999, Sleeter, 1996; Troyna, 1993), among many other challenges. So while this book is about administrators, the deeper problem revolves around students and social justice. I focus on administrators only insofar as I believe that they have the capacity to do something about the difficulties that non-Anglo students face in schools. This book explores the things that they do (or do not do) to help these students and to promote social justice and inclusion.

I chose to look at administration and diversity by using the concept of inclusion/exclusion. I believe that this way of seeing diversity is useful both in discerning problems and devising solutions. The problems associated with diversity generally involve various kinds of exclusion. At the heart of exclusion is a process that creates and assigns worth to differences. It singles out particular groups, practices and beliefs as different or "other", and then allocates a value to them. Unfortunately, this process marks many ethnic groups in the Western world in unflattering ways. One of the consequences of this is that their cultural practices are often not thought to be important enough to include in schools. So many students and their parents who do not belong to the majority culture are excluded from integral aspects of schooling. Students and their parents do not always speak the language that is favored in schools; they are often compelled to learn considerations that are foreign to them; and they have little choice but to interact with others in ways they are not always comfortable with. Students may not recognize themselves or their communities in the curriculum and in the school generally, and they and their parents may find themselves left out of the decision- and policy-making processes. They also find themselves excluded from many forms of school life, the consequence of subtle and not-so-subtle words and deeds. The solution to problems of exclusion, then, will involve efforts directed at promoting inclusion and the values that this inclusion signals. If all students are to have the same kinds of opportunities and options in school and after they graduate from school, then they need to be included and valued in the same ways as everyone else. And it is up to educators, particularly administrators, to work toward this end.

This book maps how principals promote inclusion in their respective schools. I chose to focus on principals for two reasons. The first is their influence in schools; the second is the dearth of research in the area. Despite a move in recent times to centralize control over schools in Western countries like the United Kingdom and Canada, for example, principals still exert substantial influence. While their power to control school activities may be slipping in some areas, these school leaders still have the capacity to influence the day-to-day actions of teachers and students perhaps more than any other single individual. This is particularly the case in diverse schools (Derkatz, 1996). Indeed, Troyna and Hatcher (1992) and Gillborn (1995) have shown in their research that school administrators can have a decisive effect on racist and antiracist practices in their respective schools. So it stands to reason that administrators can have an impact on inclusive practice at the school level. Unfortunately comparatively little has been written in the area of leadership and inclusion, let alone leadership and diversity. A few exceptions exist in this latter area, and these include Reyes and Capper (1991), Valverde (1988), Anderson (1990, 1996), Lipman (1998), Derkatz (1996), McKeown (1989), Dei (1996), Dei et al. (1997), Ryan (1998), Ryan and Wignall (1996), Maxcy (1998), May (1994), Riehl (2000) Winfield et. al. (1993), Young and Laible (2000), Henze, Katz and Norte (2000) and Taylor (1998), among others. Although these sources are useful, we still have much to learn about leadership, diversity, and inclusion. This book is intended to fill some of this gap.

Many academics tend to conceptualize principals' work in terms of leadership. They see administrators as leaders by virtue of positions, gifts and skills that enable them to do things that benefit their respective school communities. While I employ the term leadership, I use it in a different way in this book. Instead of conflating leadership with individual skills or formal positions, like Pajak and Evans (2000), I see it as a communal process. A series of ongoing and related practices, the inclusive leadership perspective that I employ involves many people working in equitable ways for just, democratic and inclusive schools and communities. Everyone has a role to play in this process, including principals. But the difference between this version of leadership and some of the more common ones found in the academic literature is that ordinary people can also contribute. Schools don't have to rely on extraordinarily gifted and powerful individuals to turn schools around by the strength of their wills and remarkable visions. Rather, inclusion can be achieved by people working together, accepting and acknowledging the modest but important contributions of everyone in their school communities. Needless to say, principals can make vital contributions to such a process. But principals like Kathaleen need not carry the weight of the world on their shoulders; they can and they should share leadership with others. In short, this book describes the contributions that principals can make to this leadership process.

I approached the task of writing this book in a fairly conventional way. I drew primarily from two sources. I used information from contemporary scholarly literature – both theoretical and empirical – and from my own empirical study of principals. This text, however, is not simply a descriptive account of the literature and the study. This entire project is driven by a particular bias. This bias is rooted in the desirability of inclusion. I believe that inclusion is an ideal for which all administrators should strive and I organized the book with this end in mind. This means that I look critically at what administrators do. So I point out when administrators act in ways that do not promote inclusion. While administrators do many laudable things to promote inclusion, they also do things that do not. I followed this path because I am convinced that the more we know about the ways in which administrators may or may not enhance inclusion, the sooner we can get on with the task of promoting it and of ensuring equitable education for all students in our increasingly diverse schools and communities.

DIVERSITY

Diversity is a reality for many educators. The most obvious kind of diversity is represented in the heritages, histories and cultures of the students and parents who have recently come to Canada, the United States, the United Kingdom and Australia from all over the world. This is not to say that immigration is new to these Western countries or that they were not diverse places before these recent immigrants arrived. For example, most of the people who now live in Canada or their ancestors were born in other parts of the world. Only the aboriginal people of Canada can rightly claim indigenous status. Modern immigration began as early as the 15th century and has continued through the present time. The overwhelming majority of the earlier immigrants were Europeans, and most of these Europeans emigrated from Western Europe, particularly the British Isles. For example, the United Kingdom accounted for 37% of all immigrants between 1913 and 1957 (Statistics Canada, 1993). Yet there was diversity even then. In late 19th century Upper Canada (Ontario), for example, the British majority noticed considerable differences between themselves and the recent Irish immigrants (Prentice, 1977).

Immigration patterns to Canada began to change in the 1960s. This shift came from two factors. The first was the advancement in travel technology. Mass and relatively cheap transport made it possible for people to travel to and from most parts of the world with relative ease. The other reason was the change in immigration policy in the 1960s. Before this, Canada's policies were explicitly discriminatory. They favored European immigrants over their non-European counterparts. The adjustments in the 1960s, however, made it possible for more of the latter to come to Canada. All the same, these policies – and for that matter, the immigration policies of other Western countries like the United States – still favour Europeans. With a bias toward immigrants who already have family in the country and toward those who have valued or needed skills, these policies exclude many in the Third World who don't have relatives in these positions or who have not had chances to acquire these skills. It remains to be seen how such policies will change after the September 11 terrorist attacks in New York. Quite probably, it will become more difficult for non-Westerners to enter Western countries, let alone immigrate to them. In Canada critics are resisting proposed changes in immigration policies that will make it much more difficult for unskilled or semi-skilled immigrants to enter the country (Thompson, 2002).

Despite the many obstacles, more people emigrated from non-European countries to Canada in the 1960s and 1970s. Emigration from Europe, on the other hand, declined. By 1974, immigrants from the United Kingdom comprised 17.6% of the total immigration to Canada, while places like India, Hong Kong, Jamaica and the Philippines now accounted for 5.8, 5.8, 5.1 and 4.3%, respectively (Statistics Canada, 1993). By 1989, Asian immigrants outnumbered their European counterparts by two to one. Only 7,045 emigrated from the United Kingdom (Statistics Canada, 1990). In 1991, Hong Kong was the largest source of immigrants at 9.7%, followed by Poland at 6.8%, China at 6.0% and India at 5.6% (Statistics Canada, 1993). In this same year, Canada used 126 categories to account for its various ethnic groups (United Nations Yearbook, 1994). These trends continued into the 21st century. In 1999-2000, Asian immigrants totaled 156,550, while only 45,629 emigrated from Europe. Of the latter total, 5,208 came from the United Kingdom (Statistics Canada, 2001). Varying places of birth are also a good indicator of contemporary diversity. In this regard, Asians are catching up to Europeans. The 1996 Census indicates that 2,332,060 immigrants reported their birthplace as Europe, while 1,562,770 claimed they were born in Asia (Statistics Canada, 2001). The most recent numbers indicate that from 1996 to 2001, immigrants contributed more to the increase of the national population than did "natural" births (Toronto Star, 2002).

Canada is not the only Western Anglo country that is accepting more immigrants who are not born in Western Europe. The United States, the United Kingdom and Australia are also admitting more non-Western people, and as a result, are also becoming more visibly diverse. For example, only 4,017,000 of the 19,766,000 who immigrated to the United States between 1980 and 1990 emigrated from Europe (U.S. Bureau of the Census, 1995). As of 2000, people of African American, Hispanic or Latino, Asian and American Native heritage comprised 12.3, 12.5, 3.6 and 0.9 %, respectively, of the total population (U.S. Census Bureau, 2001). In

Australia, the numbers of people coming from countries in Latin America, Africa, Southern Asia, Eastern Asia, Southeast Asia and the Middle East increased substantially between 1971 and 1991 (Australian Bureau of Statistics, 1995). Between 1995 and 1999 immigrants from New Zealand, the United Kingdom and Ireland, China, the former Yugoslav Republics, South Africa and Hong Kong constituted 17.1, 12.3, 8.0, 6.7, 4.6 and 3.7% of the total immigration population, respectively (Australian Bureau of Statistics, 2001). Many of these immigrants settle in larger urban areas. For example, 49% of the total "ethnic minority" population of England lived in London in 2000 (Scott, et al. 2001). The same holds true for Canada. In 1991, immigrants respectively accounted for 38, 30, 24 and 22% of Toronto's, Vancouver's, Hamilton's and Kitchener's total populations (Statistics Canada, 1991).

These changes are reflected in schools. In 1988, data gathered by one Toronto area school district indicated that one-third of the total day school population and two-thirds of the mothers of this same student population were born outside of Canada (Handscombe, 1989). At one school in this general area that perhaps exemplifies this diversity, a school-administered survey indicated that students self-identified with 63 different ethnicities. The largest number reported Italian (18%), Philippino (14.7%), Portuguese (9.5%), Chinese (8.0%) and Polish (6.3%) heritages. Of the 1700 who responded to the survey, only 76 reported no ethnic heritage or that their background was Canadian (Ryan, 1999). But even over the past ten years these immigrant student populations continue to evolve, although those coming from Western and Northern Europe remain few and far between. Robinson (1999) notes that in this same area where ten years ago students came mostly from countries like Vietnam, China, Soviet Union, India, Pakistan, Portugal, Greece, the Middle East and Poland, they now emigrate from areas such as Somalia, Ethiopia, Central and South America, India, Sri Lanka and Turkey.

Schools in the United States also reflect this growing diversity. The number of students classified as "minority" increased from 29.3% in 1988 to 32.7 % in 1994 (Merchant, 2000). Many "minority" students reside in the urban areas, where 54% were classified as such in 1994. On the other hand, 29.7% and 18.9% of urban/fringe and rural schools were classified as "minority" (Merchant, 2000).

Immigration, however, represents just the more obvious side of contemporary diversity. The diversity that we are currently experiencing is due to much more than simply immigration. To begin with, ethnic and/or cultural differences exist, and have existed, for some time now in all Western countries. But because some of these differences are not as apparent as those associated with the more recent immigration, we tend to take them for granted. Contemporary diversity also extends beyond ethnicity. It continues to expand with the increasing number of choices, experiences and information available to us (Ryan, 1999). Technology and the current global economy provide consumers with an unprecedented range of choices. Large-scale standardized production lines, while not yet a thing of the past, have given way to niche marketing processes that target specialized and unique populations and tastes. Now people have the opportunity to sample, purchase or experience an almost infinite range of products. The information available to most people has also expanded considerably in recent years. The electronic media, for example, have made it possible for men, women and children to acquire information on virtually anything that they are curious about – from nurturing houseplants to making bombs. This, coupled with the contemporary doubt about absolute knowledge, has made it possible for individuals to legitimately come to know things from a wide range of different and sometimes contradictory positions and perspectives. The products that we consume and the things that we know, then, influence individual identities; they help to shape who people are. So in this sense identity need not be associated exclusively with ethnicity, or indeed with one or more fixed attributes; identities are both fluid and multiple. They shift with what we know and who we think we are.

So Kathaleen would not be the only principal who has noticed increasing levels of diversity. Judging from the census data presented earlier, many administrators of schools in Canada, the United States, the United Kingdom and Australia will surely have also recognized this phenomenon. While ethnicity no doubt remains the most obvious source, other manifestations of contemporary diversity can be identified with consumption and knowledge. Regardless of the kind or origin, diversity brings with it many new challenges for administrators. Many of these challenges arise because administrators are not familiar with the kinds of situations that are associated with diversity.

THE PRESSURES OF DIVERSITY

Like everyone, administrators will routinely run into situations that they have never handled before – and the degree to which they are able to understand and deal with what they are presented with will depend on the similarities that they can see in them and the sense they can make of them. So, for example, if administrators are able in problem situations to identify familiar elements, then they will be more likely to diagnose the causes and to find workable solutions more so than if they failed to see anything familiar. The ability to identify familiar patterns in situations is a skill that is sometimes associated with expertise. Leithwood and Stager (1989) found in a study of expert and not-so-expert principals that the experts were better able to recognize familiar patterns in problem situations than the less able. Identifying patterns, however, has become more daunting for administrators as levels and kinds of diversity have swelled. Administrators struggle to understand or identify familiar patterns in at least two areas. The first concerns the people that administrators tend to identify as different, and in particular, students and parents of non-Western heritage. Many administrators find that they do not always know or understand the culture of the non-European members of their school communities. The second area with which administrators struggle is the processes associated with diversity, and in particular, racism. For example, many principals only see racism in one particular, and hence, parochial way.

Administrators of diverse schools often find that there is much that they don't know about their respective school communities (Ryan & Wignall, 1996). This is because many of them are different from the student bodies that they administer. Administrators in the study that provided the basis for this book and elsewhere are generally of Europe and Anglo heritage, while many of the students in their diverse schools and their parents are not. For example, of the 35 principals interviewed for my study, only two were not of Anglo heritage. This also holds true for other parts of the Western world. In the United States, for example, in 1994 87% of the teaching force was "White", while only 14% of principals were "minority" (Merchant, 2000).

Thus, administrators of diverse schools routinely struggle with the challenges associated with these differences. In these schools, principals and other educators find themselves scrambling to discover the identities of all these groups. This is not easy task, and it may well require time and energy that principals simply do not have. Principals may also struggle with the various sorts of diversity that they encounter. Prominent here are struggles to understand the cultures of those who are non-Western in heritage. Many more recent immigrants emigrate from non-Western countries and will regularly adhere to lifestyles distinct from those to which the mostly Anglo/European administrators are accustomed. So these administrators often find that they know little about the array of foreign religions, languages, dietary preferences, modes of dress, relationships between men, women and children, interactional styles, values and attitudes. This is not to say that these lifestyles need always be a mystery to them. Indeed, with experience, administrators can come to understand many of these practices and values and react appropriately to them. But it can be a time-consuming task to learn about and eventually understand everything about the many non-Westerners who attend Western schools, particularly when the differences are sometimes significant, and as Robinson (1999) observes, the groups regularly come and go.

Administrators may also have limited views or understandings of racism and exclusion. Unfortunately, the slim empirical evidence that does exist – most of it in studies that focus on other issues or individuals -- indicates that school leaders tend not to notice or attend to racism or issues of "race" (Taylor, 1998; Lipman, 1998; Anderson, 1990; Young & Laible, 2000). Administrators may not always comprehend the many ways in which racism works (Young & Laible, 2000), although such understanding is crucial in formulating effective strategies for preventing future racist practices (Henze, Katz & Norte, 2000). When administrators and educators do acknowledge racism, they tend to see it in one particular way (Ryan, 1999). They generally identify racism with individuals, preferring to see it in terms of the prejudicial attitudes and actions of ignorant individuals who are sometimes unaware of what they are thinking and doing. On the other hand, educators tend not to see racism as a systemic matter, as something that extends beyond individuals into the structures of the society in which they live. By adopting this parochial view of racism, however, they absolve the system of liability in racist incidents. The cause or source of these acts is seen as lying not with the system – policing, education or the state – but with a few misguided individuals. The problem, in this view, is with a "few rotten apples" (Henriques, 1984).

These two sorts of challenges differ from one another. The first – learning more about the school community – is one that administrators readily identify. Most of the administrators in the study that provided the basis for this book recognized that they knew too little about the groups that comprised their respective communities, and they felt that learning more about the community would help them do their jobs better. In some cases, such knowledge also made their jobs easier. The second challenge – understanding diversity processes like racism or exclusion – is not something all administrators acknowledge or recognize. They also did not agree with some forms of antiracism education or support principles of inclusion. So the challenge in some respects rests with the already-converted – administrators, educators, students, parents, community members and others who value inclusion – to move all administrators to first understand racism and exclusion in appropriate ways, encourage them to accept the principles of inclusion, and help them take measures that promote inclusive practices.   This book represents an effort at addressing both these challenges.

In sum, many administrators of diverse schools face hurdles understanding and dealing with racism, in understanding and reacting appropriately to what they perceive as differences, and in developing relationships with these diverse communites. In light of these challenges, administrators also need to devote time and energy to learning about these elements of diversity and to providing opportunities for others to learn. This book then focuses on these four areas. In setting the stage for this inquiry, Chapter 2 examines various approaches to diversity, while Chapter 3 reviews and critiques various approaches to leadership. The next two chapters explore how principals perceive racism in their schools and what they do about it. Chapter 4 is devoted to principals' perceptions of racism and Chapter 5, to their efforts at promoting antiracism.   In Chapter 6, I explore administrators' efforts at enhancing school community relationships. The following two chapters concentrate on understanding and responding to difference. Chapter 7 explores non-Western religions and attitudes toward schooling and documents how administrators perceive and attempt to accommodate them. Chapter 8 provides a more in-depth look at administrator attempts to understand and respond to particular diversity-related dilemmas. It looks at the efforts of two administrators as they attempt to come to terms with a gender-related dilemma and a problem that revolves around knowledge. Chapter 9 targets learning efforts. It explores the attempts of administrators to learn about diversity issues and to provide learning opportunities for their teachers. The aim of the final two chapters is to bring everything together. Chapter 10 summarizes the challenges that administrators of diverse schools face, and Chapter 11 provides some suggestions about what they might do to respond to them.

HEURISTICS

This section explores the basis for the claims that I make in this book. I take this task very seriously. Indeed the act of making claims about such an important and contested area of life should not to be taken lightly, particularly given the potential authority that such claims can assume and the manner in which they will be circulated. The claims that I make in this book are based on empirical findings and set within a particular analytic perspective. The empirical study consisted of three parts. I and other members of a research team interviewed thirty-five principals, spent time observing in a school and circulated a survey. Many of the claims I make here revolve specifically around what these administrators told us – how they perceive diversity and what they say they do to meet the challenges that arise in diverse schools. But the book is not merely a description of principals' perceptions. It is also prescriptive; I make statements about what principals should be doing. This doesn't mean that what administrators say about what they do or what should be done isn't valuable or credible, but that their statements need to be interpreted with a critical eye. This critical eye is set within the analytical perspective or framework I employ – what can very loosely be termed a "critical theory" perspective. It carries with it a number of assumptions about life and schooling, including for example, the "causes" of particular problems associated with diversity, and what needs to be done to address them. This perspective has from the beginning of the study shaped the empirical component. It initially set the stage for the research proposal, provided direction for the areas that we explored with participants and guided the ways in which the data were analyzed and employed in the book. But this influence was not just one-way. The empirical findings also prompted me to question some the original assumptions of the analytical perspective and look for various explanations of the data.

Critical Theory

The perspective or framework that I employ can very loosely be referred to as a form of "critical theory." Coined by the Frankfurt School theorists half a century ago, it has many variations, a number of which precede the critical theory designation itself. The gamut of this genre of theory runs from long standing self-estrangement theories (Fay, 1987), through traditional Marxist theories, to contemporary adaptations of Marxism (e.g., Habermas, 1986), to the more recent postmodern (Bauman, 1992) and poststructural theories (Foucault, 1979, 1980; Derrida, 1978). Many differences are evident between and among the various permutations of critical theory. They vary with respect to their assumptions about knowledge, universality, oppression and politics. The version that I employ here leans toward postmodern versions that emphasize the constructed, fluid, contested and contextual nature of life. In what follows, I sketch the rudiments of the critical theory framework that shaped this book and the empirical data that we collected. These include the concern with marginalized people, the role of domination and power in this marginalization and the kind of political action needed to work against it.

The version of critical theory that I endorse here is concerned first and foremost with promoting social justice. In doing so, it looks to improve the welfare of marginalized and excluded people. It acknowledges, firstly, that not everyone enjoys the same kinds of privileges; some people are decidedly worse off than others. This inequality, however, is not the result of chance or happenstance. Rather, there are clearly identifiable patterns in these privileges. These patterns, though, do not have their roots in human physiology or exclusively in individual behavioral traits. Instead, these differential fortunes have social causes; they are the products of enduring, yet changing, patterns of social interaction. So the causes of this marginalization and exclusion extend far beyond individuals. While individuals are nevertheless implicated in their own and others' misfortunes, they are not exclusively responsible for them. Historically evolving social practices, institutions and discourses shape, in important ways, the circumstances in which people find themselves.

These patterns of privilege are intertwined with forms of domination and relationships of power. Earlier forms of critical theory, like Marxism for example, acknowledged only one form of domination, one that revolved exclusively around the economy. It also employed a one-sided view of power. Emphasizing only its constraining qualities, Marxism favored a view of power that worked on the less fortunate working class from above, so to speak, to repress them (Miller, 1987). More recent approaches to critical theory, like poststructuralism, acknowledge more workable views of domination and power for an increasingly diverse contemporary context. The view of poststructuralism that I endorse here recognizes axes of subordination/domination other than the economy, like for example, race/ethnicity, gender, sexual orientation, religion and so on, as well as the fluid and ever-changing nature of oppressive relationships. Poststructuralists like Foucault (1980) also propose a view of power that is more consistent with multiple forms of domination. For him, power does not just suppress; it also produces. In this view, power

> does not act on people, from a distance, from the outside, but on the interior so to speak through an individual's self-intervention on social relations. In other words entrapment proceeds as we become ourselves; we are very much our own prisoners. In this sense power not only works on us, but perhaps more importantly, through us. We are not just its target, but also its vehicle (Ryan, 1998, p. 269).

This view of power provides more possibilities for political action than a view that sees power as a monolithic suppressant. Because power works through people, they have the potential to use it to their advantage, to short-circuit its oppressive effects, as it were. But individuals cannot accomplish much in isolation. In order to have an impact on oppressive situations that have their roots in wider social forms, they have to align themselves with like-minded others. Only in this way can they hope to attain any kind of emancipation or freedom from the oppression that they and others experience. The kind political activity necessary to achieve this state differs from the revolutionary tactics of the Marxists. Instead of attempting to overthrow an (alleged) universal and monolithic system, a more realistic, and in the end more effective, strategy is to resist the various contextualized and local elements of the system. But as alluded to above, this activity also needs to go beyond the local arena to target those elements that transcend these particular locales. This is why it is so important to build alliances with those in different and distant contexts.

Diversity and Inclusion

These patterns of advantage and disadvantage are evident in diverse school contexts. Generally speaking, in Anglo Western countries, those not of Anglo/European heritage do not enjoy the same kinds of privileges or successes that their Anglo counterparts do. Simply put, while it may be true that some of the former students perform well academically, many others from these same groups do not (Lee, 1996). Still, these same high-achieving students will have to face the same kinds of barriers that their lower achieving fellows do. These difficulties are not due to biological or exclusively psychological causes. They are the products of longstanding and widespread social conventions that exclude or marginalize those who do not belong to mainstream groups or subscribe to mainstream practices. This exclusion may occur in obvious and not so obvious ways. Acts of racial discrimination are an example of the former. Not so obvious exclusion may occur in testing procedures, curricular materials, teaching strategies, organizational patterns, administrative practices or other forms of interaction that implicitly ignore or devalue the knowledge, language, and values of non-Anglo groups. To change these patterns of disadvantage, then, all members of the school community need to resist practices of exclusion and to look for ways to promote practices of inclusion at the school level and beyond.

Over the years, those who explored inclusion usually did so from a perspective that revolved around student (dis)ability (e.g., Thomas et al., 1997; MacKinnon & Brown, 1994; Schaffner & Bushwell, 1996; Shanker, 1994). More recently, however, those interested in inclusion have expanded the concept to encompass not just (dis)ability, but also other axes of disadvantage such as age, gender, class, and race/ethnicity (Dei, 1996; Dei et al., 1997: Dei, 1998; Boscardin & Jacobsen, 1997). How do these scholars see inclusion? Thomas et al. (1997), for example, view inclusive schooling as total and complete accommodation. Inclusive schools welcome, accommodate and celebrate diversity, uniqueness and individuality. One way of understanding inclusion, according to Thomas et. al. (1997), is to look at it through its antonym -- exclusion. When exclusion is taken to the extreme, it leads to segregation, isolation and stigmatization of those who are deemed to be different. Inclusive practice, on the other hand, seeks to counteract all these tendencies. In doing so, it promotes and values a type of solidarity based on a complementarity of similarity and diversity (Boscardin & Jacobsen, 1997).

For Dei (1996, p.78), inclusivity means:

1. Dealing with equity. This requires attention to the qualitative value of justice.

2. Addressing the question of representation. This requires that multiple perspectives be entrenched in the academic discourse, knowledge and texts of the school.

3. Making instructional practices respond to the challenge of diversity. This requires a response to structures of domination (e.g., race, class, gender, sexual orientation, age, ability) with the school system and in the wider society.

In setting out this agenda of inclusion Dei (Dei, 1996; Dei et al., 1997; Dei, 1998) takes the concept and practice of inclusion one step further. Dei and his associates highlight the place of power in exclusive/inclusive practice. They believe that the process of teaching, learning and sharing knowledge revolves around power relationships. It is these power relationships that determine, for example, what knowledge is valued, who transmits it, and how this knowledge interchange is organized. In this view, those who favour inclusive practice do so to confront these often unequal and exclusionary relationships of power. School administrators and educators who subscribe to this philosophy need to develop a commitment to power-sharing in schools. In doing so, they will extend to students, teachers, parents and local communities, joint responsibilities over the process of education.   Such arrangements can entrench a diverse range of perspectives in the curriculum, and as a result, make schools more inclusive places. In such schools, traditionally marginalized or excluded students would ideally be provided with more opportunities, perform better, and in doing so, ultimately increase their life chances. Dei (1996, p. 79) concludes that

> inclusive schooling means opening spaces for the alternative and, sometimes, oppositional paradigms to flourish in the schools. It means ensuring representation of diverse populations in the schools. It means developing a broad-based curriculum and diverse teaching strategies, and having support systems in the schools that enhance the conditions for all students.

It is this view of inclusion that formed the basis for the concept of leadership that I employ in this book. The view of leadership that I favour is inclusive both in its nature and the ends for which it strives. Unlike many perspectives on leadership that see it in terms of gifted or powerful individuals, the view used in this book conceives of leadership as a communal process – one in which all members of school communities are involved or represented in equitable ways. The process itself is inclusive in that everyone has a right to contribute. The ends for which it strives are also inclusive. They are geared to work for inclusive, just and democratic schools and communities.

This view of inclusion and leadership set the stage for the empirical component of this book. It influenced how the study was conducted and shaped how the data were treated.

Empirical Strategies

The empirical methods employed in this study were designed to explore how administrators of diverse schools understood the diversity in their school communities, how they met the challenges that were associated with this diversity, and how they did or did not promote inclusion. The study itself was funded by the *Social Sciences and Humanities Council of Canada*. I chose methods that focused primarily on administrators. I did this for two reasons. First, it stood to reason that administrators would know more about how administrators dealt with diversity than most other people or sources. They are, after all, the ones on the front lines and presumably they spend at least part of their days thinking about diversity and devising practical strategies to help them and others through their days. The second reason that I chose administrators was to give them a voice. Too often in this day and age, other people and institutions speak for educators. We frequently find that the media, politicians, academics and other groups, often with their own interests in mind, usurp the voices of educators, including administrators, to give accounts of what they believe is happening, or should be happening, in schools. So this study is designed to give administrators a chance to speak for themselves and about the institutions in which they work.

Three strategies were employed to gather data. Thirty-five administrators were interviewed, one administrator was shadowed for two weeks, and surveys were sent to other administrators in various locations. The first tactic was to interview administrators. These interviews were semi-structured in design and qualitative in nature -- qualitative, because the flexibility in these techniques provided participants with opportunities to mull over topics that were not necessarily anticipated. Since little has been written about this area, we wanted to provide a forum that would allow new information and insights to come to light. Although we went in with domains that we wanted to explore with our interviewees, the questions that we asked were general enough for them to open up about topics that they felt were important to the topic at hand. We also felt that qualitative interviews were necessary to probe the complexities of the processes that we wanted to understand; principals needed to have the latitude to use their own words to describe phenomena that could not easily be captured in the (few) words of others. We also reasoned that doing the interviews first would provide us with ideas to explore in the observation and survey components of the study. In the end, we used the rich information we obtained in the interviews to pursue areas in the observations and to design the survey that eventually went out to other administrators.

Our administrators were selected from two large Canadian school districts that shared a common border. One district was urban, while the other had both an urban and rural component. The former was highly diverse and had been obviously so for a number of years. Even so, its diversity has continued to increase. The second district varied in its ethnocultural composition. The urban portion of the district was as diverse as the former district, while the rural part was considerably less so. The unique characteristic of this district was that this diversity was rapidly moving northwards, out from the more urban area to the rural areas. Both districts had policies that were designed to discourage racism.

We chose the schools on the basis of their diversity. While most of the schools displayed obvious levels of heterogeneity, a few, mostly rural, schools were decidedly less so. These latter schools had only a handful of students who were not Anglo. The sample included a representative number of elementary and secondary schools. The size of schools varied from small elementary schools of around 100 students to larger secondary schools with student populations of over 2,000. Although we did not initially plan for this, the gender balance of principals was approximately even. With the exception of two administrators, all were of Anglo or European heritage. The names of the administrators, schools and districts that I use in this book are pseudonyms.

The research team (a research assistant, a graduate student and me) asked administrators open-ended questions about how they dealt with the issues that accompanied ethnocultural diversity in their respective schools. Originally we attempted, using a Leithwood and Stager (1989) framework, to discover how principals made decisions in this area. We focused on how they interpreted the various issues, what goals they set for themselves, what principles they followed and what constraints they experienced as they attempted to reach these goals. We directed our questions to the areas of (1) curriculum and instruction, (2) students and teachers, (3) the community, (4) school organization and structure, and (5) resource allocation. Although we wanted to explore these areas, the questions we asked were open-ended enough to allow administrators to talk about areas of concern that we had not foreseen. Also, as the study proceeded and various other themes became evident, we pursued them. Prominent themes included racism and antiracism, cultural differences, school-community relationships and learning and professional development. We recognized after the first few interviews that these themes were important, so we followed up in the subsequent interviews.

The next phase of the study involved a two-week observation of an administrator at work in a diverse school. I felt that this strategy was necessary to get a better sense of the context in which they worked. This meant that we didn't have to rely exclusively on what administrators told us and that we might get a better sense of why administrators did the things they did. I chose one of the administrators interviewed in the previous segment of the research. This administrator was picked for the school in which he worked and his willingness to partake in the research. The school was a diverse suburban secondary school where students self-identified with upwards of sixty different heritages. I spent two non-consecutive weeks shadowing this person during working hours. I followed him during his morning and afternoon rounds, sat in on some of his meetings, lurked about his office while he did paper work and made phone calls, witnessed the informal socializing he did during the course of his day, and spent time just talking with him about his job. I also talked informally to many of his colleagues – both fellow administrators and teachers. During this time I paid close attention to issues of racism, cultural differences, school-community relationships and professional development. I would make rough notes about what I saw and heard during the day, and in the evening spend time fleshing them out. All of the qualitative data was eventually analyzed using the NUD*IST software package. Themes and sub-themes were identified and written up.

The third stage involved the development and circulation of a survey. This segment was designed to provide an idea of how principals of diverse schools in other areas of the country were approaching diversity. We used the data from the first two stages to design questions that would probe principals' perceptions of significant areas related to diversity issues. Questions were designed to elicit information about a number of areas. The first area was policy. The questions on the survey probed the nature of the diversity-related policies that were currently in place, the interpretation and/or adaptation of them, school-level policy priorities, and the policy-development process. The second area sought information about school-community relationships, and the third, racism and antiracism. The survey also probed professional development strategies and needs, perceptions and reactions to cultural differences and language issues. Some questions required respondents simply to indicate their knowledge of a topic by providing a checkmark, while others instructed them to respond on a five-point scale. As an example of the former, one question on policy perceptions asked administrators to indicate board policies that apply to diversity. A question on racism provides an example of the latter. It asked principals, "If you have ever had any occurrences of racism in your school, please indicate the form and frequency on a five-point scale." So a "1" would mean there was no racism and "5" would mean that it was pervasive. The individual items probed (1) stereotyping by students and (2) educators, (3) harassment of students and (4) educators, (5) violence, (6) graffiti, (7) name-calling, (8) exclusion, (9) fairness, and (10) classroom portrayals. Respondents were also asked to indicate the level (elementary or secondary) of their school, its size and approximate percentage of various ethnic groups. Before the survey was sent out, it was reviewed by administrators, graduate students and research officers, and subsequently altered to address their various concerns.

We chose thirty-two school districts across Canada to participate in the study. We targeted these particular districts because Canadian Census Data indicated that there was a strong possibility of culturally diverse school communities in these areas. We sent letters to the chief executive officers of these districts requesting permission to carry out the study. Twenty-two agreed to participate. We asked these districts to forward us the names and addresses of ten principals to whom we could send the surveys. We sent out 220 surveys and had 104 returned.

The data were treated in a number of ways. First, we calculated the means for each of the items. Since responses were registered on a five-point scale, the means could only run from a possible low of "1" to a high of "5." We also ran two- and three-way analyses of variance. We did this to see if there were any differences in the ways in which principals in different settings responded to the survey items. The analyses of variance were performed to establish if there were any differences between (1) the perceptions of principals of elementary and principals of secondary schools, (2) among principals of twenty-three small (85 to 300 students), fifty-three medium (301 to 800 students) and twenty-five large (801 to 2200 students) schools, and (3) among principals of school with various mixes of diversity (i.e., schools with more or less than 50% Anglo, more or less than 20% African, schools where no group was larger than 40%, and schools where Anglos exceeded 70%).[1]

This study is based almost exclusively on the testimony of administrators. In this sense it is about their perceptions of diversity and what they do about it. As described earlier, administrators were chosen as participants for the study because they are the ones who know the most about administering diverse schools. This does not mean that everyone in their respective school communities would agree with their values or their perceptions. With the aforementioned exception – the two weeks spent shadowing an administrator – we really had no way of consulting others in these schools and school communities about their claims. But even if we could have, it would be difficult for people in organizations of this size, diversity and complexity to come to agreement on any number of observations. It would also have to assume (falsely) that one real and factual situation existed quite apart of the inevitably complex and variable perceptions of the men, women and children who were associated with it. As a consequence, the claims of these administrators were taken at face value, although we were mindful that people in positions of this nature might occasionally embellish their words and deeds, simply because most school principals are likely to attempt to promote positive views of their schools (see, for example, Trnavcevic, 2000). We did nevertheless take measures to check participants' statements. For example, during the interviews we asked similar questions in different ways that confirmed and reconfirmed statements. Also we were mindful that many administrators talked about the same kinds of things, and many of these topics were not solicited. Issues of racism and learning, for example, were not something that we had solicited, at least not initially. Without prompting, many administrators spoke of these aspects of their jobs in similar ways. We also

---

[1] Three schools did not indicate size.

acknowledged that the slim evidence that did exist in literature, for the most part, supported the kinds of recollections that administrators were offering. In the end, though, whether or not others in their school communities agreed with their statements, these administrators have mined many insights that might well help other administrators of such schools to do their jobs in ways that enhance the learning that goes on in their school communities. It will be up to the reader to judge which of these practices may be appropriate for their particular situations.

CONCLUSION

This book explores leadership, diversity and inclusion in diverse school contexts. In particular, it looks at how administrators promote, or can promote, inclusion in their school communities. The position that I take in the book is that inclusion is desirable and that all administrators should work towards this end. I support inclusive practice because I believe that it is consistent with principles of social justice. Beyond that, inclusion stands a better chance than other approaches of alleviating the unfair barriers and difficulties that "minority" students face in school and elsewhere. The book revolves around an empirical study that examines the efforts of administrators in understanding and meeting the challenges of diversity. This study revealed that many administrators understand and respond to diversity in ways that were consistent with inclusion. It also indicated, however, that some administrators did not promote inclusive practice. Two significant impediments to inclusive leadership revolved around administrators' lack of knowledge of their diverse school communities and of the processes associated with diversity, like racism. This book documents the nature of these challenges and the strategies that should be taken to address them.

CHAPTER 2

EDUCATIONAL APPROACHES TO DIVERSITY AND INCLUSION

This chapter describes the various educational approaches to diversity that educators have employed over the years. Despite the considerable number of such approaches, certain broad tendencies are apparent. Most of these can be classified as conservative, liberal/pluralist or critical. In what follows, I describe each of these approaches to diversity in education, the associated explanations of student failure, and recommended strategies for success. In each case I trace how, if at all, the perspective enhances inclusion. As will become evident in the pages that follow, some approaches are more consistent with inclusive education than others. The conservative view promotes inclusive practice the least, while critical approaches support it the most. The liberal/pluralist position falls somewhere in between. All three approaches, however, display shortcomings, which I illustrate below. I also document the contemporary challenges to inclusive education. In doing so, I use some of the ideas of more recent approaches to diversity by critical multiculturalists, antiracists and postmodernists. These challenges revolve around globalization, issues of identity and recent conservative opposition to efforts to recognize diversity. Before I move on to these descriptions, I provide a brief and selective history of perceptions of human diversity.

A BRIEF HISTORY OF HUMAN DIVERSITY

Views of human diversity that have a bearing on contemporary education and inclusion have a history. They reach back to well beyond 16th and 17th century Europe. It was at this time that what came to be seen as significant differences between and among people began to take on new meanings. From this point on, such differences would occupy the thoughts and words of humanity in new ways. Of the many reasons for this, two stand out. The first is humankind's increased mobility. Advancement in travel technology, and in the shipping industry in particular, made it possible at the time for people to travel longer distances in shorter and more manageable times. The result was that the differences between and among people who lived in different areas of the world became more apparent. This differed from previous eras when people stayed relatively close to their respective birthplaces. And even those who traveled great distances did not appear to give much notice to group characteristics. Shreeve (1994) maintains that neither Marco Polo nor the 14th century Arabian explorer Ibn Battutah seldom thought in these terms. Rarely covering more than twenty-fives miles a day, it never occurred to them to categorize people in "racial" ways, or at least not in the manner in which the contemporary world does.

These differences also took on greater significance as traditional hierarchies began to break down (Taylor, 1991). Up until 16th and 17th century a European's station in life and the privileges that accompanied this position were determined at birth. So the son of a nobleman inherited advantages that a son or daughter of a serf could never in their lifetime expect. At this time, however, these long-established traditions were seriously threatened by the new and evolving economic system – a person need not necessarily be of noble birth to profit in the market. Faced with the erosion of these privileges, those of upper class standing clambered to protect this traditional hierarchy by working to ensure that they enjoyed particular advantages in the newly evolving market economy. The establishment of the nation state was one such strategy, although of course there were also other reasons for the rise of the nation state. Such a move provided an ideal legitimizing mechanism for establishing laws that favored the already privileged. So laws regarding land ownership and other resources favored those who already had the means to acquire them over those who did not.

Another strategy in safeguarding these privileges involved highlighting differences of those who were thought to be unworthy others and characterizing the differences associated with them in negative ways. Doing so, the privileged claimed, would provide a justification for treating such individuals in unfair, exploitive, and demeaning ways. These characterizations applied both to those who lived in their midst as well as those more distant others. In this respect, these characterizations had both a "class" and a "race" dimension.[1] The ruling class in feudal Europe and the later so-called bourgeoisie class in industrial Europe sought to protect their privileged positions, in part by promulgating a view of serfs and working class people as simpler and more primitive than themselves. The idea here was that these people did not deserve the same privileges as the upper class because they were somehow lesser human beings than the latter. Mathew Arnold's characterization of working class people as having no culture, as being "raw and uncivilized," and as savages, typifies this view (Young, 1995). These same kinds of characterizations also provided the owners of capital a rationale (and supposedly a clear conscience) for enslaving people from different parts of the world, and profiting from their labour. The privileged reasoned that not only was it their right, but also their duty to do as they pleased with people they believed to be "heathens", "savages" and "poor infidels captivated by the devil" (Rushames, 1962, p. 2).

The idea of "race" and associated value attributions solidified as scientists become involved. In the 18th century, employing what they believed to be scientific and thereby objective methods, scientists established two (supposed) facts about humanity. The first was that humanity was divided into distinct groups they called "races." The second fact was that each of these races had a different worth. Johann Friedrich Blumenbach was perhaps the most influential of these scientists (Gould, 1994). His theory emphasized the belief that *homo sapiens* had been created in one

---

[1] Of course, they also applied to gender, but the differential status of men and women at this time was so taken for granted that there was probably little need to justify the treatment of women.

location and then had spread out over the globe. He believed that diversity occurred as groups of people moved out from this place of origin and adapted to different climates and topographies. Nevertheless, Blumenbach did single out one group as being closest to the created ideal, and characterized all others by relative degrees of departure from this archetypal standard. His criterion for identifying this original and ideal group was physical beauty. Not surprisingly, he affirmed his fellow Europeans as the most beautiful, and those from the area of Mount Causasus the most comely of all, hence the designation "Caucasian" (Gould, 1994). At this point, however, Blumenbach faced a problem. His mentor, Carolus Linneaus, had only identified four races, and he needed an additional race to complete the transition from the most attractive races to the least. One side of the equation presented no problem; the line of departure went from the most comely Caucasians, through the intermediary North Americans to the least worthy Asians. The other side of the pyramid, however, needed an additional race to be the intermediary between his ideal Caucasians and the least attractive Africans. He solved this problem by creating a new race – the Malaysians, all in the name of science!

CONSERVATIVE APPROACHES TO EDUCATIONAL DIVERSITY

The so-called scientific research that was based on these erroneous ideas would influence approaches to the education of various groups of students and explanations for their successes and failures. Particularly influential in this respect was the connection that researchers of the time drew between what they believed to be distinct groups and their social aptitudes and cognitive abilities. Researchers were convinced that cognitive abilities were inherent, that is, they were biologically determined. To prove such claims, a number of scientists engaged in a program of research that sought to draw a relationship between brain size and intelligence. Such research, however, has long since been discredited (Gould, 1981; Shreeve, 1994). In fact subsequent analyses revealed that one of the most prominent of these scientists, Ceril Burt, actually fabricated his data (Gould, 1981). This is not the end of this story, however. Despite convincing evidence to the contrary, contemporary social scientists continue to pursue this erroneous connection between "race" and intelligence. Herrnstein and Murray (1994) are just the latest of these misguided social scientists who cling to the idea that there is a fixed connection between biology and social behaviour.

The implications of this conservative ideology for education, however, are not as clear-cut as they may seem. On the one hand, those people who had the prerogative of defining certain groups and individuals as different sought to protect their privileges, in part, by using educational institutions to eliminate what they saw in these different others as threatening. A key strategy in their drive to contain these threatening differences rested with assimilationist educational policies. The idea here was to educate different others in ways that would prompt them to accept certain values, values that they would share with the already privileged. So, for example, the school promoters in 19th century Upper Canada wanted the children of immigrants and the poor to attend school (Prentice, 1977). They believed that education would provide the means through which these young people could be taught such values as Christian love, order, the sanctity of property, and correct social behaviour. Education would encourage them to abandon their faulty habits and attitudes and to take up those more consistent with the interests of the upper classes. The school promoters were confident that their schools would discipline these groups, diffuse threats to the prevailing social order and foster good relations between immigrants and the poor, on the one hand, and the rich, on the other (see also Ryan, 1999).

The reality, however, was, and still is, according to Kalantiz and Cope (1999), that those who favored assimilationist strategies were never really serious about them. While they no doubt wanted to contain what they saw as threatening differences, most of those with privilege were not comfortable sharing their privileges with others. "The name of the game, at least in part, was a structural racism designed to keep difference the way it was" (Kalantiz & Cope, 1999, p. 249). Keeping differences the way that they were required, among other elements, the differential treatment of students. In this regard conservatives favored various forms of streaming. They had little compunction about placing different others in "lower" streams or poorer schools and accepting no blame when these students floundered. Conservatives were not at all surprised that these different others performed less well than their majority culture (and upper and middle class) counterparts. But they believed that this lack of success had little to do with this differential treatment. The reason that groups of different others did less than their more privileged counterparts was because they were presumably biologically impaired. Additional resources, special attention or uniquely crafted programs would be wasted on these students. The best teachers and resources were to be reserved for students whose superior physiologies placed them in positions to make the most of them.

While biological explanations still exist, they are, fortunately, not taken as seriously as they once were. More recently they have been replaced in conservative circles by cultural deprivation explanations. According to Erickson (1987), nurture replaced nature as the reason for school failure. "Minority" children did not do well in school, so the argument went, because their home and community environments were not cognitively stimulating (Deutsh et al., 1976; Hess & Shipman, 1965). By virtue of the cultural milieu in which they were raised, these particular students were said to be intellectually impoverished, culturally deprived and socially disadvantaged (see Erickson, 1987).

While these conservative views on difference and education continue to persist, and I allude to contemporary variations of them in the following section, other liberal/pluralist views of difference began to surface and challenge these conservative ideologies.

LIBERAL/PLURALIST APPROACHES TO DIFFERENCE[2]

Liberal/pluralist approaches to difference in education began to surface in the 1960s and 1970s. While variants of pluralism have a long history, particularly liberal versions of it, they emerged at this time as alternatives to conservative approaches. The most obvious difference between conservatives and liberal/pluralists was their view of difference. While conservative approaches revolved around a suspicion of difference, liberal/pluralist approaches valued difference. Liberal/pluralists explicitly propounded that the values, traditions, and life styles – the culture of non-Anglo groups – were to be nourished and cherished, at least superficially, and not eliminated or assimilated. They vouched for the right of different cultural groups to maintain their difference, and the corresponding obligation of other cultural groups to respect that right (Boyd, 1996). But while pluralists did not see differences as a threat in the way conservatives did, they nevertheless believed that differences got in the way of children's ability to master school curricula. Pluralists, however, did not explicitly blame the difficulties that children were having in school on their culture or nature, as conservatives did. Their explanations typically suggested that problems arose in schools because of the discontinuities between the culture of the student and the culture of the school. Discontinuities, then, rather than deficits, were the cause of academic difficulties.

The cultural discontinuity thesis provided much fodder for research in the 1960s and 1970s. Many of the researchers who pursued this line of study directed their efforts at understanding the difficulties that aboriginal students encountered in schools. These people pursued one of two paths of inquiry. One was based on the idea that the cognitive proclivities and skills of groups of aboriginal people differed in key ways from the Anglo teachers who taught them. In this view, aboriginal children experienced difficulties in school because they thought and learned differently than their Anglo counterparts. In their efforts to better understand this discontinuity, researchers probed the various dimensions of these cognitive processes. Much of this research, however, has proved to be of minimal value. Problems with it included vague conceptualizations and questionable theoretical foundations. Perhaps its most obvious shortcoming, however, was its lack of utility (Ryan, 1993). This was particularly true in the case of those who saw cognitive processes as physiological in nature (e.g., Ross, 1989; Rhodes, 1990). Racist in character (McCarty et al., 1991), this latter view left educators with virtually no room for action since there would be little use in adjusting school practices to accommodate such proclivities if these ways of thinking were in important ways already determined or fixed. Not all researchers in the area adhered to such beliefs, however. Some also acknowledged the social and changing nature of cognition (Berry, 1976). Many researchers also directed their efforts at understanding the

---

[2] May (1999) draws a distinction between liberal and corporate pluralism. In his view, liberal pluralism provides no separate standing for ethnic, religious, or linguistic minority groups before the law or government. Corporate pluralism, on the other hand, recognizes "minority" groups as legally constituted entities. Moreover, they are allocated economic, social and political awards, on the basis of their size and influence.

social and cultural discontinuities that they believed impeded the learning of aboriginal students.

The most popular of these approaches was a socio-linguistic one. It explored the idea that discontinuities in communication conventions prevented aboriginal students from understanding what Anglo teachers were trying to convey to them. One of the most cited studies of this nature was Philips' (1972; 1983) examination of the communication practices in the Warm Springs community in the United States. The basic premise of Philip's study was that communication involves more than language; rather, it always takes place within a wider set of social conventions. These conventions are generally shared, moreover, by members of particular cultural groups, who often take them for granted. In Warm Springs, for example, people had a set of expectations regarding turn-taking in communication situations. Here it was inappropriate for others to control the timing, length or direction of a speaker's turn. Participants in Warm Spring communication settings routinely refrained from interrupting speakers, requiring responses from others, and addressing particular others. Philips went on to illustrate that classroom communication practices in the local school worked in quite different ways. Operating very much like a "switchboard," teacher-directed communication patterns violated a number of Warm Springs norms. The result was that teachers misinterpreted student silences and various teacher expectations confused students. In the end, these different expectations disrupted the ability of teachers and students to communicate effectively and hindered students from mastering the curriculum.

These socio-linguistic studies proved to be of greater practical use than the cognitive-based studies. This was because educators could act on the information generated from such studies in ways that would (supposedly) smooth over various discontinuities. One of the more successful projects that employed this tactic was the Kamehameha Early Education Project (KEEP) in Hawaii (Au, 1978). Educators in this setting promoted speech situations in reading classes that were consistent with the ways in which students spoke at home and in their communities. The result was that students participated more enthusiastically in these lessons and their understanding of texts increased. Nonetheless, successful examples of this sort were rare. Groups of "minority" children generally tended to do less well than their majority counterparts, critics asserted, because the socio-linguistic explanation ignored the wider power relationships between the respective groups. I will address this in greater detail below.

"Culture" assumed an important role in discontinuity explanations and associated prescriptions. Advocates of this approach found it particularly useful in identifying unique groups of people who tended to struggle in educational institutions. Drawing on various anthropologically-based versions, advocates used the term culture to refer to the various forms of lifestyles, values, rituals, knowledge, and so on, that set groups apart from other groups and from the majority Anglos. This appeared to present few problems in the case of the aboriginal people. For Anglo researchers, the obvious differences between themselves and aboriginal people made it a relatively straightforward matter to identify the latter. Of course, many of these people overlooked the considerable differences between and among the many different aboriginal groups in North America and elsewhere. Identifying distinct groups, however, would become more complicated as researchers attempted to use this concept to identify other groups of people, and as these researchers began to take the idea of difference more seriously, exploring it from more than just an ethnicity perspective. Even so, this idea of culture now had a secure foothold and would become a mainstay in explanations and strategies for dealing with associated differences in education. In fact, the most popular contemporary approach of this sort, multiculturalism, actually incorporates the term.

Multiculturalism is a much-contested term; it has many meanings and many applications. One must distinguish between multiculturalism as a term that describes the general condition of a population and as a strategy for dealing with the conditions that accompany diversity. Some use it to describe what they see as the increasing diversity in contemporary life. While most see this diversity in terms of ethnicity or heritage, others also distinguish other forms of difference such as gender, class, sexual orientation, age, ability, as well as many other more ephemeral differences. The other general use of this term is as a strategy for dealing with this diversity. There is, however, no agreement on the related explanations, rationales or practices. The meaning of multiculturalism frequently differs from area to area. In the United Kingdom, multiculturalism was generally identified more with a liberal/pluralist orientation, while in the United States it was used to refer both to pluralist and critical approaches to diversity.

The version of pluralist multiculturalism that I outline here represents perhaps the most widespread articulation of this particular approach to diversity. It is what often comes to mind when people think of multiculturalism as a form of education. It has also been referred to as "benevolent" multiculturalism (Gibson, 1976; Troyna, 1993; May, 1994). In the pluralist tradition, advocates of this version of multiculturalism believe that the differences associated with various "minority" groups should be intrinsically valued and pursued for their own sakes. The differences that are deemed to be important in this regard are those that could be captured by the term culture. Multiculturalists of this persuasion feel that what needs to be honored is the respective "minority" groups' cultures. The way to do this is to provide the opportunity for all students to learn about the culture of these groups in the classroom. So, not only would students be exposed to the various traditions, rituals, knowledge, values, lifestyles, customs, dress and so on of the respective groups, they would also have the chance to read books written by members of these groups. Such measures, its proponents articulate, would enable members of both "minority" and majority groups to better understand one another. It would also increase the compatibility between "minority" homes and school, elevate previously marginalized students' academic achievement and self-esteem, improve their life chances, and reduce incidents of racism.

Proponents tended to see this version of multiculturalism as apolitical. For them, multiculturalism is political only by virtue of the fact that it is a means of promoting social cohesion and harmony. They believe that acknowledging the importance of various groups by including aspects of their respective cultures in classroom activities would be enough to quell social unrest in those communities that felt something needed to be done to ameliorate their children's persistent difficulties at school (Tryona, 1993; McAndrew, 1987). For these multiculturalists, achieving equality is a matter of making technical adjustments to school programming so that all students would have the same kind of opportunities. In this regard, multiculturalists see schools not just as neutral sorts of institutions but as beacons of hope for the marginalized members of "minority" groups. The fact that schools (or the wider economic and political environments) are part of the problem would never occur to them. As far as these people are concerned, most schools' inherent organizational patterns, pedagogy, curricula and assessment practices are the means for guaranteeing equality of opportunity for all students. While there might be a need for some adjustments in these aspects of schooling, like exposing students to other cultures in the classroom, this caveat is as far as any critique might have gone. The problems that persist, like racism or poor achievement, are believed to be psychological in nature, not social or institutional. Multiculturalists of this persuasion maintain that individuals, not systems, fail or commit acts of racism.

This version of multiculturalism surfaced in academia, in state sponsored reports, government policy and, of course, in classroom practice through the 1970s and 1980s and into the 1990s. State involvement was more evident in Canada, the United Kingdom and Australia than it was in the United States throughout this period. Responding to changing social conditions, increasing levels and awareness of diversity, and demands to meet the challenges that accompanied this diversity, the governments of Australia (Rizvi, 1992), the United Kingdom (Troyna, 1993) and Canada (Moodley, 1995) authorized at various times reports that looked into problems that were associated with these changing conditions, and issued recommendations, some of which found their way into policy. In Canada, where virtually all educational responsibility for education rests with the individual provinces, the federal government instituted a policy of multiculturalism early in the 1970s. In introducing the policy to parliament, Prime Minister Trudeau said that

> We believe that cultural pluralism is the very essence of Canadian identity. Every ethnic group has the right to preserve and develop its own culture and values within the Canadian context. To say that we have two official languages is not to say we have two official cultures, and no particular culture is more official than another. A policy of multiculturalism must be a policy for all Canadians (Mazurek & Kach, in Boyd, 1996, p. 614).

While the Canadian federal government has only limited responsibilities in the area of education, it did provide funds to support multicultural initiatives, although according to Anderson and Frideres (1981), the total budget proved to be "relatively modest." Nevertheless the provinces and individual school boards did take advantage of some of these opportunities. The policies and practices adopted by the various Canadian provinces and individual school boards varied considerably, however. The support, moreover, for multicultural initiatives from provincial governments like Ontario changed over the years as different political parties came to power. The multicultural policies of the Progressive Conservative government of the 1970s and the antiracism policies of the New Democrats of the early 1990s were rolled back in the later 1990s as a right-wing conservative party came to power.

Despite the well-meaning intentions of liberal/pluralists, only small gains were made on the part of members of marginalized groups. Many young people of these same groups were still experiencing problems in school. Of the various critics of this approach, one group maintained that the reason that "minority" children continued to do poorly in school was because the key causes of the problem had not been correctly identified. Advocates of a critical approach, for example, maintained that the problem with education was systemic; it was the system that was responsible for these patterns of school failure, and not the individuals in the system.

CRITICAL APPROACHES TO DIFFERENCE

Advocates of critical approaches to difference took issue with pluralists on a number of accounts. For one, they challenged pluralist explanations of student failure and strategies for improving the academic achievement of students. They did not believe that cultural discontinuities between students and Anglo teachers and practices were the primary reason these students had difficulty mastering the curriculum. Nor did they accept that smoothing over these discontinuities or incorporating the culture of some of these groups into the curriculum or classroom practice would improve their academic achievement. Instead these critics maintained that the causes of these problems extended far beyond schools and the individuals associated with them. For critical scholars, the problems were systemic in nature. In their view, student fortunes were dictated, in large measure, by the unequal power relationships embedded in social structures that transcended schools, families and individuals. This general approach followed two different lines of inquiry. One was reflected in the work of Ogbu (1982, 1987, 1992), the other in the analyses of antiracists.

Ogbu's theories on school success and diversity evolved from his early ethnographies of diverse schools. It developed in response to empirical findings that indicated that not all "minority" students did poorly at school. Noting considerable diversity among these groups of students, Ogbu also emphasized that some of these students did reasonably well at school despite considerable differences between students' respective cultures and the culture of the school. For Ogbu, this meant that there was more to the cultural discontinuities explanation than mere incompatibilities at an interactional level suggested. Much of his subsequent work has aimed to explain this differential success.

Ogbu's major contribution to the study of "minority" students' achievement is his typology of groups. In his early research, he observed that the various levels of success among students were not random; there were distinct patterns of achievement among such students. These patterns of achievement provided the basis for his division of students into groups of autonomous, voluntary and involuntary minorities. Ogbu did not go into depth with the first group, the *autonomous minorities*. He remarked that they were "minorities primarily in the numerical sense" (Ogbu, 1992, p. 8), and included groups like Jews, Mormons and Amish. His most significant contribution came from the distinction he drew between voluntary and involuntary minorities. According to Ogbu, *voluntary minorities* come to the host country from abroad. They choose to do this because they believe that there is a chance for a better life in the new country. This group would include people from India, South America, and Africa, for example, who immigrate to the United States. His third group is the *involuntary minorities*. Unlike voluntary minorities, involuntary minorities do not, and did not, have the same option to exercise their will in such matters. They were either enslaved, as in the case of African Americans, or conquered, as in the case of Native Americans. Ogbu contends that voluntary minorities do consistently better in school than involuntary minorities, but his explanation departs from the well-established cultural differences explanation that anthropologists of the time favored.

Ogbu does not completely abandon the cultural discontinuity hypothesis, however. He does not discount altogether the idea that cultural discontinuities may impede educational success. What he does do is break down cultural differences into two different kinds. The first is what he refers to as primary, those differences that existed *before* the two groups came in contact. So for example, the traditional Kpelle culture had no measurements of weight, area, speed and temperature. These differences existed for many years before the immigration of the Kpelle to the United States. At some point, during their American education, Kpelle students' understanding (or rather lack of understanding) of these concepts impeded efforts to learn the formal curriculum at school. Ogbu maintains that while these differences can initially cause difficulties, they can eventually be overcome, that is, if students are motivated to do so. And he contends that voluntary minorities are so inclined. They are motivated to overcome these obstacles because they have accepted the folk theory that success at school can guarantee good jobs when they finish. Ogbu contends that they have little reason to believe otherwise.

Ogbu's involuntary minorities do not share this same faith in the system. Having experienced a long history of unfair treatment at the hands of the dominant majority, they do not buy into the meritocractic beliefs of their voluntary counterparts. They have learned that they will not automatically have access to good jobs when they graduate, even if they possess the educational qualifications to qualify for these positions. A history of racism has produced a job ceiling – those who control the jobs tend to favour members of their own majority group over members of minority groups. According to Ogbu, students are well aware of this sense of hopelessness. So unlike their voluntary counterparts who devote themselves to mastering the school curriculum, involuntary minorities engage in other sorts of activities. Adaptive in character, these behaviors tend to be geared toward meeting other needs such as forging a positive identity in institutions where they are regularly devalued. These activities, however, generally do not assist them in their academic pursuits. This is because they are, by and large, oppositional or deviant. These behaviors constitute a key element in of Ogbu's "secondary discontinuities." In contrast to primary discontinuities, these secondary discontinuities have developed over time in contact situations where the dominant group exercises its power over other groups in ways that penalize the latter. And unlike voluntary minorities, who see advantages in overcoming primary discontinuities, involuntary minorities think that they have more to gain in maintaining these secondary discontinuities. Deviant and oppositional activities offer them opportunities to create positive identities and links with their similarly oppressed peers, while conforming behaviour leaves them with nothing.

Although insightful in many respects, Ogbu's framework displays a number of shortcomings. I will mention two. The first is his oversimplification of the degree of diversity, not only among groups that constitute both voluntary and involuntary minorities, but also within them. It is difficult to accept the proposition that students from Africa, South America, and Asia would generally display the same kinds of behaviors in North American schools, and fare equally as well. For example, there is substantial diversity among groups that normally are identified as "Asian," and their performance in school also varies considerably. Some of these students may also engage in the type of oppositional behaviour normally associated with involuntary minority students (Lee, 1996). But it is not just so-called voluntary minorities who display such diversity. So do involuntary minorities. Indeed, some of these students do well in school (Erickson, 1987). Refugees also do not fit easily into Ogbu's typology. While they may look forward to life in a new country, the trauma that many will have experienced may sometimes affect their school efforts. The essential point here is that there is more to success and failure in school than Ogbu's typology is able to capture.

Another weakness of Ogbu's framework is that it is exclusively explanatory. That is to say, he employs it to explain why certain groups of minority students don't do as well as other students. However, he fails to critique or challenge in a meaningful way the system that is responsible for the unequal power relationships that persistently disenfranchise minority students. According to Levinson (1992), Ogbu does not challenge capitalist relations *per se*, despite employing the concept of a job ceiling. Whatever changes he does recommend are pragmatic rather than fundamental; they remain exclusively within the framework of current mainstream educational and social arrangements (see, for example, Ogbu, 1992). Lost in all of his explanatory detail is that both voluntary and involuntary students are subject to systemic racism. Whether students are new to the host country and full of hope or their communities have been conquered or enslaved, they all face persistent obstacles in school and in life. Overcoming these obstacles often requires that they work harder than those who are not subject to racist practice (Ryan, 1999). Because Ogbu is so preoccupied with understanding why some groups do better than others, he fails to attend to this persistent injustice, and as a consequence, misses the opportunity to confront it.

Not all those who approach difference from a critical standpoint overlook systemic racism. In fact, one group, the antiracists, take racism as their starting point for explaining what happens in schools and for doing something about it. Antiracist approaches in education emerged as an alternative to multicultural education. They represented a reaction to conservative responses to increasing diversity and also to the apparent failure of multicultural approaches to improve the academic achievement of groups of "minority" students.

As one might expect, antiracists highlight persistent and widespread racist practice. They believe that racism is responsible, in large measure, for "minority" students' difficulties in school and in life. While drawing on previous conceptions of racism, antiracists in education nevertheless also take issue with them. They dispute views of racism that depict it as an individual and psychological phenomenon that shows up in personality traits, attitudes, and behaviour. Antiracism advocates believe that racism goes beyond individual and intentional acts of prejudice that are perpetrated by misguided men and women. For them racism is systemic; it is part of the persistent, pervasive and often taken for granted patterns by which most people live their lives. They do not, however, completely accept the institutional views of racism that display deterministic tendencies and ignore the role of individual subjects. Instead, antiracists acknowledge both the "behavioral" and "structural" nature of racism. West (1994, p. 18), for example, maintains that "structures and behavior are inseparable, that institutions and values go hand in hand. How people act and live is shaped – though in no way dictated or determined – by the larger circumstances in which they find themselves."

Antiracists take issue with the claims of liberal/pluralists, and in particular, multiculturalists. They do not accept the idea that cultural differences *per se* cause certain students to fail in school. They also dispute the claim of liberal/pluralist multiculturalists that incorporating the cultures of particular groups of students into classroom practice will improve student performance or their eventual life chances. For them, school failure (and the position of ethnic minorities generally) is ultimately tied to enduring patterns of subordination and domination that characterize the relationships between White middle-class groups and non-White ethnic groups. The real problem is not that various groups are different, but that certain groups are subject to systemic racist practice both in school and out. The problem antiracists have with multiculturalists is that educators' emphasis on such surface cultural or lifestyle phenomena such as "saris, samosas and steel bands" (Troyna, 1993) tend to deflect attention away from the structural inequalities that drive racist practice, inhibit school achievement and inevitably diminish the life chances of many already marginalized students. They say that we could not expect any meaningful changes in student outcomes or in their life chances without changes in the structural patterns that provide obstacles for certain groups of students. Most certainly, superficial changes to school practices will not be enough to guarantee a fair chance to succeed.

Despite advances over the pluralist positions, the first antiracist approaches displayed their own weaknesses. One of these was that early antiracist thinkers tended to reduce racism to a "black/white" issue. This is something that more recent antiracists have criticized. Gillborn (1995), for example, cautions against oversimplifying what he believes to be a complex phenomenon. He maintains that racism takes shape in complicated relationships that revolve around more than simply a "black/white" dichotomy. In this regard, critics have also claimed that some antiracists tended to "essentialize" certain groups, a charge that would also apply to some multiculturalists. They maintained that antiracists (and pluralists) viewed groups in terms of what they believed to be their fundamental, immutable and enduring characteristics. Rattansi (1992), for example, maintained that by focusing on the "Black Struggle," antiracists reified the notion of community. While representing an often successful alliance against racism, it nevertheless presented a unified conception of the experiences of this group. In doing so, it tended to homogenize different histories, cultures and needs, and excluded groups not captured by this characterization. This antiracist position overstated the importance of culture, while at the same time understated the fluid nature of inter- and intra-group relations (May, 1999). Critics of essentialist positions claim that group cultures are perpetually being made, re-made and negotiated in the contexts in which they exist.

CONTEMPORARY CHALLENGES

More recently, those who have adopted a critical perspective have moved beyond these earlier positions. "Critical multiculturalists" (May, 1999), "critical antiracists" (Gillborn, 1995: Carrim & Soudien, 1999), and (critical) "postmodernists" (Rattansi, 1992, 1999; Ryan, 1999) have employed new ideas and concepts in their efforts to come to grips with the limited successes of previous approaches to diversity in realizing inclusive education. Differences appear among these positions, but so do similarities. One significant similarity is their attention to the many contemporary challenges that threaten inclusive approaches to diversity. These include the rise of globalization, the complexities associated with identity, and recent conservative efforts to contain diversity.

Globalization

Globalization presents many challenges for those interested in promoting inclusive education. In some ways, the meaning of the term globalization is self-evident, referring to the world becoming smaller; our community is no longer local, but global. In a sense, though, this global world is not new. For many centuries now, humanity has been aware of what has been happening in distant parts of the world. What has changed, though, is the ease with which travel and other forms of communication occur. So now, Africa, for example, is much closer to North American than it once was. Travelers, that is, those privileged enough to afford the fare, can fly between the two continents in a matter of hours, while the latest communication technologies can beam almost simultaneously distant images into people's homes. What also makes these phenomena global is that they threaten the integrity of that which we have come to regard as national. Contemporary corporations, various forms of communication, and to an extent, real people, can permeate the borders of countries in ways that these national entities have either little incentive, or power, to prevent. This continues to have significant consequences for diversity in the contemporary world.

One of the most obvious forms through which globalization occurs is the economy. Some (e.g., Sklair, 2001) go so far as to say that the economy is the most powerful global system. Whether or not this is the case, the world's largest companies strive to transcend national boundaries. While they may be tied to various countries in any number of ways, a consequence of having to do business in the real world, their interests do not coincide with any national interests. Rather, they are private, motivated by a desire on the part of the owners and managers of these corporations to turn a profit. These people operate with the mindset that in order to turn a profit their companies need to globalize (Sklair, 2001). This is because globalizing provides these corporations with a number of advantages. No longer bound to particular locations in ways that they once were, these corporations can move with relative ease in order to avoid such problems as tax burdens, strong labour movements or unfavorable local laws and regulations. So when wages become too high in North America, a company like Nike can pick up and move its production to South East Asia where it can pay workers substantially lower wages.

Increasingly, local communities are forced to make themselves attractive to such corporations by offering them tax breaks; front-line workers find that they must accept either short-term or contract positions; unions are rendered less powerful; and local enterprises realize that they are not able to compete on an equal footing with these larger organizations. Hardest hit in all of this are the world's subaltern populations. Whether they reside in North America or South East Asia, these already marginalized groups are becoming increasingly subject to the whims of global capital which unceremoniously tramples their culture and interests. They are also finding they can depend less and less on the shrinking public purse to provide them with the opportunities to improve their situations, whether it is through public education or other arenas.

Other dimensions of globalization are at least in part products of this expanding economy. The new and unpredictable flow of people, money, technology, media images and ideas are made possible by, and make possible, the global economy. Immigration patterns, for example, have changed over the past twenty to thirty years, particularly with regard to the United Kingdom and its former colonies. This has happened as travel has become cheaper, more accessible and faster, as Europe and the West have opened their borders to more immigrants than they had previously. Now people from many non-Euopean countries in Asia, Africa and South America come to settle in the United Kingdom, Australia, the United States and Canada in unprecedented numbers. The result is that these countries have become more visibly diverse, and most people are acutely aware of this diversity. Schools have also become more diverse in this respect, particularly those in and around larger cities. But where once school communities were populated by two or three different groups, many find themselves constituted by upwards of sixty different groups (see for example, Ryan, 1999).

Enhanced communication flows have also had an impact on diversity. While people still communicate with each other in face-to-face situations, they are nevertheless relying more and more on electronic mediating devices. Today most people (in the Western world) spend substantial periods of time watching television, viewing movies in theatres and in their homes, surfing the Internet and sending and receiving facsimiles and emails. As far back as 1987 almost 100% of Canadian households had televisions (Young, 1989). In the United States students will have spent more time in front of a television than in the classroom by the time they graduate (Apple, 2000). These forms of communication know few borders. Satellites receive and transmit signals to and from all parts of the world in seconds; people from all parts of the world can visit the same website simultaneously, and they can email and use other forms of chat environments for instant communication, regardless of where partners in conversations are physically located.

The impact of this electronic medium on diversity is not straightforward. Some might jump to the conclusion that these electronic media are reducing diversity, making us more like one another. In one sense, this may be true. Morely and Robbins (1995) cite the case of the BBC. They write that it initially linked individuals and families to a shared centre, providing the British with common view of themselves as members of a national community. It would be a mistake, however, to believe that everyone shares, or will share, a common culture.

Communication processes are too paradoxical in character for that. Rather than inhibiting diversity, the integration associated with the contemporary global village actually promotes it. Even though more people will be connected to one another, the sheer number of these interdependencies increases exponentially the potential for diversity. Perhaps the greatest potential for diversity, however, rests not with the quantity of these relationships, but with their character. The potential play of differences that accompanies these electronic representations allows for multiple interpretations of them (Ryan, 1999).

The tensions that globalization presents for inclusion are many. One of the most persistent of these is associated with the global economy. As mentioned above, marginalized groups are becoming increasingly subject to the whim of global capital. They now find that their interests are increasingly being trampled by the global capital juggernaut, and they are less able to depend on the financially strapped public institutions like schools to protect these interests. Another challenge is the rapidly expanding nature of diversity. The sheer number and ephemeral nature of these differences will make it difficult to identify, let alone include and represent, them fairly in school activities.

Identity

Issues of identity present challenges for inclusion. While those concerned with diversity issues have in the past attended to these issues, particularly with regard to how groups were identified, they did so in ways that glossed over the associated complex processes. So, for example, some multiculturalists and antiracists preferred to see groups unproblematically as undifferentiated wholes with solid roots or foundations. They did so because it suited their analytic or political purposes at the time. Most of these scholars, however, failed to acknowledge the complex ways in which individuals and groups came to be (re)presented and the effects that these representations had on them and others. This oversight is now being addressed by researchers in the field (e.g. Rattansi, 1992, 1999; Ryan, 1999; McCarthy, 1993). Representation has become a particularly pertinent issue today because of the ways in which the electronic media multiply and distribute these images.

Many of those who currently study identity emphasize the complexity of the processes associated with it. This complexity is due, in part, to identities being social in nature. They take shape in the various social circumstances that people find themselves in. Two consequences follow from this. One is that identities are perpetually changing. This malleability departs from some multiculturalist and early antiracism positions that depicted groups and the individuals associated with them as displaying more-or-less fixed characteristics or cultures. If we accept the idea that people become what their social circumstances allow them to be, then the ever-changing situations that people find themselves in will shape, in important and rapid ways how they will evolve individually and as groups. They will adapt to the inevitable new circumstances, using the resources that they find at their disposal to help them meet their immediate and longer term needs. This means that people will as a matter of course   adopt new forms of language and communication, new ways of interacting, thinking and valuing, aspects of life that some would refer to as culture. It will also mean that they may abandon other aspects of their respective lifestyles. So groups and individuals are not static, nor do they have some enduring essence. Rather they continue to evolve in unpredictable ways as they negotiate their respective existences in different and changing contexts.

Another implication of this view is that people and groups will adopt many, sometimes conflicting and contradictory, identities. So in this regard, ethnicity may become but one of many identities that people assume, even though it remains a powerful, explosive and durable force, particularly at the collective level (May, 1999). Men, women and children will also adopt one or more of many potential gender, class, spiritual or sexual identities. They may also see themselves and others as family members, wage earners, students, friends, gangbangers, jocks, residents, citizens, skinheads, professionals, activists, rappers, druggies and so on. Indeed, the number of identities that we can assume are limitless. This is at least partly a consequence of the ever-increasing discourses and lifestyle images to which we are exposed in the media and elsewhere, stimuli which we use as resources for constructing identities. Still, while assuming various identities may in some ways be enabling, the acts associated with them can also be oppressive; by assuming an identity, we subject ourselves to the logic associated with the accompanying discourses. Given the source of these discourses and the interests that they serve, they can be debilitating both to oneself and to others. While taking on a "druggie" persona may endear oneself to (some of) one's peers, the practices associated with it can interfere with both mental and physical health, as well as a range of other life chances. Those who assume skinhead identities, on the other hand, may find themselves endorsing and circulating sexist and racist discourses that are quite obviously harmful to many people.

Contemporary identities are a challenge for inclusive-minded individuals and institutions. Plainly put, identities are much more complex today than they were assumed to be in the past because there are now more opportunities for constructing different identities. Today individuals and groups display identities that are multiple, fluid and contradictory. A consequence of this is that people belong to many groupings or categories, which may shift regularly and may not be consistent with one another. This makes it difficult to include a full range of contemporary identities in school activities. It is no longer, as if it ever were, a matter of simply identifying homogeneous groups, learning about their respective cultures, and changing structures to make them part of school operations and activities. Educators will have to be sensitive to the nature of contemporary identities and use their imaginations to accommodate them fairly in schools. This will not be an easy task, however, for there are many contemporary forces at work that discourage such accommodations. One of these has emerged in the form of recent conservative views on diversity.

Conservative Challenges to Diversity

Contemporary conservatives see certain kinds of diversity as a threat to themselves and their communities. There are no doubt many reasons for this attitude, including, among others, the uncertainty that comes from economic reorganization, downsizing and instability, the increased competition for scarce resources and the loss on the part of a beleaguered middle class of what were once unquestioned privileges (McCarthy & Dimitriadis, 2000). The discourse that many worried conservatives appeal to revolves around a concern with the preservation of their community in light of perceived threats to it. They tend to believe that an increased recognition of diversity represents a serious threat to a community's cohesion. In their view, any serious deference to diversity can only result in fragmentation and conflict. In the United States Schlesinger (1991) believes that what he refers to as the contemporary "cult of ethnicity" will leave his country "a society fragmented into ethnic groups." This is because acknowledgement of this diversity "exaggerates differences, intensifies resentments and antagonisms, drives deeper the awful wedges between races and nationalities" (p. 58). Such a course risks "the disintegration of the national community, apartheid, Balkanization and tribalization." [3]

This talk of patriotism, nationhood and nationalism is what some refer to as the "new racism" (Short & Carrington, 1999; Rizvi, 1993). No longer needing to rely on claims of biological or cultural inferiority, these discourses nevertheless are just as much about exclusion as inclusion. Talk of home and homeland, what Morely and Robbins (1995, p. 89) refer to as *Heimat,*

> is about conserving fundamentals of culture and identity. And, as such, it is about sustaining cultural boundaries and boundedness. To belong in this way is to protect exclusive and therefore excluding, identities against those who are seen as aliens and foreigners. The "Other" is always and continuously a threat to the security and integrity of those who share a common home. Xenophobia and fundamentalism are opposite sides of the same coin. For indeed *Heimat-* seeking is a form of fundamentalism. The apostles of purity are always moved by the fear that intermingling with a different culture will inevitably weaken and ruin their own.

Advocates of these discourses conveniently overlook a number of points, however. First, as May (1999) points out, there is not, nor has there even been, such as phenomenon as a homogeneous common culture. Nation states have always displayed wide arrays of diversity. Indeed the idea of a common culture as something attached to a particular place was a German innovation, a reaction to the disintegration of traditional forms of life brought on by the spread of commercial values (Fuller, 2000). The rise of the nation state was, at least in part, an effort to stem this apparent disintegration. It provided leverage for those who felt threatened by these changes to force large numbers of different people and groups to abide by a common law, language and culture. And it was easier to act on these individuals and groups if they felt they shared a common stake in defending what was now their state. May (1999) also points out that conservative ideologues mistakenly believe only in an "either/or" scenario – either give up ethnic identities or jeopardize social cohesion. Often for these people, there is no in-between. But ethnic differentiation need not always and inevitably lead to conflict and fragmentation. There are many positive alternatives to these gloomy forecasts. Finally, May (1999) notes that national integration is rarely, if ever, achieved. What usually happens in these sort of drives is that inequalities are sustained, if not exacerbated. Such arguments,

---

[3] For a Canadian version of this see Bissoondath (1994).

however, generally do little to dislodge conservatives from their appeals for a cohesive (and exclusive) culture.

Inevitably these discourses find their way into school policies and practices. Conservative ideologues have recently aligned themselves with other groups, forming what Apple (2000) refers as the new power bloc, a group that has managed to exert considerable influence on contemporary schooling. Besides conservative intellectuals, this alliance consists of neoliberals committed to marketized solutions to educational problems, authoritarian religious fundamentalists worried about the preservation of their traditions, and a professional middle-class that favors techniques of accountability, measurement and management. Recent efforts in Western countries to introduce a market element to schooling have done little to encourage diversity in curriculum, pedagogy or the organization of schooling. Instead this practice has produced a new element of stratification. To make themselves attractive to clients – that is to students and their parents – schools in quasi-market situations tend to favour those students whose performance is likely to enhance their respective images. Consequently, they devote much of their efforts and resources to the academically more able students already enrolled and tend to admit only those students who they feel will be able to excel in this way. The results of this practice do not generally work in the interests of marginalized groups. In England, for example, these practices have resulted in an alarming number of students of color being excluded from school (Apple, 2000; Whitty, Power & Halpin, 1998). Administrators of schools that find themselves in market situations may even go so far as to enunciate their preferences for (and against) students of certain ethnic backgrounds (Trnavnecic, 2001).

Conservative discourses have also influenced efforts to centralize and control what happens at the school level, despite the rhetoric about self-managing schools and the free market. Apple (2000) declares that there is a connection between the free market and the increased surveillance in the educational arena. Efforts at marketization inevitably go hand in hand with policies for the "producers," motivated in large part by a mistrust of the latter. These often take the form of accountability measures or standardized testing for both students and teachers. Unfortunately, standardized testing hits already marginalized students the hardest. In Texas such testing has actually widened the gap between the quality of education for poor and "minority" students and those more privileged students (McNeil, 2000). It also drastically reduces community input into schools. In England, Gilborn and Youdel's (1998) study of the effects of benchmarks indicates that some areas have seen a widening of inequalities. This has occurred between students, schools and ethnic groups, and is especially the case for White and Afro-Caribbean students.

DIVERSITY AND INCLUSION

A starting point here is that the interests of groups of students who are identified as "different" or "minority" will best be served in schools that employ inclusive practices. Inclusive schools welcome, accommodate and celebrate diversity, uniqueness and individuality. Those who value inclusive practice, though, need also to give credence to the role of power. Since inclusion/exclusion is a product of prevailing power relationships, the argument can be made that educators and school administrators need to develop a commitment to power sharing in schools. This requires that they extend to students, teachers, parents and local communities, joint responsibilities over the process of education. Such arrangements can, among other possibilities, entrench a diverse range of perspectives in the curriculum, and as a result, make schools more inclusive places.

Strictly speaking, not all theories of, and strategies for, diversity are helpful in promoting inclusive practice. The least helpful in this regard are conservative approaches. Earlier versions that assumed "different" others were biologically or culturally inferior actually promoted the opposite – exclusion. They also provided a rationale for devoting fewer efforts and resources to their education. Why, for example, pay more attention to these students if they were inherently incapable of doing well in schools? More recent conservative views and alliances with other groups are no more helpful. Although they do not rely on charges of inferiority, their emphasis on cohesion, nationhood, common culture and the market translate into the same kind of practices in schools. For example, market-conscious schools tend to devote more of their time and attention to academically-inclined students capable of enhancing their respective images at the expense of less gifted, sometimes ethnically "different" students. On the other hand, standardized testing has been shown to be of little benefit to marginalized students. In some areas, it has actually aggravated the gap between poor and "minority" students and more privileged ones.

Liberal/pluralist approaches to diversity promote inclusive practice on more counts than conservative approaches. First and foremost, they value the perceived differences in non-Anglo groups, and as a result, favour the inclusion of these groups' respective cultures in school activities. Doing so, proponents believe, will improve the self-esteem of these students and overcome the cultural discontinuities inhibiting their academic performance. This approach displays weaknesses, however, as advocates of critical approaches correctly point out, for the forms of inclusion that pluralists recommend are superficial; these practices do little to address the more extensive patterns of inequality that critical advocates believe are responsible for the difficulties that students experience in school and in life. Effective and sustained patterns of success can only be achieved if the various forms of systemic racism are exposed and overturned. And this requires that educators face up to issues of unequal power.

Critical approaches advocate for a more comprehensive type of inclusive practice than do liberal/pluralists that includes taking stock of the relevance of power differentials. Proponents of critical approaches campaign openly for inclusion, maintaining that it can only be achieved when people recognize, understand and change the structures that constrain and exclude individuals and groups from the privileges that others enjoy. Earlier approaches to diversity, like some versions of multiculturalism, nevertheless presumed an unrealistic static notion of groups. More recent versions of critical antiracism, multiculturalism and postmodernism, however, have begun to address the critical issues of representation and identity. These issues are particularly relevant in today's global village where individual and group identities will continue to evolve in complex and unpredictable ways. Critical approaches to diversity have much to offer principals in their quests to promote inclusion in schools. Among other things, the insights that the critical perspective provides can help administrators understand how they can best contribute to leadership processes that enhance inclusion. In the next chapter on leadership, I develop a concept that is consistent with the pursuit of inclusion in diverse school contexts.

CHAPTER 3

LEADERSHIP AND INCLUSION: A REVIEW

The previous chapter examined various approaches to diversity. In it I concluded that not all of these approaches were consistent with inclusive educational practice. In this regard, critical perspectives proved to promote inclusive practice the most, while conservative approaches were the least helpful. Liberal/pluralist positions fell somewhere in between these two options. This book, however, is not just about general approaches to education and inclusive practice. It explores the work of administrators. My task in this chapter is to develop an approach to leadership that is consistent with critical approaches to diversity and to inclusive practice. Towards this end, I survey and critique various approaches to leadership. I conclude in the end that administrators interested in pursuing inclusive education will profit most from an emancipatory approach to leadership, an approach that differs markedly from more popular views. The most significant variation is that leadership is conceptualized not as a set of traits or actions associated with a particular individual, but as a communal process.

THE LURE OF LEADERSHIP

The idea and practice of leadership continues to be as popular as it ever was. This preoccupation with leadership and leaders is reflected in the words and actions of politicians, captains of industry, educators, academics and media personalities, among others. Their articles show up regularly in newspapers, magazines, journals and books, just as their speeches and casual conversations win wide audiences. Many practicing executives, managers and administrators read these offerings, others attend seminars and sessions, while those who take what these leadership gurus say seriously may eventually attempt to incorporate recommended forms of leadership into their own practices.

Why are we so preoccupied with leadership? The answer lies, in part, with the deeply held cultural belief (Gronn, 1996; Lakomski, 1999) that certain individuals can help us out, particularly in times of uncertainty or change. We continue to subscribe to the notion that particular men or women who are endowed with special skills have the capacity to act so as to profoundly influence future courses of events. And we continue to hold onto the hope that humanity will profit from the words and deeds of these gifted individuals. On the other hand, we also fear for our future in the absence of these sorts of leaders. Loeb (1994), for example, lamenting the apparent dearth of contemporary leaders, asks "Where have all the leaders gone?" He claims that wherever one goes in business and in government, people are perpetually asking where these unique individuals are. Loeb laments that we can no longer name larger-than-life-leaders, like De Gaulle, Roosevelt or Churchill, who seemed to arrive on the scene just in time to pull the world through a crisis. For Loeb, the consequences for industry of this lack of leadership are all too real – as the icons of the business world fall, so do their corporations.

Loeb (1994) and others imply that leaders are needed most when there is a crisis in human affairs, when things seem to be slipping out of control, or when rapid changes render current organizational arrangements obsolete. If we accept the notion that leadership is important, then it would seem that some form of leadership is required for our rapidly changing contemporary social landscape. However, it also may be the case that current and accepted leadership practices and approaches are not appropriate for evolving social conditions. As the context for leadership changes, new or different leadership ideas, approaches, concepts and practices may be in order. This is as true for educational institutions as it is for any other sector of our contemporary world. And like these other areas of life, education in the Western world faces conditions that differ from those of fifteen and even ten years ago. Not least among other priorities, leaders of today's schools must work with school communities that continue to display increasing levels of diversity. This chapter outlines an approach to leadership geared to help school communities cope with the demands associated with diversity and to work towards inclusive forms of educational practice. Before moving on to this task, I will first address the meaning of the term leadership.

THE MEANING OF LEADERSHIP

Those who introduced the concept of leadership into the administrative and organizational lexicon did so with the idea that it would eventually be helpful in improving what organizations do. Over the years, however, the term itself has taken on many different meanings (Gronn, 1996; Leithwood, 1999; Yukl, 1994). Those who explore this concept will not always use this term in the same way. Yukl (1994) has assembled a number of different "definitions" of leadership that scholars have developed over the years. Other scholars go so far as to dismiss the concept of leadership as meaningless. Lakomski (1999, p. 36), for example, maintains that the "concept of leadership is without a referent," suggesting that "there is no natural object of this kind in nature to which leadership refers." Yet others refer to its vagueness (Leithwood, 1999). Despite the complexities associated with the concept, however, many – but not all – who use the term would probably agree that leadership refers to the ways in which processes of influence work between and among individuals and groups. Yukl (1994, p. 3), for one, maintains that "most definitions of leadership reflect the assumption that it involves a social influence process whereby intentional influence is exerted by one person (or group) over other people (or groups) to structure the activities and relationships in a group or organization."

The differences in conceptions of leadership that are relevant to inclusion revolve around the kinds of relationships among individuals and groups and the nature of the influence processes. Those who write about leadership inevitably make assumptions about how people in organizations relate or should relate to one another.

Approaches to leadership also differ with respect to the ends to which leadership efforts are, or should be, directed. Finally, those who study leadership also vary in their beliefs about the best procedure to improve practice. Some scholars make contributions to practice by making more or less explicit prescriptions for leadership practices or by adopting stances that suggest or outline particular inroads for approaching practice. Other scholars contribute to practice in more indirect ways. These people may look to devise concepts to help us understand leadership and organization outcomes or to conduct empirical studies to help describe the behaviour of people in leadership roles and their impact on others.

Each of the approaches outlined below assumes a position on the various elements of leadership, as the term is commonly conceived. Advocates of managerial/technical, humanistic, transformational and emancipatory forms of leadership all take a position on the relationships among organizational members, the form that influence takes, and the ends to which leadership efforts are directed.[1] They also approach leadership from either an explicitly prescriptive stance or one that attempts to explore leadership from a more neutral position. Some, however, are more appropriate than others for contemporary contexts of diversity and for inclusive education.

MANAGERIAL/TECHNICAL LEADERSHIP

Like assorted other forms of leadership, managerial/technical leadership encompasses a number of different approaches that themselves display some common characteristics. Thus, advocates of the managerial/technical approach (Simon, 1957; Fiedler, 1967; Evan, 1973; Katz & Kahn, 1978) assume that there are unique individuals in formal positions of responsibility who are quite distinct from the people who work under them (Callahan, 1963; Perrow, 1986; Gronn, 1996; Vanderslice, 1988). The division between leader and follower is exclusively a function of an individual's place in the organization. Those who see organizations in this way believe that the superiority that accompanies leaders' formal positions entitles them to act in ways that will ultimately influence their followers and benefit their respective organizations. Vanderslice (1988) goes on to say that this hierarchical view of leadership revolves around the idea that a large part of the leader's role is to behave in a manner that best controls or directs the behaviour of the followers. Those who subscribe to this approach believe, as Gronn (1996) observes, that there is a causal connection between what these leaders do and what eventually happens in organizations.

---

[1] Each of these types can be considered "ideal types" in the Weberian sense. They represent "pure" forms. As a consequence, none of the examples cited may conform in every respect to the type with which they are identified. They might just as easily display characteristics from two or more of the other forms of leadership. This typology derived very loosely from other reviews of leadership approaches (e.g. Heck & Hallinger, 1996; Leithwood & Duke, 1996; Richmon & Allison, 2003), traditions in social science and knowledge (Habermas, 1971) and traditions of inquiry in the field of educational administration and leadership. The crucial point here is not that this typology has a firmly anchored foundation but that it makes sense to readers, and in doing so, helps them gain insight in the study and practice of leadership in contexts of diversity.

Pioneers of technical approaches to leadership were motivated by a desire to provide leaders with sure-fire strategies for accomplishing organizational goals. In doing so, they sought to reduce the options for leader decisions and ultimately reduce the chances for leader error. These strategies flowed from the way in which advocates of this approach conceptualized the nature of the influence that leaders used to direct their followers. While those who favored technical forms of leadership believed in the leader/follower dichotomy, they rejected the idea that influence did or should originate with the force of the leader's personality, as in the case of charismatic leaders. Instead, they felt that people in leadership positions could be more effective if they could tap into what they believed to be the more powerful and predictable underlying social processes that dictated what people did in organizations. In this view, both leaders and followers were caught up in causal networks of relationships, and it was up to the leaders to put into place those triggers that would engender desired outcomes. Searching out the appropriate triggers, however, was not to be the task of leaders. Rather, this job fell to social scientists. Their empirical studies were to provide information about the ways organizations worked, and this information would eventually find its way into the hands of leaders who would be expected to act on it. Thanks to social scientists then, leaders merely had to pull the levers and push the buttons that they knew would lead to desired outcomes. Illustrating this point, Greenfield (1986, p. 65) draws on Campbell and Lipham's comparison of the science-supported leader and the bush pilot who

> now finds himself in the pilot's chair of a monstrous flying machine of untold power and dimensions. The social scientist tells us that there are buttons to push, levers to adjust, gauges to watch, beacons to reckon, and codes to decipher. He tells us that one cannot fly this craft by the seat of the pants, but that certain buttons and levers, when actuated, produce specific and predictable results in the performance and the posture of the craft.

This technical ideal took a few years to emerge. Indeed, many would probably agree that the first scientific approach to leadership was not scientific at all, even though it emerged under the banner of "Scientific Management" (English, 1996). It did, however, feature systematic study of the workplace by observers. This approach is best reflected in Frederick Taylor's time and motion studies. His investigations were designed to calculate the most efficient ways of performing tasks (Callahan, 1963). Taylor believed that his studies would provide the basis for leaders to design job tasks in ways that would result in the highest levels of productivity. Other early social scientific efforts at providing advice for administrators were also criticized as not being scientific (Simon, 1957). Henri Fayol and others who worked in this tradition simply outlined principles for leaders to follow. Derided by critics as merely "proverbs," these principles basically advised leaders to plan ahead, pay attention to coordination, refrain from wasting time on routine and established functions, and deal with exceptional cases (Perrow, 1986). In time, those dissatisfied with what they believed to be these unscientific approaches, like Herbert Simon, appealed to more formal models of social science to help leaders do their jobs.

Simon (1957) provided a framework for serious social scientific explorations of organizations that would assist leaders in doing their jobs. His idea was that social scientists should not offer prescriptions for actions because these principles were value-laden and not consistent with an objective scientific exploration. Instead social scientists were simply to explore how organizations worked. They were to uncover the inherent causal networks that were embedded in all organizations, supply the results of their studies to leaders, who were then to act on them. Of the many leadership studies done in this tradition, perhaps Fiedler's (1967) contingency theory of leadership is the best known. Fiedler sought to match leader activities with organizational conditions. He maintained that the effectiveness of leadership style depends on the climate of the organization. For example, emphasis on tasks would work best in some situations, while a relationship orientation would work better in others. What style was more effective would depend on the leader-member relations, the positional power of the leader, and the task structure. Fiedler believed that an ideal fit between leader and organization would best be achieved, however, by adjusting the organizational context to suit the leader's style.

Managerial/technical approaches to leadership continue to appear both in management studies (Gronn, 1996) and in educational administration (Leithwood & Duke, 1996). The former revolve around efforts to cope with an increasingly ambiguous and complex strategic decision-making environment. This is done by systemizing this complexity, by among other strategies, matching structures and roles, and ensuring that individuals with appropriate skills occupy these roles (Gronn, 1996). Managerial/technical approaches in educational administration, on the other hand, focus on the functions, tasks or behaviors of the leader. They are based on the assumptions that these functions, if performed competently, facilitate the work of others in the organization, that organizational members behave rationally and that authority and influence are commensurate with formal positions in the hierarchy. Leithwood and Duke (1996) outline ten such sets of managerial tasks that leaders commonly carry out.

Conceptualizations and empirical studies based on managerial/technical approaches to leadership may not always be helpful to school communities in contexts of diversity. In particular, the leader/follower duality, the concept of influence employed, and the ends to which leadership efforts are directed may not serve diverse communities very well because, among other things, they are not consistent with inclusive practice. As alluded to above, the leader/follower duality is central to a managerial/technical view of leader and organization. The idea here is that it is necessary for someone superior to direct others so that the latter will be able to contribute to organizational goals. The justification for such an approach is based on the notion that

> People are tractable, docile, gullible, uncritical – wanting to be led. But far more than this is deeply true of them. They want to feel united, tied, bound to something, some cause bigger than they, commanding them yet worthy of them, summoning them to significance in living (Bendix in Perrow, 1986, p. 58).

Vanderslice (1988), however, takes issue with the idea that organizations need to subscribe to hierarchical roles if they are to achieve their goals. She believes instead that not only is it possible for organizations to function without static formal leadership roles, but that there may actually be negative consequences that flow from these sorts of arrangements. Vanderslice (1988) contends that research findings indicate that the differential power arrangements that are embedded in traditional hierarchical organizational forms may undermine the goals that leaders hope to achieve and limit rather than maximize the motivation, creativity and productivity of those in low power roles; power differentials may also generate negative consequences for followers' self-concept, task-related behaviour, verbal behaviour and assumption of responsibility. She goes on to illustrate by way of her description of a case study of a cooperative venture in a restaurant – one that includes everyone in the operation and management of the enterprise – how non-hierarchical arrangements can work to the benefit of organizations.

Managerial/technical approaches to leadership also present an unrealistic view of influence. Those who subscribe to this approach presume that the strategic manipulation of underlying mechanical social processes can produce desired effects in workers. This view of organizations and social processes has long since been discredited. In educational administration, Greenfield (Greenfield & Ribbins, 1993) was the first to take on what was the orthodoxy at the time. He maintained that unlike some physical processes, men and women were not always predictable, and as a consequence, were not the appropriate subject matter for a science geared to explain the physical world. But even if one does not accept entirely this existential critique of positivist social science, it is plain that no universal principles of organization have emerged in the interim that would allow people to accurately predict future events in them. The central point here is that whatever influence so-called leaders will have over other organizational members, it won't be the result of the former's scientific manipulation of the latter.

Managerial/technical approaches to leadership also gear their efforts toward ends that may not be appropriate for contexts of diversity and inclusion. Invariably, advocates of this view favour the arrangements that they do because they believe that they are the best way to achieve organizational goals. These goals are generally directed toward fairly narrow ideals of productivity. Proponents of this view believe that the best way to achieve these ends is to find ways to get employees to do things that managers want them to do. This is particularly true for business types, although as we have seen above, hierarchical arrangements may not necessarily be the best way to achieve such ends. While educational varieties of this approach do not pursue quests for productivity in the same way or with the same vigor, they nevertheless stress the importance of organizational goals, like student achievement scores. What they tend to ignore are goals that target wider social issues, like working for changing unjust social structures and forms of community (Foster, 1989). A tight focus may prevent them from directing efforts toward global change or ensuring that marginalized community groups receive fair, equitable and inclusive treatment in schools and beyond. Concentrating exclusively on making sure that student marks are as high as they can be may deflect attention away from these more global social issues of equal or greater importance, and inevitably defeat efforts to meaningfully include these communities in the life of schools.

HUMANISTIC LEADERSHIP

Humanistic approaches to leadership appear in many different forms. But unlike managerial/technical leadership, which is a fairly standard category for classification in reviews of leadership (see for example, Leithwood & Duke, 1996; Gronn, 1996; Yukl, 1994), the humanistic category that I describe here is, in some ways, unique. It represents parts of what other reviewers would classify as moral (Leithwood & Duke, 1996), political-conflict (Heck & Hallinger, 1996), and constructivist (Heck & Hallinger, 1996). This approach took shape, in part, as a response to managerial and technical approaches to leadership. While it shares with the latter an acceptance of the division of leader and follower and, in some approaches, the ends to which leadership efforts are directed, it differs with respect to the nature of the influence which leaders are thought to exert on their followers and in the way in which some – but not all – scholars generally approach the study of leadership.

The humanistic approach to leadership represents a basic shift in the way in which social life is conceptualized. Where managerial, and in particular, technical approaches assume in their models that human life is determined from without, humanistic social scientists believe that social life springs from within. They assume that organizations and the leadership that is exercised within them are the accomplishments of human beings rather than the product of social or natural forces. Taking their cues from elements of the human relations school, the work of Chester Barnard (1938), interpretive social sciences and forms of conflict theory, advocates of this perspective seek to explore leadership from the ground up – in terms of the stuff of everyday life. First and foremost, they are concerned with exploring and clarifying the perceptions of individuals, the frameworks with which they interpret life, the values that motivate their actions, and the ways in which power and politics both enable and constrain the things that they do and say. While some of these people are preoccupied with exploring and describing leadership conceptually and empirically (Hodgkinson, 1978, 1983; Greenfield & Ribbins, 1993; Blase, 1993; Ball, 1989), others are more prescriptive in their orientation (Sergiovanni, 1991).

Advocates of humanistic approaches to leadership feature issues of meaning. They do this because they believe that what people do in organizations is intimately tied to their perceptions. But unlike other approaches to the study of human life, like behaviorism or some forms of deterministic social science, this one does not sanction the idea that individuals' surrounding environment merely impresses itself on them in a uniform way. Rather, social scientists of this persuasion acknowledge that all human beings must interpret what goes on around them, confer meaning on these goings-on, and then act on the basis of them. The complicating factor here – one that confounds approaches that presume uniformity in organizations – is that not everyone interprets life in the same way (Greenfield & Ribbins, 1993; Ryan, 1997). These interpretations depend, among other things, on an individual's biography and the social context within which sense is made (Gronn & Ribbins, 1997). Despite the variability of meaning-making in organizations, social scientists posit that leaders can influence followers by manipulating this symbolic universe, that is, managing meaning (Anderson, 1989). One way they can do this is through their (symbolic) actions. Sergiovanni (1984), for example, contends that what a leader stands for is more important than what he or she actually does. Another route through which leaders can influence followers is by the manner in which they "frame" meaning (Gronn, 1996). Those leaders who are able to make sense of things in ways that appear to favour followers' interests are more likely to be able to get the latter to accept their version of events, and thus influence the way that followers perceive things and eventually act on them.

Those who subscribe to a humanistic approach to leadership also elevate the importance of values and ethics. Taking their lead from the work of Chester Barnard (1938), they maintain that moral issues are an integral part of organizational and administrative life. Hodgkinson (1978, 1992) and Greenfield (Greenfield & Ribbins, 1993), two of the pioneers in this area, take issue with attempts by positivistic social scientists, like Herbert Simon, who encourage scholars to refrain from exploring the value side of administration, in hopes that research into this area can be more objective, and thus more scientific. They argue that it doesn't make sense to eliminate values from organizational and leadership processes because they believe that people's actions spring from their (subjective) values. Thus, what leaders and followers do and say is intimately and ultimately tied to their values. Values, however, can be both a source of influence and a source of conflict. They can be a source of influence when leaders can articulate defensible conceptions of right and wrong (Leithwood & Duke, 1996), prompting followers to accept such positions. But they can also be a source of conflict when individuals' values differ from others. When such conflict does occur, the outcomes are inevitably determined by power and political processes.

In addition to issues of meaning and value, advocates of humanistic approaches to leadership believe that organizational members are also subject to political and power brokerings as they go about their daily business. Rejecting the structural functionalist notion that order in organizations is a product of common value orientations, they see what goes on in schools and other workplaces as the result of negotiations between and among competing individuals and groups. Who gets and does what depends on what kind of power these individuals and groups can mobilize. School organizations resemble more closely battlefields than instruments of order (Greenfield, 1975). So advocates of this position look at a leader's influence in terms of the power that he or she can bring to bear on his or her followers. This relationship is a reciprocal one, as Greenfield and Hodgkinson note. What's more, Greenfield (Greenfield & Ribbins, 1993, p. 166-7) agrees with Hodgkinson's view that leadership is "a matter of will and power, of bending one's will and of being bent in turn by others." Research has described some of the strategies that leaders employ to influence followers in these ways. Blase (1993), for example, maintains that the principals he studied most often employed manipulative rewards that involved prestige, rituals and rewards to influence teachers to achieve goals upon which they agreed.

Humanistic approaches represent a different and, in some ways, a more constructive, approach to leadership than managerial/technical approaches. In particular, their more "realistic" portrayal of what goes on in organizations provides a firmer foundation for understanding life in organizations than the illusory managerial/technical framework. However, like their managerial/technical counterparts, they have limitations when it comes to providing appropriate leadership for contexts of diversity and inclusion. While they nevertheless subscribe to the values and interpretations that necessarily intrude into the research process, most humanistic approaches attempt to distance themselves from explicitly advocating for a particular position. Greenfield's position on this perhaps typifies such stances. On the one hand, he criticizes technical forms of leadership for attempting to eliminate values from inquiry. Yet, he also takes critical theorists to task for adopting explicit value positions (Greenfield & Ribbins, 1993). Others follow this same path. Hodgkinson (1991) implores leaders and social scientists to acknowledge values, yet avoids prescribing value positions, other than encouraging people to adopt reflective stances towards values.[2] Blase (1993) is content simply to describe the power and political processes associated with leadership and school organizations generally. The problem with such a stance, however, is that its preoccupation with a form of neutrality reduces possibilities for doing something about issues that specifically concern diversity and inclusion. If leaders and the social scientists who explore leadership do not incorporate a particular position on inclusion into their practices and studies, then the chances of them achieving anything in these areas is naturally reduced. Not all social scientists, however, adopt this more-or-less neutral position. Sergiovanni (1991) for example, prescribes a number of measures he claim leaders should take to improve their schools. All the same, his general exhortations rarely address diversity-related issues. When he does mention a helpful concept like democracy, Sergiovanni's belief that it should occur with "a framework of shared values" misconstrues the context within which diversity operates, and thus proves to be of little practical help.

Like many managerial/technical approaches, humanistic approaches to leadership also assume that leaders are distinct from followers and that their relationship is a hierarchical one. Those who adopt this perspective often see leaders as occupying formal positions. Hodgkinson's reference to power illustrates such a stance, although I believe that he and Greenfield would not necessarily advocate that leaders bend others to their respective wills, as Blackmore (1996) seems to imply. Rather, the statement reflects their desire to simply describe the *real politik* of school organizations.[3] Even so, this duality has its limitations, just like the managerial/technical and transformational perspectives do, for leadership practices appropriate for contexts of diversity and inclusion. Simply describing rather than challenging structures that inhibit inclusive practices limits possibilities for action.

The way in which humanistic social scientists conceptualize influence is also inadequate for those who seek appropriate ways to lead in contexts of diversity and inclusion. The concept that many of these people employ to understand this influence relationship is power. Unlike managerial/technical advocates who provide little room for the exercise of human agency in their perspectives (see Gronn, 1996), social scientists of the humanistic persuasion go to the other extreme. For many of these people, power is an individual quality. It is exercised by individuals on other individuals. More often than not, analyses concentrate on how individual leaders exercise this power to get their way with followers (e.g. Blase, 1993). Unfortunately conceptualizations of this sort cannot hope to capture the complex and wider social forms of power that generate patterns of inequality that work against the interests of

---

[2] Some might also argue that Hodgkinson does favour transrational values over other types.
[3] Furthermore, in an earlier work, Greenfield (1981, p. 27 as cited in Gronn, 1983) endorses a type of anti-leadership, stating that "we are all leaders."

certain communities of people in diverse contexts. They cannot, for example, explain or acknowledge how power works in more global ways through discourses (Ryan, 1999) or social structures (Troyna, 1993; Dei, 1996) to offer advantages for some students and not others. This also means, unfortunately, that this view of power limits what "leaders" can do to improve the situation of disadvantaged groups. Seeing power as simply a product of individual action restricts educational leaders' scope for action, and thus limits their capacity to counteract a social form that transcends individuals.

TRANSFORMATIONAL LEADERSHIP

Transformational leadership has emerged more recently than either managerial/technical or humanistic approaches, at least in educational circles, although its roots harken back further than either of these two approaches (Gronn, 1995). It has arisen in part as a reaction to the determinacy of the former and the descriptive/analytic stance of the latter. It is appealing to some because it taps into the romantic idea of the hero/leader and it is particularly timely for those who believe we are in need of a savior for what they see as our contemporary beleaguered institutions (Gronn, 1995). Even though it represents a fairly recent gloss on leadership, this approach nevertheless draws on the long tradition of interest in distinguished (charismatic) people (Bass, 1985; Avolio & Bass, 1988). This tradition includes the portrayal of celebrated people in ancient myths, and later, in the arts. Here, narratives revolved around heroes who accomplished great feats and delivered their people from calamity (English, 1996). As the 20th Century dawned, those interested in leadership approached the study of accomplished leaders in more systematic ways. Taking their lead from Max Weber (1947), who employed the term charismatic to refer to gifted leaders who could, among other things, counteract the paralyzing effects of bureaucracy, researchers directed the first systematic empirical study of leadership to the exploration of the traits that leaders were presumed to possess. Those who conducted these studies believed that good leaders were blessed with characteristics that enabled them to perform feats that would benefit organizations and humankind. These attributes, they concurred, were an integral part of who these people were, and as a consequence, could be designated or identified in advance of leaders occupying formal positions. In other words, people were believed to be natural leaders – they were born and not made. Explorations of these traits, then, were designed to provide more information about them and thus help organizations choose their leaders. Such characteristics evolved over the course of these inquiries from explorations of physical characteristics, personalities and abilities to more specific traits such as intelligence, alertness to the needs of others, understanding of the task, initiative and persistence in dealing with problems, self-confidence, and desire to accept responsibility and occupy a position of dominance and control (Yukl, 1994).

While charismatic leadership (House, 1977) and transformational leadership (Burns, 1978; Bass, 1985) are not necessarily identical, they share many characteristics. In fact, charisma is often treated as a component of transformational leadership (Bass & Avolio, 1993; Bass & Avolio, 1994). Approaches to transformational leadership also share elements with managerial and humanistic approaches. In particular, these three approaches are similar in the way they conceptualize leader/follower relationships. In some renditions, though, advocates of transformational leadership see a more pronounced division between leaders and followers. In their view, leaders are gifted in ways followers are not, and as a consequence, it is their responsibility to inspire these less skilled individuals to reach greater heights. Indeed, leaders are expected through their actions to raise the "level of human conduct and ethical aspiration of both leader and led" (Burns, 1978, p. 20), thus transforming both. According to Bass, transformational leaders provide: (1) inspirational (charismatic) leadership, and thus increase follower motivation; (2) individual consideration to followers, and thus cater to their individual needs; (3) intellectual stimulation, and thus influence followers' thinking and imagination; and (4) idealized influence in ways that prompt followers to identify with the leader's vision. Leaders who are able to accomplish these feats are believed to be able to enhance the resources of both leader and led, by raising their levels of commitment to mutual purposes and by further developing their capacities for achieving these purposes (Leithwood & Duke, 1996). Conducting much of the research on transformational leadership in education, Leithwood and associates have identified eight dimensions transformational leadership, including building school vision, establishing school goals, providing intellectual stimulation, offering individualized support, modeling best practices and organizational values, demonstrating high performance expectations, creating a productive school culture and developing structures to foster participation in school decisions (Leithwood, 1994; Leithwood, Jantzi & Steinbach, 1999).

Although some aspects of transformational leadership may prove helpful for leaders who work in contexts of diversity and inclusion, other dimensions are not as useful. Its normative (Gronn, 1996) quality, its focus on a number of useful strategies for leaders, its broad goals, and its inspirational character may help any leader or perspective leader in their work. All the same, the mode in which advocates of transformational leadership conceptualize the relationship of leaders and followers and nature of influence associated with this relationship may offset helpful leadership practices in these contexts. While managerial, humanistic and transformational advocates all favour making a distinction between leaders and followers, this tendency is perhaps strongest among the latter. While they do allude to an interactional component, these scholars nevertheless emphasize the stand-alone, solo performances of leaders who exercise their considerable talents to raise everyone's performances. Unfortunately, this scenario does not allow for alternate leadership arrangements. In particular, it cuts off efforts to imagine or recognize leadership as a collective endeavor (Gronn, 1999).[4] This is unfortunate, for as Vanderslice (1988) and Gronn (1999) have aptly illustrated, collective leadership practices can be very effective. Collective leadership ideas and practices are also ideal for contexts of diversity and inclusion. They make it possible for a range of members of school communities to be involved meaningfully in decisions about fundamental schooling matters.

---

[4] There are exceptions. See Avolio & Bass (1998).

The manner in which transformational leadership conceptualizes the nature of influence between leaders and followers is also problematic. The tendency of advocates of this approach to attribute influence to the force of a leader's personality, skills or any part of what he or she stands for assumes undue causal agency (Gronn, 1996). They take for granted that (some) individuals have the power to affect widespread changes in organizations and their members. Unfortunately, few individuals possess such powers, and thus it is unrealistic to expect people on their own to have such an impact on organizations. What happens in organizations is more likely the consequence of more collective forms of actions, long standing traditions, and cultures or wider social patterns than the result of the actions of a single individual, no matter how remarkable his or her qualities may be. Although mixed, most research in this area illustrates this very point. A comprehensive review of this research shows that the direct effect of leaders in formal positions of authority on organizations is "relatively small" (Hallinger & Heck, 1998, p.157).[5] What influence this single individual has is usually indirect, that is, it is mediated by other organizational conditions. The point to remember here is that what individual leaders do and the impact they have on others will depend ultimately on the social context within which they work. This context generates both opportunities and constraints that both limit and enable what a person is able to do. Foster (1989, p. 44) contends that

> Leadership is always context bound. It always occurs within a social community and is perhaps less the result of "great" individuals than it is the result of human interactions and negotiations. Roosevelt and Churchill, to take two often-cited examples, took advantage of what might be called "a corridor of belief" which already existed in followers. Each leader did not so much create a new and idiosyncratic universe so much as enter these corridors and open various doors.

While Roosevelt and Churchill did accomplish great things, it was the nature of the social conditions in which they operated that allowed them to have the impact that they did. Because such conditions were favorable to them, they were able to engineer favorable results. The corollary to this is that unfavorable conditions would not have allowed them to do what they did; their extraordinary gifts would have been powerless in such situations. And no matter how much they exerted their will, imagination and skill, they would not have been able to pull off comparable feats. Churchill in fact experienced this change of fate: after the war he quickly faded from public life.

The transformational approach to leadership also has other shortcomings. One is that providing conditions that allow for the unrestrained actions of one individual, however limited, can be unhelpful and even dangerous. While there may be many gifted and virtuous people who, when placed in positions of power, may bring about good results, there are also those who may wreak havoc. Another problem is the vacuum in an organization when a gifted or charismatic leader moves on. Because an organization may depend so heavily on one individual rather than on more collective practices or established procedures, organizations may flounder when this

---

[5] Some research does show that leadership has more of an impact than Hallinger & Heck (1998) claim. Leithwood & Jantzi (1999a, 1999b, 2000), for example, maintain that leadership accounts for three to six percent of the variation in student engagement and up to 40% of the variation in school conditions. These findings are the exception rather than the rule, however. See also Gronn (1996, 1995).

one person leaves.[6] Also when so much is invested in one person, the voices of other less prominent individuals and groups tend to be lost, even though transformational leaders may work toward empowering followers and including them in decisions. This may be a problem when it comes to providing accounts to diverse communities. What is being accounted for may reflect only what the transformational leader believes is important, and the forms that these accounts take may not be of the kind that best reach these communities. Ensuring that communities that differ from dominant communities have the same opportunities requires that their desires, knowledge, languages and so forth become part of the school curriculum and that they have the power to voice what they believe. As a consequence, it is important that community members have as many opportunities to take the lead in matters as any formal or informal school leader. Assuredly, this is not always easy in contexts where school communities look to charismatic leaders for direction.

EMANCIPATORY LEADERSHIP

Like the above approaches to leadership, emancipatory perspectives do not constitute a unified movement, and differences among the alternative varieties are manifold. Even so, many similarities loom. Generally speaking, they all take their inspiration from critical traditions in social science. These traditions include, among others, Marxism, neo-Marxism or Critical Theory, feminism, and poststructuralism. Those who work from these perspectives draw on a version of what Fay (1987) refers to as self-estrangement theory. This theory revolves around the idea that humans have created forms of life for themselves that are both frustrating and unsatisfying. Moving beyond these circumstances requires that they find ways to understand their situation so they can throw off the shackles that bind them. The version of this theory appropriated by critical social scientists generally focuses on the plight of the marginalized. These social scientists contend that human beings are responsible for constructing forms of life that routinely provide advantages for some, while at the same time penalizing others. Doing something about this state of affairs requires that they move through three phases – enlightenment, empowerment and emancipation. Knowledge plays a pivotal role here. The idea is that once people are provided with knowledge about their disadvantages, they will be in a better position to intervene in the affairs of the world. This means that their acquired knowledge will empower them (and others) to alter the current unjust social arrangements so that the latter will unfold in everyone's favour (Ryan, 1998). The version of leadership described here advocates for providing the means for educational communities to work toward altering these unjust patterns in schools and in the world generally so that all groups of students will be able to do well in schools and live satisfying lives once they graduate.

---

[6] While transformational leaders may attempt to "build capacity", their departure may have negative consequences for the organization, particularly if they were influential. In Richmond Road School in New Zealand (May 1994), for example, after Jim Laughton, the visionary principal, passed away, school practices reverted back to what they were before his tenure, even though attempts were made to institutionalize the changes.

These emancipatory or critical approaches have evolved over the years. Proponents of the more recent approaches, like poststructuralism for example, have criticized the more traditional Marxist and neo-Marxist approaches. They take issue with the notion that there is a clear division between so-called oppressors and oppressed and that reason paves the way for changes in current unjust social arrangements (Ellsworth, 1989). Poststructuralists contend that domination does not simply allow one group to get its way with another. This is because men and women assume a variety of fluid and shifting identities – from the more enduring yet changing forms of racial/ethnic, class, gender, sexual, religious and other identities to those associated with family, social and work roles, to those ephemeral consumer-driven identities (Ryan, 1998). Thus a so-called oppressor in one situation may become the oppressed in another. One consequence of this complexity is that poststructuralists avoid calls for revolution. Instead they believe that resistance to particular and contextual oppressive patterns offers a more realistic strategy for achieving equity (Foucault, 1980; Ryan, 1998). These ends, though, are not to be achieved through the employment of enduring forms of reason. Rather those interested in equity will find that any change in unfair practices will require they mobilize power through such strategies as forging affinities and alliances with others (Ellsworth, 1989; Ryan, 1998).

Emancipatory and critical approaches to leadership offer more possibilities for contexts of diversity and inclusion than the previous three approaches mentioned above. One reason is that emancipatory perspectives generally emphasize inclusion. Proponents of emancipatory leadership approaches advocate to include everyone, particularly those who are not normally included, in the content and process of schooling. This would mean that they would look for routines to include the perspectives of diverse community groups in the curriculum, and in doing so, reveal their accountability not just to the majority cultural groups but also to all groups. Those who see leadership as a means of achieving these ends do so in the way they conceptualize the relationship between and among individuals in organizations, the nature of influence in organizations and the ends to which they believe leadership should be directed. These approaches are also explicitly normative. They do not attempt to hide their intentions to improve the prospects for marginalized groups.

Emancipatory leadership represents a kind of "anti-leadership." It is "anti" in the sense that it opposes most conventional views of leadership. Instead of viewing leadership as a set of skills or activities associated with a single individual, proponents of this approach prefer to conceptualize leadership as a collective or communal process, that is, a set of evolving patterns and practices that involve a few or many people (Pajak & Evans, 2000). Unlike most other students of leadership, proponents of this approach do not see leadership as something invested in a single and unique individual acting in ways that will best motivate or coerce those for which he or she is responsible. Rather, they question the individual nature of leadership and the division of organizational actors into leaders and followers. They acknowledge the limited power of a single individual acting alone. As Foster (1989) aptly illustrates above, what individual so-called leaders are able to accomplish depends to a large extent on the context in which they are working. They are only able to open those doors which the "corridors of belief" offer up to them at a particular time. In this regard, groups of people are able to accomplish more than most individuals. Emancipatory advocates also do not see a rigid demarcation between leaders and followers. They do not believe that leadership roles should be allocated on the basis of organizational position or assumed personal characteristics or skills. Instead they favour a view that sees the respective roles of leader and follower as interchangeable; leaders can become followers just as followers can become leaders. In practical terms, this means that all members of diverse school communities have opportunities to take part, or be represented, in leadership ventures, regardless of ancestry, ethnicity, social class, gender, education, language, age, and so on. In this sense, this form of leadership is doubly inclusive. It includes everyone equitably in a process that also works for inclusion.

The ways in which proponents of emancipatory leadership see influence may also assist diverse community groups. They acknowledge that influence operates through power relationships, and that these power relationships occur in two significant arenas. The first of these arenas is global in nature. What happens in schools is ultimately associated with power relationships that extend far beyond them. These more global influences find their way into schools, setting the conditions in which varieties of disabling practices occur. So occurrences of racism or that students who belong to certain groups routinely do poorly is not something unique to particular schools or schools generally, but the result of wider relationships of power. But power is not simply a negative thing – something that constrains or oppresses. It also can be positive, that is, it can produce things (Foucault, 1980; Ryan, 1998). So in this sense people can use power to help them resist social forms that place them at a disadvantage. The best way to do this, emancipatory advocates portray, is not through the actions of one individual, but through collective communal processes (Pajak & Evans, 2000). They prefer to see influence not as something that one or more individuals exert on others so that they can get them to achieve organizational goals, but as something that finds regular expression in collective endeavors such as various sorts of coalitions of like-minded people who organize to work for common goals. Leadership here does not revolve around single people we refer to as leaders who wield power, but around community-centered enterprises that mobilize to resist unfair practices and pursue worthwhile social goals.

A key aspect in this approach is dialogue (Smyth, 1989; Lipman, 1998; Maxcy, 1998; May, 1994; Bogotch & Roy 1997; Tierney, 1993; Short & Greer, 1997; Robinson, 1996; Ryan, 1999). In order for diverse community groups to become involved meaningfully in their schools they must be able to communicate with each other and with educators. Toward this end, proponents of emancipatory leadership believe that leadership efforts both depend upon, and should work toward, dialogues of respect and difference (Tierney, 1993). Those immersed in leadership efforts can do a number of things to help support successful communicative relations over time. For example, they might attend to nurturing what Burbules (1993) refers to as communicative virtues. These include, among others, qualities such as tolerance, patience, openness to give and receive criticism, a willingness to admit mistakes, a desire to reinterpret one's own concerns in a way that makes them comprehensible to others, self restraint, a willingness and ability to listen thoughtfully and attentively, and a willingness to re-examine one's own presuppositions and compare them with others. Burbules (1993) goes on to recommend a number of practical strategies that complement these virtues. He maintains that doing such things as restating what one's partner has said, using analogies that resonate with others' experiences, internal cross-referencing with the conversation, using vivid imagery, employing humour and volunteering new information can help involve people in the dialogue (Ryan, 1999). Such strategies are bound to go a long way in including diverse communities in the lives of their respective schools.

Proponents of emancipatory approaches also make little effort to disguise their intentions. Abandoning all pretenses of neutrality, they fully acknowledge their interest in achieving certain ends. But in contrast to those who are concerned with reaching comparatively narrow organizational goals, emancipatory advocates make no attempt to conceal their emphasis on wider social issues and concerns. Their concern with social justice prompts them to look for measures that will allow them to combat social ills such as poverty, hunger, racism, sexism, political oppression and various other forms of exploitation. Taking action requires first, though, that people recognize and understand unfair practices. Toward this end, emancipatory advocates (Foster, 1989, Smyth, 1989) believe that leadership practices need to be educative in nature. They contend that leadership activities ought to revolve, at least in part, around efforts to help people understand how their own and others' freedom is being denied. Included here are systematic efforts to critique the status quo. Such a strategy would involve taking a step back from many of our taken-for-granted practices, placing them under a microscope and subjecting them to a critical gaze (Foster, 1989). Only in this way can we come to live with the ways in which people are unfairly treated, challenge these injustices, and take concrete steps to change them. Doing so will go some distance toward ensuring that all community groups will be equally served by the schools their children attend and the society in which they live.

INCLUSIVE LEADERSHIP

Not all approaches to leadership are equally equipped to promote inclusive educational practices. Approaches that favour distinctions between leaders and followers, see leadership in terms of solo performers and performances, rely on manipulative forms of influence that call on either technical or personal forms of power, focus on comparatively narrow organizational goals, and assume forms of neutrality, will not guarantee that diverse groups will be included equitably in the content and processes of schooling. Granted, many of the practices and concepts that managerial/technical, humanistic and transformational approaches to leadership advocate and/or employ to understand and improve schools will not serve all school communities equally. Emancipatory or critical forms of leadership, however, show more promise. This is because they are inclusive both in the kinds of relationships they envision and the ends for which they strive. Advocates' emphases on communal rather than exclusive and individual action, inclusive forms of practice, and attention to global forms of power and justice, critique, action and dialogue will help, rather than hinder the opportunities and life chances of traditionally marginalized groups.

Those interested in promoting inclusive schools need to see leadership as a collective process. Associating leadership with an individual by virtue of his or her hierarchical position of power in an organization will not further the cause of inclusion. So the mantle of leadership should not fall naturally and exclusively to the principals on the basis of their officially designated roles. There is more to be gained by promoting a process of leadership that involves or represents everyone equitably and consistently. This does not mean that principals will have less to contribute to such a process than others. Certainly principals will have much to contribute at the school and community level. This is because the power they derive from their organizational position, their experience and their knowledge will in most cases make them more influential than any other single individual in their school communities. They can use this power to initiate, nurture, and sustain a leadership process that works for inclusion in ways that most other members of their school communities cannot. The rest of this book explores principals' efforts to do just this. It will show how they contribute (or do not contribute) to this inclusive leadership process. The next two chapters probe how principals perceive and deal with a significant impediment to inclusion – racism.

CHAPTER 4

ADMINISTRATOR PERCEPTIONS OF "RACE" AND RACISM

This chapter explores the issues of "race" and racism. In particular it examines administrator perceptions of "race" and racism. It is difficult for administrators to ignore issues of "race" and racism, particularly if they work in diverse contexts. Like everyone else, they look at the world through "racial" or "racialized" lenses. In other words, their world views are ultimately tinged or tainted by their attitudes towards "race." These perceptions will inevitably dictate how they respond to various situations, and even though administrators may choose not to acknowledge issues of "race" or racism, their (sometimes unconscious) views on them will dictate what they do. Issues of "race" and racism are intimately linked to inclusion. Racism is by its very nature exclusionary. Its multiple forms routinely exclude or marginalize those who are subjected to them. Both personal and impersonal kinds of racism methodically place their targets at a disadvantage – whether at school or in the world outside of school. So, if administrators are to promote inclusive practices in their schools, then they need to be able to understand issues of "race" and racism in ways that enable them to do something constructive about racism. Unfortunately, this understanding is not always prevalent, as this chapter will illustrate.

THE CHALLENGE OF "RACE" AND RACISM

School leaders of today face many challenges. Prominent among these challenges is the task of ensuring that all – and not just some – students perform well in their respective institutions. This is no small task, given the history of variable student achievement and the reality that this variability is not random. Compelling evidence now exists that shows that student success and failure follow particular patterns. One of the most noticeable of these patterns revolves around "race" and ethnicity. In Western countries like Canada, the United States, the United Kingdom and Australia, students who do not belong to the dominant ethnic (Anglo) group routinely have to overcome significant barriers if they are to succeed in the educational institutions of these countries. These systematic barriers are in some ways associated with a phenomenon we have come to refer to as racism. Some scholars go so far as to say that racism and issues of "race" are the main reason why students of colour do poorly in schools (Young & Laible, 2000; Ogbu, 1994). While racism has undoubtedly always existed in some form or another in schools, it has become more obvious in recent times, particularly with the increase in diversity in Western countries. Many researchers (e.g. Alladin, 1996; Dei et al. 1997; Gillborn,

1995; McCarthy & Critchlow, 1993; McLaren, 1999, Sleeter, 1996; Troyna, 1993) have documented its pervasive presence in educational institutions.

Against this backdrop, racism ought to be a serious concern for educational leaders, particularly those who hold positions of responsibility in schools, like principals and head teachers. This is because the place where racism is often most evident is at the school level. It is here that the various and complex forms of racism emerge in their obvious and not so obvious guises – in the name-calling, harassment and the interpersonal conflict, in the subtle stereotyping and taken for granted understandings and practices, and in curricular and organizational patterns. It is also at this site, despite efforts in recent times to (re)centralize control over schools in Western countries (such as the United Kingdom and Canada) that principals and head teachers exert substantial influence. While their power to control school activities may be diminished in some areas, school leaders still have the capacity to influence the day to day actions of teachers and students perhaps more than any other single individual. Indeed Troyna and Hatcher (1992) and Gillborn (1995) have demonstrated in their research that school administrators can have a decisive effect on racist and antiracist practices in their schools. This is why it is so important for them to acknowledge the presence of racism in their schools and to understand it in a way that provides a basis for constructive responses to it. Unfortunately, the slim empirical evidence that does exist – most of it in studies that focus on other issues or individuals – indicates that school leaders tend neither to notice nor to attend to racism or issues of "race" (Anderson, 1990; Lipman, 1998; Taylor, 1998; Young & Laible, 2000). This evidence also indicates that administrators do not understand the many ways in which racism works (Young & Laible, 2000), even though such understanding is crucial in formulating effective strategies for preventing future racist practice (Henze, Katz & Norte, 2000). This chapter documents how school administrators – principals in this case – perceived racism in their respective schools. It maps the extent to which these administrators believe racism exists in their schools and the ways in which they understand it.

RACISM, EDUCATION AND ADMINISTRATORS

Racism is a much-contested concept. Over the years, scholars, practitioners and policy makers have attributed a number of meanings to it. Of the many different understandings of racism, two stand out. One views racism as a form of individual prejudice. The other considers racism as a more global, systemic phenomenon. Many advocates of the latter perspective also acknowledge that racism is both individualistic and systemic. This territory has been covered extensively over the past few years (see, for example, Gilborn, 1995; Henriques, 1984; Rizvi, 1993a; Shohat & Stam, 1994; Troyna & Hatcher, 1992; Troyna, 1993; West, 1994). These and other scholars have identified these two versions of racism, mined their respective meanings, and drawn out the consequences of adopting them. The reason that I revisit these issues, as will become apparent below, is their relevance to the ways in which administrators of schools (and students and parents) perceive racism. Administrators' preference for one particular understanding of racism will inevitably have significant consequences for what they do about the actions associated with racism.

Inquiry into "race" and racism in education has a comparatively short history. In the United States some of the earlier research was conducted by Coleman et. al. (1966). More sustained efforts to explore the area were carried out by researchers in the United Kingdom. Much of this research was quantitative. While earlier inquiries of this sort (e.g. Keysel, 1988; Maughan & Rutter, 1986) were misleading, subsequent advances in quantitative research (e.g. Smith & Tomlinson, 1989) made it possible to delineate in clearer ways the interaction of selected and student achievement (Gillborn, 1995). The problem with some of this research, however, was that it saw racism in terms of the "overt" variety, ignoring the more subtle and widespread forms. This also was one of the criticisms of multicultural education at the time. Troyna (1984; 1987), for example, argued that attention to the more superficial aspects of "culture", and a view of racism as a form of individual prejudice deflected attention away from the more enduring, insidious and less visible effects of racism. Despite the shortcomings, this and future research would document the inequities between dominant and non-dominant ethnic groups in educational institutions.

More recently, scholars have explored racism in schools from a perspective that acknowledges its systemic and subtle character. They have probed the implications of the study of racism and practice of antiracism in education (e.g., Dei, 1994; Gillborn, 1995; McCarthy & Critchlow, 1993; McLaren, 1999; Troyna, 1983). Academics have also conducted empirical studies that have explored, for example, racism in children's lives (Short & Carrington, 1999; Troyna & Hatcher, 1992), the perspectives of Black students and parents (Dei et al., 1996; Dei, 1996; Gillborn, 1995), the attitudes and views of White teachers (Sleeter, 1994), racist discourse in curricular materials (Johnston, 1996; Ryan, 1999) and issues of language and identity (Ibrahim, 1999). But while scholars have attended to the perspectives of students, teachers and parents, they have largely ignored educational administrators. With a few exceptions of inquiry into administration and diversity (Anderson, 1990, 1996; Derkatz, 1996; Lipman, 1998; Maxcy, 1998; May, 1994; McKeown, 1989; Reyes & Capper, 1991; Riehl, 2000; Ryan, 1998a; Ryan & Wignall, 1996; Valverde, 1988; Winfield et al., 1993) little, if any, attention has been accorded to "race" or racism and administration. The few articles that do address racism/"race" and administration, often as a peripheral issue, as mentioned above, indicate the tendency of administrators not to recognize racism in their schools (Anderson, 1990; Lipman, 1998; Taylor, 1998; Young & Laible, 2000). And for those administrators who do acknowledge its presence, evidence suggests that it is crucial that they understand it in a way that is helpful in eliminating or reducing its effects (Henze et al., 2000; Solomon, 2001).

THE PRESENCE OF RACISM

Many principals in my study were reluctant to acknowledge that racism occurred in their schools. Those who did acknowledge it, moreover, tended to emphasize its insignificant nature. This was true for those administrators who were interviewed, just as it was for those who completed the surveys. One of the survey respondents actually wrote in "No incidents" on his form. The results of the survey perhaps testify more eloquently to the general ambivalence towards racism. The best indicator of this was in the responses to the query "If you have ever had any occurrences of racism in your school, please indicate the form and frequency of occurrence on a five point scale." The mean response was 1.9, which in this case roughly meant between "none" and "little." While this figure in itself is revealing, the difference between the mean response to this question and the other questions in the survey that dealt with issues other than racism, was even more revealing. This is because all other means were at least 3 and some were as high as 4.

Given the diverse nature of most of these administrators' schools and the documented nature of racism at both personal and systemic levels, these responses are both puzzling and troubling. Why is it that principals are reluctant to admit to the presence of racism in their schools? There are several plausible explanations. One is that administrators simply could not see racism or issues of "race" in their respective schools. This phenomenon is not something that is necessarily unique to these principals, however. In an American context, Anderson (1990) documents the inability of the administrators in his study to notice what he perceived as pressing issues of race in their school communities. He maintains that they were conditioned to ignore the constraints that worked against students of African heritage and to believe in the promise of upward mobility for all students. The result was that they did not – nor could not – acknowledge the presence of these students nor the injustices that were associated with them. Anderson (1990) also notes that this is a problem that goes well beyond schools. He argues that, with a few exceptions, Black Americans have been rendered invisible throughout American history. But this is not something that remains in the past. Anderson (1990) contends that while racism continued to be perhaps the most pressing contemporary social issue in the United States, it rarely formed part of any public discourse.

This process continues unabated today. The United States, however, is not the only country where threatening issues like racism are ignored or swept under the carpet. In some places, particular agencies may actually take an active role in rendering these issues invisible. In Ontario, Canada, for example, the current conservative provincial government has engaged in such a practice. Upon taking office in the mid 1990s, it proceeded to dismantle the anti-racism unit established by its predecessor. It also went about purging words like "equity" from government documents and policies. Government officials did this on the pretext that racism was not a problem, that is, it did not exist, at least in sufficient portion to warrant attention, in Ontario schools. These officials also believed that a preoccupation with concerns like equity would get in the way of their agenda of standardizing schooling for all children in the province. The government took these actions despite the fact that the province continues to become more diverse by the day – more immigrants than native born citizens now call its largest city home – and compelling evidence that non-Anglo groups face substantial barriers in their education (e.g., Dei, 1996; Ryan, 1999; Paquette, 1989, Canadian Council on Social Development, 2001).

At least two more explanations can be cited for administrators' failure to acknowledge racism. The first revolves around the implications of acknowledging racism in schools. Most principals may feel obliged to convey a positive image of their respective schools to parents, the larger community and the district office. Acknowledging the presence of racism or other undesirable elements like violence, for example, risks characterizations of their school as racist or violent. Such labels may inevitably reflect badly on the principal him or herself and the school community generally. Acknowledging racism, however, may also convey an unrealistic image of the school. This image consciousness is perhaps even more pronounced in those places where market or quasi-market conditions exist, as in England or say, Slovenia. In these places, schools (and administrators) are under considerable pressure to construct images of their schools that would motivate potential clients to choose them over others (Ball, Bowe & Gerwitz, 1994; Trnavecic, 2000). Potential clients would quite possibly be less willing to select schools that were perceived as racist or violent. But even where boundaries and clientele are for the most part fixed, as in Ontario for example, administrators may still feel the pressure to present an unblemished image.

The last reason that principals may not acknowledge racism in their schools is in the narrow way in which they view racism. There is evidence in their interview responses to indicate that this may be the case. Their statements reveal that administrators generally equate racism with individual acts on the part of people who they believe are malicious, ignorant or not capable of exercising good judgement. In other words, most administrators do not see racism as systemic. This contrasts with accounts of how students and parents may see racism.

ADMINISTRATOR PERCEPTIONS OF RACISM

Those administrators who acknowledged the existence of racism in their schools identified a number of its forms. They maintained that racism emerged in incidents of harassment, in situations associated with the school, and in graffiti and other similar forms of representation. Administrators also acknowledged the presence of stereotyping, but generally did not equate stereotyping with racism. In all of this, they saw racism primarily in terms of individual actions or isolated incidents.

Harassment

A number of administrators identified acts of harassment as occurring in their schools. In the survey items, the mean response (on a 5 point scale, 1 meaning never, and 5 frequently) for harassment of teachers was 1.6, for students, 2.3, and others, 2.0. Harassment of students was significantly higher ($p = < .05$) in schools with an Anglo population of 70% or larger than in schools of different mixes. Incidents of physical violence and name-calling were also significantly higher ($p = < .05$) in these particular schools. These findings are similar to findings in a study conducted by Verma et al. (1994) in the United Kingdom. This study found that there were higher levels of name-calling in schools where one group predominated. Furthermore, it was the non-Anglo groups who generally reported this abuse.

Incidents of abuse were significantly lower in schools that were truly multi-ethnic, that is, where no one group was clearly the numerical majority.

A few administrators – mostly at the secondary school level – recall occasions where more serious kinds of harassment have taken place. These incidents required that administrators call in the police. In these cases gangs of students had verbally and physically assaulted individuals. Like Troyna and Hatcher (1992) discovered in their study, the more common incidents involved name-calling. Most administrators believed that much of this name-calling, although it may involve references to "race," heritage or background, was not racially motivated. They didn't believe that perpetrators initiated such actions to play out their racist beliefs. Rather, they contended that individual students used racial name-calling as a tool to lash out at other students in the heat of the moment. Tom, for example, an administrator of a diverse elementary school, maintained that racial comments are often

> made simply out of frustration – so you attack the person, the colour of the person, or whatever. And oftentimes it's done in the fashion of "it's the only mechanism that I have to get back at this person, so I will do that." It's not done in an ongoing sort of way, and I think there's a difference there … it's very easy to target someone's skin colour because it's right there at your fingertips.

Administrators' reluctance to acknowledge the presence of racism is typically reflected in Tom's view and in the views of many others in this study. These administrators believed that racist name-calling is not actually racist, but a tactic used by children who don't always understand what they are doing to get the better of their protagonists in a conflict situation. In their study, Verma et al. (1994) also had this sense. They reported that students used racial/ethnic names as weapons or reinforcers in the context of student-student abusiveness. The names happened to be just one of many potential resources for these students, and they put them to use in the heat of the moment. While this may be true in some cases, it need not apply to all situations. In another study conducted in the United Kingdom at the elementary level, Troyna and Hatcher (1992) found that name-calling occurred in a range of settings – from situations where some children employed deliberate, "cold," repeated harassment of Black children to assert dominance over them, to situations where children used it much the same way as described above. To be sure, some children expressed regret afterwards and others insisted that they used racist language as a means of defense. But whether or not the intentions of the children are "racist" or not, they nevertheless draw on an already available racist repertoire or racist ideologies (Troyna & Hatcher, 1992) to help achieve what they want. And in doing so, they continue to breathe life into this racist culture. Additionally, despite some perpetrators' wishes for the name-calling not to be "racially hurtful," it is difficult to temper the effects of this sort of practice. Edward, for example, maintained that any kind of racial name-calling, whether or not it is employed with racist intent, is hurtful to some of his students. He is the principal of a high school that serves a handful of Native students, and contended that name-calling has a particularly negative impact on his Native students.

> My Native students are most sensitive about anything that could be construed as name-calling, some sort of put down…. At the same time … that's also an issue for my non-Native students. It seems it's almost a way these days for kids to be hurtful of others. So it's kids in general … But

it seems to be heightened when you bring in the culture because right away the Native student
will say, "They name-called me because I'm Indian."

This feeling coincides with the impact that name-calling had on the some of the students who participated in Dei et al.'s (1997) study of Black high school students. Students were particularly disillusioned by these name-calling experiences and frustrated when little or nothing was done about the harassment. This is an experience not shared entirely by Anglos who administrators say are sometimes the objects of racist name-calling. They refer to this as "reverse" racism. Noreen, who is principal of a large and diverse high school, explained that

We've had several reverse racial comments. We find Black students calling our kids names – "honkies", things like that. You know mostly you concentrate on the White kids calling Black kids names; that's kind of the traditional white racism. We get more the other way and our kids are really surprised by that and have hard time with it. They don't really know how to deal with it because it's never happened to them before.

Despite the fact that Noreen believed that "our (White) kids" have a "hard time" with being called "honkies," it is difficult to equate their experience with harassed Black students. To begin, the former's heritage or lineage is never really threatened. It is continually reinforced through institutionalized practices and discourses, through the media and in personal interaction. So aside from a personal affront that could come from any confrontational interchange, the effects of being called a "honky" are likely not to go much beyond the situation. From Black students' perspectives, however, hearing racist and derogatory comments from fellow students only builds on the obvious and not so obvious negative images that they encounter in the media, in the school curriculum, and from countless other sources and situations. These reinforce for many of these students the negative or not-so-positive attributions they continually hear about themselves and the groups to which they belong in other aspects of their lives. This does not mean that racist name-calling directed at White students should be condoned, or that such charges by these students be ignored or minimized (see for example, Gillborn, 1995). Rather it merely signifies that racist name-calling will produce different effects on those who belong to traditionally marginalized groups than it does on those who identify with dominant and privileged groups.

"School" Racism

A few administrators acknowledged forms of racism that originated with the school – whether it was in the curriculum or in the actions of educators. These administrators spoke mainly about students and parents who accused the school of being racist. They rarely referred to incidents where they believed school personnel acted in a racist manner. When they did, it was either in very general terms or they attributed the actions to aberrant individuals. In this sense, it is typical of the kinds of reactions that Sleeter (1996) observed of teachers in her research. She found that White educators were generally reluctant to address issues of White racism. To do so might undermine their secure positions of privilege and also cause them a certain amount of personal discomfort. For many White people, it would simply be easier to side-step or ignore such issues, and in doing so, preserve images of themselves as good people.

A few administrators in the study acknowledged the presence of racism in their schools. Peter conceded that some teachers in his diverse secondary school may be racist. He said, "I think we just assume that our teachers are okay, that we don't have racist teachers ... and it's wrong to do that. It's wrong to make that assumption about our teachers." Mary, an administrator in a large and diverse secondary school, also noticed racism among some teachers. She said that "we had a few teachers make some fairly derogatory remarks about East Indian students." She remembered one teacher in particular who would

> do things like call down to the office. I remember this one time [when she said] "I want the [vice principal] up here. There's a number of East Indian students in the hall." I mean she would call us if "There's a number of Black students bugging my kids. There's a number of Italian people in the hall." You know, when you think of all the things, it sounds ludicrous, but she didn't mind saying that in front of her whole class, over the PA. And she mentioned today this little girl came back to class and "Oh she was wearing all these robes," she said and, "Oh God, she smells."

The characterization of racism in this and other cases is in terms of acts perpetrated by individual teachers who are mistaken and perhaps malicious in their intentions. In the latter case, this particular teacher possessed racist attitudes that led her to say and do things that were harmful to individuals and groups. Mary, the administrator, makes an obvious effort to distance herself from these views and actions, implying that she or the school does not sanction them. In subsequent dialogue, however, she said little about how she deals with the actions of this teacher or others like her.

When administrators spoke of school racism it was usually in the context of describing the charges of racism by students and parents. Most of their talk about racism revolved around their concerns over student and parent beliefs that the school was racist. Administrators said they often have to deal with the accusation that they are picking on certain students because they are Black. Larry, who is the principal of a diverse high school, said that he has heard many times the statement, "You're picking on me because I'm Black." He believed that these charges are "ploys" to get school officials to back off. He recalled one student who regularly took this tack.

> My vice principal has dealt more with him ... I just remember my vice principal mentioning it to me once when he was dealing with him over something, not terribly serious, just pesky behaviour that was inappropriate and taking up the teacher's time, and maybe people aggravated at him sort of thing ... Every once in a while he goes too far with his comments or whatever and he puts them off. But I suspect maybe this was just a ploy that he was using, too, that maybe he thought we would back off if he used this statement.

It is little wonder that the members of the Black/African community feel somewhat oppressed, and as a consequence, believe that educators react negatively to them on the basis of their "race." There is little question that they are the objects of both subtle and more obvious forms of racism. Among other setbacks, Black students are the specific target of stereotypical discourses in schools. In a study of a diverse school (Ryan, 1999) both teachers and students saw Black students, particularly the males, as "threatening" and "violent." They also opined that Black students – both male and female – were less academically able than other students. These views – supplemented by other similar views circulating in the wider society – affected the way in which these educators subsequently interacted with students. For example, some teachers would be more likely to suspect Black students who do well on tests to achieve this standing by cheating. One student in this study eloquently described how she had to work much harder than other students to achieve the same standing as they achieved (Ryan, 1999, p. 105). One only has to read a few of the statements of the high school students who Dei et al. (1997) interviewed to get a sense of the desperation, frustration and hopelessness that Black students feel as a result of the unfair treatment they received in schools. Accordingly, while there may be some instances where Black students use the "picking on" charge as a ploy, it is easy to understand why many others would legitimately make such a claim. These claims are a response not only to individual situations but to a whole range of situations and patterns that penalize them specifically because they are Black. Thus students of colour may well be in a better position to ferret out the racist implications and meanings of particulars words and actions than more naïve or less informed teachers and administrators (see also Gillborn, 1995; Solomon, 2001).

All the administrators who brought these issues up reacted in similar ways to the accusations, generally dismissing them as inaccurate, and insisting that they are addressing the students' behaviors only. Larry, for example, said that he responds to students by saying

> It has nothing to do with what colour you are. It has to do with your behaviour and you're being treated the same way as everybody else here. We have a code of behaviour and we have expectations. We expect people to live by it and live up to it.

Like many of the other administrators with whom we spoke, Larry maintained that he was colour-blind when it came to dealing with students who were not White. This belief is something that is not unique to these administrators, as I observed above. Studies of teachers (Rist, 1978; Sleeter, 1993, 1996) indicate that many educators believe that they are also colour-blind. This view assumes that there is no difference between black and white, that people are all the same under the skin (Henriques, 1984). It also assumes that "race" plays no part in the way people perceive things or in the actions they take that flow from these perceptions. Considerable evidence exists, however, to the contrary. As West (1994) maintains in the title of his book, "Race matters." What happens with these administrators, as with the teachers in Sleeter's (1993, 1996) study, is that they try to suppress negative images that they commonly associate with people of colour, an exercise that according to Sleeter, requires considerable energy. The result is that they adopt this colour-blind discourse to justify their actions, even though their perceptions and actions are ultimately "racialized."

One of the most striking aspects of administrators' talk of charges of racism is how they differ from the ways in which students and parents see racism. Administrators, as presented above, tend to view racism in terms of mistaken, intentional and/or malicious acts perpetrated by individuals. Student and parent complainants, on the other hand, take a more global view. They identify systemic patterns in the ways in which the school (and society) treats them. This was also found in another study (Ryan, 1999). In that study, a student of African heritage eloquently described the treatment that he and his friends received as systemic in nature. He believed that racism was part of a system that provided advantages for some, while "keeping minorities down." It seems that those who are the objects of oppression are often better able to gain insight into the manner in which they are oppressed than those who are not or those who, however unwittingly, are part of that system of oppression (see also Nieto, 1999 and Taylor, 1998). It is apparent that administrators may not be able to appreciate references to systemic forms of disadvantage. In the following passage Pat, an administrator in a secondary school, was unable to understand what some students mean by their references to "we." He said

> I have a real concern that the Black kids in this school feel alienated and feel that "we're" out to get them. And when we ask them who's the "we", they don't have an answer. So it's vague – "There's somebody out to get us; they want to get rid of "us" from the school."

Pat acknowledged that Black students in his school felt alienated, but he had difficulty understanding their articulation of the source of this alienation. One way of interpreting this impasse is to see it in terms of the different meanings that the two parties associate with "we/them." On the one hand, the students' "we" can be understood as an attempt on their part to identify the source of their feelings of oppression. Their vagueness need not necessarily be seen as an inability to understand what it is they are experiencing, but an effort to articulate a complex system of oppression that goes beyond those individuals who are merely its messengers, a system that is "at once grindingly quotidian and maddeningly abstract" (Shohat & Stam, 1994, p. 23). While individuals may be part of this persistent pattern of oppression, their acts need not always be overtly racist, even though when combined with other series of acts, they may well have the same effect as more explicitly racist acts. Pat, on the other hand, questions the vagueness of the students' "we". He believes that the students are vague because they lack credibility. For him, identifying racism means fingering those individuals who are responsible for perpetrating specific and identifiable acts. And because students cannot do this, he believes that there is no racism in his school. For him, racism is exclusively associated with misguided or malicious individuals, and not with wider and more subtle practices and patterns.

Graffiti

Although not common, a few administrators also note the presence of racist graffiti in their schools (mean = 1.9). The presence of this graffiti was significantly greater (p = < .05) in schools with an Anglo population of at least 70% than in schools with other mixes of school populations, in larger rather than smaller schools, and in secondary, as opposed to elementary schools. The symbol that appeared most on the walls and other surfaces, according to these administrators, was the swastika. Many were not sure, however, whether those who drew them were aware of their significance. Mary, an administrator in a diverse secondary school, for example, didn't "think that these people know what it means... [To them] it's just a symbol, and they're really doing it backwards, too, which leads me to believe that they don't really know what they're up to. But it is a symbol of hatred and that is worrisome." Cathy, another secondary administrator, also described a situation in which she believed the offender didn't know what the swastika meant. She said that "one of the kids one time drew swastikas on a paper he handed in to his Jewish teacher and she was devastated. And it really hurt because she thought this was a nice kid who really liked her." Cathy discovered in conversation with the young man that he didn't know what the symbol stood for, and as a consequence, was very upset when its significance was explained to him.

Administrators identified other sources of racist representations. Pat told of the time the student newspaper in his school published a story that he considered racist. Although the paper was usually checked for potentially offending pieces by the school staff, the article slipped by them on this occasion.

Stereotyping

Administrators also referred to issues of stereotyping in the interviews. Most, however, did not consider stereotyping as a form of racism. Many administrators believed that stereotypes were mistaken beliefs that distorted how people perceived certain groups of people. A lack of knowledge or understanding, in their view, prevented men, women and children from seeing groups and the individuals associated with these groups as they really were. There were a few administrators who denied that stereotyping was a problem in their schools. Noreen, for example, an administrator in a diverse elementary school, said that "we don't find it [stereotyping] here in terms of racial groups, cultural groups." She did admit, though, that it may be lurking "below the surface" although she had not "picked up on it." She also maintained that her staff tells her that "we don't have things like this happen in our school." The surveys, on the other hand, reveal that administrators believe that stereotyping practices occur in their schools. They also indicated, however, that the levels of stereotyping were low. Administrators said that there was very little stereotyping on the part of teachers (mean = 1.8). On the other hand, they felt that stereotyping was more common among students (mean = 2.4). The findings also reveal higher incidents (according to administrators) of stereotyping in larger and medium sized schools than in smaller ones ($p = < .05$). The latter would seem to support the notion that stereotyping does not occur as much in contexts where people have the opportunity to get to know one another, as would presumably be the case in smaller schools. Nevertheless, there is also evidence, presented below, that knowing someone is not always sufficient to counteract stereotypical views.

Administrators' perceptions of stereotypes in their schools follow familiar patterns. They spoke of groups who they believed were unjustly depicted, as less intelligent and more violent than others. They also spoke, with concern, of "positive" stereotypes, groups who they saw as being portrayed as more athletically or academically gifted than others. They are correct to be concerned about such positive stereotypes, because the consequences that result from their use are not always as obvious as those associated with negative stereotypes. Their use assumes an unnatural commonality among members of the group associated with this stereotype; individuals who employ this generally overlook the diversity within such groups. This is particularly true when it comes to depictions of the "model minorities." In this vein, with his study of Asian students in the United States, Lee (1996) unravels the stereotype associated with this model minority. He documents the diversity within this group, dispelling among other things, the myth that all of these students are ideal students. While some of these students perform well academically, others do not. Still others are engaged in resistant activities not normally associated with Oriental students. The problem for the less able students is that they may have difficulty living up to unrealistically high expectations placed upon them by teachers and others. These students may feel undue pressure and experience frustration at their inability to achieve levels beyond their capacity (see also Ryan, 1998b, 1999).

Administrators also alluded to those "hidden things" – things of which we are not always aware – that lead us to view people in mistaken and harmful ways. Pat, for example, said that "there are all sorts of hidden things that we do in dealing with races different than us, and we've got to be cognizant of them." He doesn't elaborate any more on this process other than to say that we need to know about them, to understand them, and presumably ourselves. His views coincide with the views of other administrators who believed that stereotypes result from ignorance. Diane, for example, maintained that "a lot of stereotypes come about because we don't understand. And it's that fear or ignorance that creates negative stereotypes." Diane adds the element of fear to the mix here, believing that fear and ignorance prevent understanding and in the process, create harmful stereotypes. The implication is that the understanding that would come from knowing more about the group or groups in question would help those in educational communities to see the truth and penetrate these stereotypes. Understanding would, as one administrator affirmed, result in "people who are looking at people as individuals" and not as members of stereotyped groups. Administrators, however, also pointed out that this would be no easy task, given the static nature of their teaching staffs. While the student population over the past few years has become increasingly diverse, the teaching staffs have not changed a great deal. They are still primarily composed of Anglos who often know little about the many groups of students they teach. Larry, for example, maintained that "the teachers here ... have been here for quite awhile. There probably should have been more staff turnover, but there hasn't been. And so they haven't had a lot of experience with other groups of nationalities." Verma et al. (1994) describe similar things in their study in the United Kingdom. They found that teachers tended to concede to their lack of knowledge of students' cultural backgrounds, regardless of what they were. Furthermore, school staff did not know enough about the demographic profiles of their student intakes.

While some administrators in the study recognized the harmful effects of stereotyping, most did not see this as a form of racism. Yet the effects of stereotypes can be even more devastating than the more explicit forms of racism. This is because stereotypes can easily become taken for granted and an accepted way of life; they can be harder to recognize and, ultimately, to challenge than more obvious forms of racism.   However, the view of stereotypes that many administrators take – that of mistaken images – is not particularly helpful in combating them; it assumes that representations should (and should be able to) accurately portray the designated group as it really exists.   Unfortunately, such a stance ignores the perpetually evolving character of groups, the diversity between and among group members and the social and political nature of the construction of group images.   Quite simply, it is impossible to expect to be able to portray an entirely accurate representation of a group of people either in words or images.   It is also equally unrealistic to expect that these images will be inherently positive (Ryan, 1998b; Shohat & Stam, 1994).   A more sensible view is to see images of groups as the products of politically-grounded sense-making frameworks or discourses.   The task for educators then is not to attempt to supply illusory accurate information, but to construct and circulate discourses that work in the interests of groups who most often are stereotyped.

CONCLUSION

School leaders have an important role to play in the battle against racism and exclusion.   Principals, in particular, are in unique positions to influence the course of events at those sites where racism most often shows itself.   But to contribute to such an enterprise, they must be capable of acknowledging the presence of racism in their respective schools and to understand it in a way that enables them to do something constructive about it.   As the results of this study show, however, this is not always an easy thing for administrators to face up to.   While there were exceptions, many administrators were reluctant to acknowledge the presence of racism in their schools, and if they did, preferred to minimize it.   And, when they did make reference to racism, they generally saw it as a form of individual prejudice.   These findings are not unique to this study, however.   The slim evidence that does exist in other inquiries (Anderson, 1990; Lipman, 1998; Taylor, 1998; Young & Laible, 2000) also suggests that administrators tend to overlook issues of "race."   Many may have difficulty even saying the word "racism" (Rizvi, 1993b).   In this and other studies there is also evidence that indicates that there are administrators who do acknowledge issues of "race" and are able to see past the more superficial manifestations of the conflict in their schools that are associated with it (Solomon, 2001; Henke et al., 2000).   There were also a few administrators in this study who were able to also do this.   Regardless of how they understood "race" and racism, many administrators in this study spoke of the things that they did to combat racism. The next chapter documents these efforts.

CHAPTER 5

ANTIRACISM: STRATEGIES FOR COMBATING RACISM

Racism is not consistent with inclusion. At the very least it is exclusionary – racism marginalizes groups of people, depriving them of the privileges that others routinely enjoy. To ensure inclusive practice in schools then, educators need to work toward eradicating all forms of racism. This requires that they plan and put into practice antiracism programs. Antiracism consists of forms of thought and/or practice that seek to confront, eradicate, and/or ameliorate racism. It implies the ability to identify a phenomenon – racism – and to do something about it (Bonnett, 2000). As we have seen, however, racism can take many forms and it can be defined in different ways. Inevitably, how people see racism will dictate the nature of the antiracism practices that they favour. If, for example, educators perceive racism in terms of personal prejudice, then the actions that they endorse will be designed to eliminate this kind of racism, frequently at the expense of other broader forms of racism. This was the case in this study. Because many administrators saw racism as individual prejudice, the kind of antiracism that they sponsored in their schools was designed, for the most part, to eradicate this specific form of racism. While some administrators did refer to measures that targeted broader and subtler forms of racism, most concentrated their efforts on eliminating or discouraging prejudice that they believed originated with particular individuals.

Administrators described a number of measures that their schools took to combat racism. These measures included two kinds. The first was proactive. Administrators adopted these strategies to ward off potential racism. Toward this end, they sought to tutor their school communities and to develop policies. The other strategy was reactive, taken after the fact. Its components included dialoguing with students and parents and punishing offenders. As alluded to above, these measures were by and large designed mostly to deal with only one kind of racism – individual prejudice. Both the preventative and reactionary strategies targeted, for the most part, individual acts of discrimination, while failing either to acknowledge or address racism as a systemic phenomenon. Some administrators, however, did talk about strategies for dealing with some of the more subtle forms of racism like stereotyping, but without necessarily acknowledging them as examples of racism. The measures that they recommended were designed to help people understand stereotyping and the nature of the groups in question.

PREVENTION

Administrators believed that it was important to have strategies that prevent racism. Toward this end, they talked about putting in place measures to ensure that racism

75

would not occur in their schools. They employed programs designed to enhance understanding and knowledge, instituted school codes and rules and introduced conflict mediation. While these strategies are to be commended for addressing forms of individual prejudice, they are, for the most part, ill equipped to deal with the subtler and more global forms of racism.

Promoting Understanding

Administrators valued strategies that helped students, teachers and administrators understand the processes associated with racism and stereotyping, understand one another and understand one self. They believed that sponsoring various activities would educate members of their school communities in ways that would help them understand these phenomena, others and themselves.

Administrators favored measures that would allow their teachers to understand more about issues of racism. One particularly effective way to do this, they believed, was to get students to talk about it in front of teachers. Administrators spoke of how effective theatrical presentations proved to be for both students and staff. Referring to one such event, Noreen said "It really ... opened their eyes. The staff told me that for some that was a real eye-opener, that these things really happen to our kids." Noreen described in detail the interactive theatrical presentation, an event that they had to raise money to sponsor:

> With very limited props, just enough to suggest something, as opposed to being in full costume, ... they asked students to come up from the audience and share a scenario where either they had been discriminated against or they had discriminated against someone else, or they had observed discrimination. And they came up and told their story to the actors and to the moderator and, in effect, to the whole audience. Now you would think that adolescents would be hesitant to go up and talk.... What they did was they described the scenario and then the actors, using, as I said, a minimum of props, acted it out. And then they went back to the person and said, "Is that what you were talking about? Is that what happened?" And the one who was telling the story from the audience could then direct, modify what they had done. "No, it wasn't quite like that," and then they would do it again. "Should it be more intense? Should the people be more angry? Should they be less complacent?" or whatever. And the kid actually got to direct it.

Administrators also sponsored panel discussions and town-hall meetings, and invited guest speakers to talk to students and teachers. Respondents to the questionnaires, however, believed that these measures were less effective than others in combating racism. Although seen as generally somewhat effective, sponsoring discussion forums (mean = 2.84), inviting guest speakers (mean = 3.06), and sponsoring theatrical productions (mean = 3.21) were all situated at the lowest end of the effectiveness scale. Respondents indicated that the former two were more effective ($p < .05$) in secondary and larger schools. Even so, some administrators who were interviewed talked about the benefits of these strategies. Kevin, for example, maintained that his school has had "assemblies where we'll have a panel of kids and they'll talk about racism and what it feels like to be different from other people." Pat employs another strategy, sponsoring town-hall meetings where he encourages students to talk about things like whether there was any racist behaviour in the school. Administrators believed that this kind of strategy is important in educating educators about their own stereotyping tendencies. Noreen said:

One of our Black students talked about being in gym class where they were playing basketball, and as they were playing he talked about trying out for a hockey team that weekend, and two other boys in the class said to him, "What are you talking about? Blacks don't play hockey!" That was the scenario presented ... It's using kids to educate the staff, because the staff were in the assembly – this staff who for the most part tells me, "We don't have things like this happen in our school." Now, perhaps that's not a major racial incident, but nonetheless we're talking about stereotyping.

Administrators also talked about other ways to hear what students have to say. Kevin said he likes to have other kinds of feedback from students, like forms that students fill out. At the time of the interview, his school was piloting this feedback process. The idea with this and other strategies is to give voice to those not normally heard from. Doing this, these administrators believed, would provide others – teachers in this case – with a view of a side of life that they did not normally have access to. While they did not indicate that student perceptions were to be valued more than teachers' – in Kevin's case he felt that for student opinion to count, it had to be expressed by more than a few – they nevertheless regard student perspectives as providing teachers with valuable information both to understand what some students experience and to do something about the injustices associated with these experiences. Hearing from students also provides administrators with the opportunity to legitimate and circulate discourses or ways of making sense that are not normally in circulation, at least in some circles. So, for example, this is an opportunity to spread the idea that it is commonplace for young Black men to play a variety of sports, or that young Black men do more than just play sports. Kevin provided a flavor of the kinds of things he thought his school community should know:

We have wonderful Black kids who can't play basketball. It's expected that everybody who's Black can play basketball. We have lots of them who can't. We have lots of kids who are Chinese who are not great ping-pong players. We have Chinese kids who are good basketball players. We have Black kids who are extremely good in calculus.

Administrators also surmised that familiarity with others can dispel negative stereotypes. Kevin, for example, believed that when you know someone

You can't think of stereotyping or you can't be prejudiced or you can't dislike another group if the person who is sitting beside you in your office, and is probably one of your best friends in that office, is a member of that group. We judge, I think, ethnocultural groups by the people within them that we know. And I think society does that. ... They tend to judge the Canadians of Caribbean origin from those ones they happen to see on the front page of the *Sun*, who just shot the policeman. ... But when the people you're seeing from those groups are professionals like you, or are fine people, then those stereotypes quickly go away.

Other administrators favored other ways of becoming familiar with individuals and groups with whom they do not normally have immediate contact. Cathy, for example, provides opportunities for students in her school to attend various kinds of celebrations. One group, she noted, attended a Chinese New Year celebration last year. Others have in the past had the opportunity to participate in many other feasts and celebrations. Students and parents have the opportunities at these functions to meet others they wouldn't ordinarily have interacted with, and to get to know them.

Kevin and Cathy are echoing a common refrain here. It goes something like this. The images of members of particular ethnocultural groups that we see from afar, like those on the front page of newspapers, are sometimes negative. But even though they are negative, they are also powerful because they influence the way in which many people view these groups. People tend to make up their minds that all people who belong to these groups are like the ones who grace the front page. We do not always know any different because we know few, if any, members of this group personally. The only information we have of them is through these sources. If only we did know these people better, we could understand that they are really not like the characters in the newspaper. Knowing them on a personal and individual basis would allow us to understand the group as a whole, knowing full well that they are "okay" – that "they" are, in many respects, just like "us." The reality is, though, that "they" are not all just like "us." In fact various ethnocultural groups – of which Anglos are one – differ in many respects from other groups. This does not mean, however that they are naturally "good" or "bad." Moreover, it is not realistic to expect the former – that all members of such groups are "fine people", as Kevin believes. This myth reduces the complexity and diversity of such groups to a point that is difficult to accept. As a matter of course, there will be some who depart from prevailing norms. This happens with all groups. Also, knowing people more closely or being in closer physical contact with them will not always guarantee a more positive attitude toward them. In fact, in some cases it may accentuate already negatively formed views (McCarthy, 1990).

Steve takes this familiarization process perhaps further even than Kevin and Cathy. He stressed the importance of getting to know unfamiliar others on an *individual* basis. Getting to know people individually, he said, would allow people to penetrate group stereotypes. He maintained that it was important to deal with students individually rather than as part of groups:

> What happens when you deal with things … in a group is they tend to roll off. "It's the other person that's doing it, not me. I would never do that. It's the other person." And so you deal with it individually. If somebody says, "Well you know, this group is strong mathematically." No [you can't say that].

Where Kevin maintained that getting to know individuals was a good way to understand what groups were really like, Steve discounts groups altogether. Echoing liberal sentimentality, he believed that the only fair way to treat people was individually, denying any potential group affiliations. Acknowledging links with groups, he appraised, would unfairly penalize those who were associated with them. Engaging in such a practice, as illustrated above, however, is to deny the role of ethnicity and "race" in the lives of students and teachers. The views and actions of all those in educational communities are "racialized," that is, modulated by the ways in which people see issues of "race" and ethnicity. Whether people want to admit it or not, they treat individuals on the basis of their perceived group memberships. Student fortunes are in important ways tied to these group memberships. While it may be laudable for Steve to want to avoid the negative consequences of associating unfounded general assertions and stereotypes with certain groups, denying the role of "race" in people's fortunes and opportunities is not helpful either.

Administrators also thought that it was important to provide opportunities for both teachers and administrators to reflect on their often taken-for-granted attitudes and practices. Some of this occurs "naturally" in the course of people coming to terms with their changing situations. Larry, for example, said that some of his teachers have had to examine what he believed to be their unconscious stereotypes:

> I think that our staff is an experienced staff and I think it has had to go through the growing pains of being more aware of the various groups. But they're pretty sensitive [to their own thinking about their expectations]... and I think [they will] step back from themselves occasionally and will ask themselves the question ... and looking at kids and saying, "Is there something in my thinking, just because that's the way I am, that is putting a false expectation on a child?"

Other administrators divulged that teachers and administrators may not always engage in reflection on their own. As a result, it helps to provide opportunities for them to do so. Diane felt that in order to deal with destructive stereotyping practices, educators need to pay attention to what they do, what they use, and how they think. She maintained that this would "involve staff talking about their own feelings and some of our own stereotypes." Others felt that it helps when people can get others to help them look at their practice. A case in point would be Pat, who said that he found it useful for his fellow administrators to share their critical feelings with him. He told us the story about how his co-workers noticed that he treated Hong Kong families differently than South African families (see chapter 9). This was something that surprised and shocked him, prompting him to admit that, whether we realize it or not, we all have racist tendencies. Here Pat illustrates the importance of reflection. Indeed, it was this collegial critique that prompted him to reflect on his own taken-for-granted attitudes and practices. Engaging in reflection can be useful because it provides educators with an opportunity to get past one of the more insidious aspects of stereotyping practice – its taken for granted nature. Stereotyping is part of a process in which we engage order to make sense out of our experience (Ryan, 1998, 1999). We draw on pre-existing frameworks that assist us in this sense-making endeavor. But these frameworks can become so ingrained that we rarely pause to think about them. In order to give us a chance to pause and reflect on them, we need to problematize them. An effective way to do this, to help people step back from their taken for granted practice, is to have someone else take a look at this practice, much as Pat and his colleagues do. They critically appraise one another's practices, letting one another know things that they may not easily be able to recognize without this sort of help. If Pat's story is any indication, then this mutual reflection can assist educators to recognize and avoid stereotypical practices.

Interpreting and Enforcing Board Policy

All the school districts for which the administrators in this study worked had some form of antiracism policy. Administrators generally found that these policies were helpful. They provided both guidance and support for them in dealing with diversity and "race" issues. Janice, for example, maintained that

> It's good to have something that you can look at and talk to the children about, and even, in the case of this one parent who was in talking about wanting her child in a class of her own kind, if you can refer to something and say, "This is what our Board believes and this is what we believe. And we're trying to teach our children, and that saying goes against line three here, or whatever." It's something tangible.

Some administrators preferred to talk about people rather than policies. They preferred to take direction or advice from these individuals from the central office rather than review pieces of paper. Most found that they were very constructive in clarifying policy and providing support for these policies. Not all found central office administrators helpful, however. Wilbur, for example, told us that one of his superintendents often frustrated his efforts. He maintained that this individual "became panicky when any racial or cultural issues comes up."

While most school administrators felt that board policy was generally facilitative, they also indicated the processes associated with the recognition, interpretation and implementation was far from straightforward. To begin with, school administrators may not always be aware of the existence of certain policies that concern diversity or antiracism. The survey portion of this study confirmed this impression. It indicated that there was virtually no agreement among administrators who worked in the same district about the existence of such policies. It was rare that any two administrators would identify the full range of policies that existed in their board. Another source of ambiguity in the policy process revolved around administrators' personal biases. Some principals felt that they had a duty to implement board policy regardless of how they might feel about it. This meant attempting to put their personal biases aside if they did not coincide with board policy. Diane said

> I have to recognize some of my prejudices. And I feel strongly as an employee, whether it's this board or anywhere else, there are times when you have to leave your personal feelings at the doorstep because it's my responsibility to ensure that board policy is implemented. That's my responsibility. And that makes me face my prejudices and put them on the back burner.

While Diane perceived a need to transcend personal feelings, others acknowledged that interpreting board policy always involves something personal. They believed that personal biases and world views will inevitably have an impact on how the policy is interpreted and thus the way it will be implemented in the school. Larry said

> With over a hundred elementary schools out there, you get various principals interpreting these directives and saying, "Hmm, I guess that means such-and-such," or "Oh, that means such-and-such." And principals are very individualistic and strong-headed types and proceed to implement how they see what it means.

Implementation often involves translating these more general policies into school policies and regulations that are appropriate for the local school contexts. So the way in which policy gets translated in different contexts may vary considerably. And this variation will inevitably be associated in some way with the principal's values.

Developing School Policy and Behaviour Codes

Administrators in this study were convinced that developing school policies and instituting behaviour codes were effective ways to prevent racism. These policies were often guided by board-wide policies or arose as schools attempted to realize their own particular goals. Al pointed out that his school policies were closely related to Board policy. He said, "we basically have a Board policy called XYZ that outlines what the schools, teachers, and students use in terms of antiracism. Our particular school policies flow from that."

Most of the policies that dealt with antiracism and diversity revolved around behaviour codes. Administrators believed that these codes were the most effective way of preventing racism. This is confirmed in the survey portion of this study. Respondents to the questionnaire believed that this practice was more effective than any other method (mean = 3.99). Administrators who were interviewed were also enthusiastic about behaviour codes. For example, Randy felt that spelling out expectations and consequences for violations can act as a deterrent for racism. He said, "I haven't had a single complaint that I can think of in the last two years. I think it's having kids know they [racist acts] will not be tolerated. If something does happen, you treat it very strongly and the kids will accept that." Diane, on the other hand, believed it important that each student know what to do when they experience racism. She said that the procedure in her school "spells out very, very carefully what you do and how you go about it, and if in fact you feel you are being discriminated against, and it spells it out for student, for staff member, for parent, for anyone." Diane also put a priority on emphasizing not only rights but also responsibilities for everyone in the process. She said

> I personally have difficulty with the fact that we always emphasize rights, and I believe in rights strongly, but I believe in responsibility first and foremost. So we as a staff ... with the kids and through the [school council], we try very hard to address "What are your responsibilities and what are your rights regardless of race, religion and sex?" And we talk about the responsibilities, so that even if you're the one who has been harassed or whatever the incident is, you still have certain responsibilities.

For the most part, administrators believed that it was important to include fellow administrators, teachers, other school staff, students, parents and community groups in the development of school policies, and in particular, behaviour codes. Diane formally involves the community, through the Parent Council, in the process of developing and reviewing codes of conduct. Mark also involves others in the development of his school's student code of conduct. He said it

> became very much a community partnership development, with an eight member writing team – two parents, two students, two teachers and two administrators. And the eight people wrote together, wrote the code of conduct, having gone back to various groups and for all kinds of input along the process. So we ended up with a code of conduct that was very much a partnership, consensus-building, basically.

Mark's school was not alone in its quest for consensus. The survey indicated that policies were generally determined at the school level as a result of consensus (mean= 3.78) rather than other methods. Consensus, in Mark's case, was reached with difficulty, however. It was not an easy matter to get some of his "conservative" teachers to agree with students who had "some very left-wing attitudes." He said that eventually after "a lot of political maneuvering" and with a bit of give-and-take, they managed to hammer out an agreement. He felt that the whole process, although difficult at times, was worth it "because out of it evolved a code of conduct that was acceptable to everyone. They could live with it." Mark is one among many in the study who recognize the importance of this broad-based input. Gillborn (1995) and Corson (1996) also endorse this kind of process. Gillborn (1995) writes that one of the schools that he studied sought wide input from all groups, including students. Corson (1996) also recommends an inclusive approach to policy development through the various stages, including problem identification, a tentative policy stage, error elimination, adoption and implementation.

Other principals in the study also found it particularly useful to have students included in the policy development process. Diane makes it a point to involve her student leadership group in the development of school policy. She said "The leadership group is involved in any decision-making, whether it was a homework policy for the school or a behaviour code for the school – and all those things are reviewed annually." Paul also includes students when putting together and reviewing student codes of conduct. He said the students were comfortable in the process. Paul expected to encounter unhelpful forms of resistance, but instead found that students took the whole process very seriously and made constructive contributions.

On occasion, development of these codes may be motivated by specific problems, while at other times these specific situations may require additional consideration. When Noreen recognized that her school needed something to deal with unacceptable behaviour at sporting events, she met with her coaches. She said:

> This year we sat down with the coaches and we talked about safe coaching. How do you coach properly? What do you do if a fight breaks out? Is there any name-calling back and forth? As coaches what do you do? How do we make sure our kids are safe? How do we teach our kids to respond to name-calling? And we developed a guideline for that.

While school policies and codes of conduct may cover a wide range of areas, they inevitably overlap with antiracism efforts. Peter's school now advertises its antiracism policy in various venues. He said, "We have a now-articulated race relations policy which we send out and which we use. It's written in our discipline code, it's written in our student handbooks, it's on the wall out there." Concepts like respect, harmony and equality surface regularly in these statements. Wilbur said that his school's code of conduct firmly specifies "that everybody's to be treated equally, with the same kind of respect." Al's elementary school, on the other hand, promotes an atmosphere where "putdowns" are actively discouraged. He told us a story about how many of his students were shocked at the behaviour of politicians in the House of Commons when they traveled to Ottawa. He said:

> I think the most telling fact that it [respect for others] had been internalized was when we took the grade eights to Ottawa about three years ago and they were fortunate enough to see Question Period in the House. And they were totally shocked, totally amazed, at how the "put-downs" were done to the Prime Minister. And [they said], "That's a put-down sir!" That told me that the kids understood.

Janice publicized at her school a statement called "The Blueprint for Harmony." She said that it is basically "try and get along with everybody, no matter what race or sex or whatever. And it's based very much on the race relations policy." Typical of statements like these are the document that Al's school circulates. It is entitled "Vision for Fairness," and runs as follows:

WE, THE STUDENTS AND STAFF OF TOWNVILLE PUBLIC SCHOOL, WILL:

- Respect the rights of all people who enter our school regardless of race, religion, gender, language, culture, age and ability.
- Recognize the strengths and talents of each individual.
- Recognize stereotyping and prejudice as destructive.
- Recognize ethnic, sexist and racist jokes as hurtful.
- Recognize the misuse of peer pressure and the misuse of physical violence and social avoidance as destructive.
- Use language that respects the equality of the sexes.
- Encourage all people to express themselves in a polite and responsible manner sensitive to the feelings of others.
- Provide a warm and inviting atmosphere to students and staff – particularly to those new to our school.

These administrators rightly emphasize the importance of integrating codes of conduct that address racism into the school regulations. Clearly spelling out the consequences of certain actions can be a powerful deterrent to racist activities. For the most part, however, the regulations that these administrators describe are designed to address individual/group and overt acts of racism. With exceptions, they are developed to deal almost exclusively with the more obvious and easily identifiable prejudicial activities. They are generally directed, moreover, at one group – students. Little in these codes allows the school to address some of the more subtle manifestations of a phenomenon that are systemic or institutional in nature. Although the codes may have some success in preventing one kind of racism they will do little to stave off some of the more pernicious and widespread forms of racism that penalize students at least as potently as the more overt forms do.

Worth noting are examples of school policies that do address more systemic and institutional forms of racism. One of the schools that Gillborn (1995) studied directed antiracism policies at much more than just student behaviour. To begin, this school's policy committed itself to practices and philosophical positions that clearly reflect a determination to recognize and oppose racism, and to address cultural diversity in as positive and rigorous a way as possible. More specifically, it made recommendations for the system of appointments and promotions, highlighted the need for increased awareness and training across the school, and laid down guidelines for the curriculum. It also recommended various forms of student and community consultation and committed the school to the continual monitoring of examinations, assessments and "testing for bias."

Curricular Representations

Probably because of their tendency to see racism in terms of obvious acts of prejudice, administrators who were interviewed spoke little of racism in the curriculum. Their preoccupation with these things and the accompanying inability to identify some of the more subtle manifestations in pedagogy or curricular materials as racist perhaps explains why they did not spend much time talking about the curriculum.   Nevertheless, respondents to the questionnaire indicated that incorporating antiracism ideas into the curriculum was a reasonably effective way of preventing racism (mean = 3.48). Ironically, though, they believed that sponsoring a program of antiracism education was the second least effective means of dealing with racism (mean = 3.0). This would seem to indicate that administrators would be more comfortable incorporating select ideas rather a wholesale program of antiracism. Indeed a piecemeal type of approach would not be as threatening to the current program as would a more systematic one. Unfortunately, this approach goes against current thinking in the field. Effective antiracism and diversity programs require whole-school approaches (Gillborn, 1995; Troyna, 1993; May, 1994; Nieto, 1992).

Some administrators said in the interviews that it was important that the resources that they employed be free from stereotypes. These people encouraged librarians and teachers to look for harmful stereotypical images in books and bring them to administrators' attention. Cathy is one administrator who took action to eliminate unacceptable books from her school's library and replace them with others. She said that when

> I was first a principal, I went into a school that had textbooks that were from the late 60s because the previous principal didn't believe in spending money on books. He was very frugal with funds and he felt that things like history never changed, and so we had "perfectly good, intact history books. We don't need to buy new ones." Except our views of what's acceptable in books has changed, and staff would bring me some of these books that would refer to the Indians as savages – that sort of thing. I went to my superintendent and said "I need some money!" and I said, "Look at what we have here to work with." And he gave me some money and we bought some new books.

Cathy has also taken other measures to ensure that students have appropriate materials with which to work. She said that she recently purchased

> Some Clip Art for the computer and I was looking at it, realizing this is great. We now have some people around here that are Oriental and Black and just part of the little pictures and things that you can add into things, whereas before you wouldn't have found it so you might not even have thought of using it. But once it's there it's handy and readily acceptable. If you're looking for a picture of a parent and a child, okay, you take it and you don't worry about the race or whatever, and you don't have to search for something different.

It is important to include a wide variety of images and narratives and to exclude stereotypical and negative images or narratives in curriculum materials. It is virtually impossible, however, to eliminate the latter as well as potential interpretations of other images and narratives that work against groups of students. So the screening of materials needs to be supplemented by a critical approach to all curricular materials. In this regard, educators need to be able to recognize oppressive images and discourses in curriculum materials when they see them, understand their genesis and production, contest them and provide alternate ways of making sense of the material (Ryan, 1999). Teachers and administrators need to be both willing to engage in these tasks and to possess the considerable skills that it takes to engage in such an enterprise.

Mediation

More typical of administrators' concerns than curricular issues were disruptive situations and behaviors that they associated with prejudice. To head off such occurrences in the future, some administrators introduced conflict resolution programs. Tom said that his school had implemented a conflict mediation program where students act as mediators and attempt to help other students get through conflict situations. He related that these mediators have a standard set of questions

> to ask persons in conflict, and they go through a series of questions. It's really a self-resolution of the conflict as you work through these questions, and it works very well. It helps to diffuse it … and that way if the issue happens to be racial and religious, it doesn't matter because the children are still working through to get the key problem, "he took my ball," so they can get to the bottom of it. If that's not a solution for them, a resolution, then it's brought to the office.

Diane, an elementary school administrator, puts another spin on the conflict management program. She prefers to call it, "'I care' helpers." She said:

> We started out with "I care" language when we discovered – that it wasn't just a multicultural thing – that the kids were fighting and we were putting out the fires. It took us an entire year to really be able to identify what the problem was and the problem was that the kids couldn't verbalize what was bothering them, so they were much quicker with their hands and their feet. So that's how we developed "I care" language, so that if you hit me I would say to you first, "When you kick me that really made me angry and I want to kick you back. Would you please stop it?" Now that also tied into racism.

Educators and students who use peer mediation to diffuse conflict – racial or otherwise – generally like it (Samuels, 2000). It has been effective in some situations, in part, because it empowers students to take action themselves. Peer mediation, however, is not a panacea; it has a number of limitations. It should not be employed in cases where conflict is "serious" because it places much responsibility on students, and it may deal with some of the more superficial aspects of deeper forms of conflict without addressing the latter. So, for example, those involved in conflict resolution may be so concerned with ensuring that the parties in a racial conflict situation get along that they may overlook the role of "race" or racism in the conflict. By smoothing over the more superficial aspects of racial conflict, they may not diagnose, address or contest the racism that lies at the heart of it.

REACTIVE MEASURES

Administrators take action when incidents of racism are brought to their attention. Generally speaking, administrators maintained that they adopt "zero tolerance" policies to combat racism; they simply don't tolerate what they perceive as such action. Tom, for example, maintained that in his school "It's a zero tolerance policy if the situation becomes that of a racial slur nature." He and his staff take immediate action in such cases. "We tend to deal with the child on the basis of discussion and the inappropriateness of the action and so on." Other administrators also noted that they react not just to racist put-downs, but to all sorts of such actions. Jerry said that he deals with "non-racial put-downs" just as seriously as he does with the racial

ones.   Administrator or school reactions generally fall under three categories:
dialogue with students, dialogue with parents, and sanctions or punishments.

Dialoguing with Students

The first action that administrators usually take in cases where they believe racism is
involved is to bring in the alleged offender or offenders and victim or victims to talk
with them.   A first order of business is to find out the facts of the case.   This,
however, is not always a straightforward matter, as the participants often present
different versions of the facts.   At times, particularly when younger children are
involved, the offender will not know the significance of his or her words.   Steven
relived that this sort of experience is common, citing the time when he asked a boy

> why he'd said that. He didn't really know. He called the boy a nigger and he really didn't now
> why he'd called him a nigger. And I said, "Well, where did you hear that word?" "I heard it on
> television." "Do you know what it means?" "Well, no. It just means Black." But I said, "Do
> you think it's a favorable comment to make to somebody? Is it a compliment?" He said, "No."
> He knew it was something negative. He didn't quite know what it was.

Steven believed that an important part of his job was clarifying racist incidents
for the involved parties.   In this case, he saw his mission as clarifying for the
perpetrator the meaning of the words that he used.   Other administrators also
believed, particularly with younger children, that they had a duty to convey to them
the significance of their actions.   Sometimes this meant going beyond those involved
in the incidents to talk to other children.   Larry has done this on more than one
occasion.   He feels that it is important for him to help not just the students who are
involved in the racist incident to understand what has taken place.   He said that
educators also

> need to make sure we're addressing what the real problem is, and with a little kid that's
> sometimes hard. And it needs some addressing, in the way of speaking to the rest of the children
> and making sure they understand that they're being cruel by calling names or whatever.

Administrators may also attempt to bring offenders and victims together.
Edward adopts such a strategy, but only in appropriate circumstances.   He said:

> It's a case where we take a couple of tracks and it depends what stage the students seem to be at.
> But at some point we've got to counsel them individually and bring them together and form
> apologies, make them understand what was hurtful about what they said, make them understand
> that they better not say it again.

Jerry also attempts to bring students together when racial incidents occur.   He
believed that these meetings present opportunities for students to problem-solve for
themselves.   He felt this way because he acknowledged that there will always be
things that occurred in such situations about which adults will never know.   He
maintained that

> When you bring them together and they accuse one another of these things, you do a lot of
> counseling and problem solving. You can't necessarily prove that one person said this and
> another said this, or you usually find if someone's complaining that a racial put-down happened,
> then I hear the other child saying, "But you yelled in front of everybody that I was fat and that
> really hurt! So I found something that hurt you back." And it might have been something else.

We spend an enormous amount of time dealing with stuff that no adult's heard, but helping kids to problem solve.

Some administrators thought that extra work may be needed with the victim. Edward, for example, observed that sometimes it is necessary to spend time with a student who has been victimized. He asserted that it helps to "separately work with the student on the side and try to show them that they (the offenders) didn't really do it because you're (a member of a visible minority group); they were just putting people down and they're not right doing that." While Edward is right on one count here, he is mistaken on others. It is important to spend time with victims of racism, but not just after they have been subjected to more obvious racist acts. It is necessary to continuously respond to their unique needs – needs that arise as a result of their experiences in a world where they are routinely marginalized. Telling these young people that their membership in a particular group has nothing to do with being the object of racist acts, however, is not helpful either. While being a member of a group certainly does not cause racist practice, saying that group membership has nothing to do with racism is not exactly accurate. Those who are members of particular groups are frequently the objects of racism. Racism exists and it punishes members of certain groups. The clearer we are about this, the sooner we will be able to get on with doing something about racism. So educators would be better off not glossing over or covering up racist practice, but helping others understand it, acknowledging the injustices associated with racism, and working with others to do something about this racism.

Dialoguing with Adults

Many administrators contact parents when their children are involved in racist incidents. Diane is one administrator who will "automatically call you as a parent" in these cases. She maintained that she will say to the parent, "I notice Johnny makes a lot of comments, such-and-such. Can you help us?" Diane also noted that in such cases, "there's a letter that is sent home, [outlining] what kind of, say, racial slurs or whatever kind of behaviour occurred that's not acceptable... So that you make parents very aware of that." Jerry uses what he referred to as "specific language" in his notes home. He does this because he wants parents to "understand what we're dealing with here; we're not dealing with soft issues here, we're dealing with very hurtful things."

Not surprisingly, parents react differently when informed of their children's inappropriate behaviour. Cathy, for example, maintained that not all parents are supportive of the school's response to racist acts. Routinely, she brings

in the parents and says, "Your child's saying these kinds of things that aren't acceptable, are hurtful"... When I've dealt with this kind of thing in the past, sometimes the parents are horrified to hear their child saying that sort of thing and you know they will be well counseled at home. Other times parents are not so supportive and you have to work on the parents, too, and say, "We're not going to accept this. We want an apology, or we'll have to look at stronger measures."

Cathy is not the only administrator who has encountered parental resistance to antiracism measures. Others admitted that they have had to deal with parents who do not support their school's approaches to issues that involve students, as well as a range of related matters. Wilbur proposed that, for the most part, kids handle diversity better than their parents. Administrators spoke of parents who phone them to complain about such things as students being required to take French, wanting their children to be in classes "of their own kind," and objecting to their children having lockers beside other students who have different skin colours. Administrators maintained that they took tough stands on these matters, refusing to give in to parents who they believed held racist views. Wilbur said:

> I had a parent phone me and say [that] she's really disturbed because her White daughter was going to have a locker with a Black girl. And she said, "I don't want this to sound the way it might sound." And I said, "Madam, there's no way you can't make it sound the way it might sound. Any way you put this, it sounds blatantly racist." And she accepted that. And I said, "I understand your concern, but the reason we're doing this is because kids have to learn to get along, so you run with it for now. This is what we're going to do. I'm not going to move your daughter; we're not going to change lockers. If there's a problem that arises, then we'll deal with the problem, and if we need to change lockers we will.

Jerry also discussed the range of responses he gets from parents. Regardless, he believed that in the end parents will go along with school decisions if they understand that these decisions are based on a caring for their kids. He suggested that sometimes

> The parents are upset, and you get a range of reactions. You get some parents who support the school and are just totally embarrassed and ashamed, and are very supportive and use it as a teachable moment. And you get some parents who just totally disagree with you that that should be something that you would suspend a child for. And some people are in-between. But you work with parents, and one of the things we do here is spend a lot of time in direct contact with parents. I think if parents think you care about their kids and you want to help them work this thing through, that you're in touch with them, that caring is also part of your discipline and that you discipline because you have to accept consequences, but you're going to also teach and build on that, we've gained a lot of ground.

The testimony of administrators indicates that racism is something that extends beyond the confines of the school. In fact, some administrators find that dealing with racism in the school requires that they also deal with it in the community. Racist attitudes are sometimes apparent in the encounters that administrators have with parents. The administrators who talked about this issue maintained that they stood firm with parents on these matters, just as they would with students. Once again, though, administrators saw the racism that required their responses as generally overt in nature.

Sanctions and Punishments

Administrators also indicated that they punished those who commit racist acts. Many took a hard line in applying these sanctions. Tom said that

> as far as the students go, certainly the one emphasis we have in this school is clearly that we do not, in any way, use ethnic slurs and, generally speaking, that does not happen. But if it does, we are very, very strict in enforcing suspension for those students. So there's clearly no tolerance, zero tolerance, for that kind of thing.

Other administrators do not automatically suspend students for their racist acts. Jerry usually gives them a warning before he suspends them from school. After their first offense, he tells students that "It's not acceptable, it will not be tolerated, and therefore you have a warning. And the next time, you're suspended." Edward, on the other hand, employs a range of measures in situations that involve racism, including "loss of privileges, loss of time, detentions, writing lines, writing notes of apology." Administrators also believed that punishing offenders will deter other students from committing acts of racism. Barney claimed that it is important to make an issue of racist acts. He felt that highlighting such incidents would act as a deterrent. He held that

> We are very, very strong on racial incidents and I said we haven't had any. Maybe it's because five or six years ago when we did have a few, we went at them very strongly. I reacted so strongly that the kids were in shock. They couldn't believe that I reacted that strongly. I pulled out everything. I was going to throw them out of the school. I suspended them for a very long time. Like, it wasn't just a matter of three days or something. I think I suspended them for ten days. And I made them go through almost a re-education and I made a big deal out of it, to the extent that they say, "Jeez, I don't want to go through that again!"

The distribution of punishment follows a familiar theme; administrators sanction individuals who clearly display overt racist behaviour. While this is something that is obviously necessary, there is little evidence that many of them are either aware of, or have sanctions or disincentives set up to counter some of the more subtle forms of racism. Most administrators are concerned exclusively with overt acts of racism. Furthermore, they clearly direct sanctions at one group in their school communities – the students. Few mentioned the possibility that there might be a need to take action in situations where educators are the perpetrators of overt acts of racism – something that does occur in schools in this study and elsewhere (Ryan, 1999) – or that the system victimizes certain students.

ANTIRACISM AND INCLUSION

If schools are to be inclusive places, then they need to practice antiracism. Antiracism, however, need not be seen merely as the opposite of racism – a negative of a negative, so to speak. It can also be seen as "positive," that is, as a set of policies and practices that enhance the welfare of all groups of students. By working *against* debilitating practices that penalize groups in the school community, antiracism works *for* them. In doing so, it strives to include all groups, their values, knowledge, practices, and so on, in schooling processes. Virtually all administrators in this study identified the destructive nature of racism and the positive consequences of working against it, and although they generally wouldn't characterize their institutions as racist, they talked about the steps that they took to eliminate or discourage racism in their respective schools. They spoke about the preventative measures that they took and the ways in which they reacted to racist incidents after they had occurred. In attempting to prevent racism, they sought to help people understand racism, understand others and understand themselves. Administrators also spoke of developing policies, behaviour codes and mediation programs, as well as scrutinizing curricular material. They also talked about what they did after-the-fact, including dialoguing with students and parents and punishing offenders. Many of the antiracism strategies that administrators employed were consistent with inclusive practice. Not all were, however, for the practices that many administrators recommended only addressed individual or personal elements of racism. To ensure that antiracism strategies are successful and consistent with inclusive practice, administrators need to see racism for what it is – individual *and* systemic phenomena. They need to find means to incorporate this view into a whole school approach that features educative as well as policy aspects.

To increase their prospects for success in the battle against racism, administrators need to employ whole-school approaches (Gillborn, 1995; Troyna, 1993). They need to involve the entire school community in the development of antiracism practice. This strategy entails making antiracism an essential and routine part of educational practice in forms that ensure its longevity and protect it against wider changes in educational policy. Although the administrators in this study realized the importance of working against racism, their attitudes and the practices they put into place did not always favour whole-school practices. This was particularly apparent in the responses to the survey. Respondents believed that antiracism programs were the second least effective means of combating racism. Also, many of the administrators who we interviewed directed their efforts at eliminating individual indiscretions and not at systemic or institutional racism. They tended, moreover, to focus on only one segment of their school community – the students. This delimiting did not apply to all study participants inasmuch as some championed aspects of whole-school approaches. The best chances for success rest with initiatives that integrate all segments of the school community in an antiracism program that targets both individual and systemic racism, and acknowledges that everyone – and not just students – can be implicated in racism.

In an earlier study (Ryan, 1998), I provided an example of how a school community can work together to battle racism. After a student had been subjected to particularly demeaning and obviously racist treatment at the hands of other students, he wrote down his account of what had happened in moving and lucid detail. He then approached a staff member with the idea of publicizing what had taken place. After hearing the student out, the teacher went to the principal, and together principal, teacher and student worked out a strategy. The plan was for the (anonymous) account to be circulated to each homeroom class where teachers would read it. All teachers went along with the plan and in many classes discussions of racism took place. As it turned out, the reading of the account and the subsequent discussions of it had a marked impact on both students and teachers. Many were angry about what had happened and they were spurred on to search out various forms of racism and to work against them. In this case, the principal let the student and staff member lead the way. He endorsed their ideas for handling the situation and made it possible for them to carry out their plan. The strategy worked, insofar as it motivated the school community to look for ways to battle racism beyond reactionary responses to prejudice. But a whole-school approach also needs to involve both a policy and an educational component.

The argument here is that antiracism practice needs to be entrenched in policy. Such a situating is key because policies provide coherence and legitimacy for antiracism programs and guidance for those who put them into practice. They also make it possible for the whole school to become involved in antiracism efforts. Virtually all administrators in this study indicated that their respective school had policies that targeted racism. While some aspects of the policy processes of which they spoke and the content of these policies were consistent with whole-school and inclusive practice, others were clearly not. The positive aspects of the policy process included the manner in which administrators attempted to involve their school communities in the development of the policies, in much the same way that Gillborn (1995) and Corson (1996) endorse. Many administrators attempted to include all key stakeholders in this process by finding ways to get input and feedback from them. This included students, parents, community members, teachers and non-teaching personnel.

The content of the policies of which many administrators in this study spoke, however, was not consistent with whole-school enterprises. The policies often took the form of codes of conduct for students. If policies are to address whole school issues, then they must be directed not just at particular individuals, but also at systems and institutional practices. The policies that Gillborn (1995) describes at the schools he studied did this in a more appropriate way. They encapsulated a wide range of processes that need to be targeted and monitored, including, among others, hiring and promotion, education and professional development, assessment and curricula.

Whole school approaches also require an educational component. I describe the educative aspect in greater detail in Chapter 9. For now I want to emphasize that all members of the school community need to know more about one another and about racism. It is not just students who need to acquire understanding; so do administrators, teachers, students, and parents. Some administrators in this study acknowledged the need to promote this kind of understanding. It should be noted, however, that "understanding" has its limits. No guarantee exists that we can achieve "authentic" understanding of different others (see Chapter 8) or that this understanding will always engender a positive view of others (McCarthy, 1990). Thus, while understanding in this sense is important, educational efforts need to go beyond this.

Gillborn (1995) notes that inservice must be a key part of a school's antiracism agenda; it should not be piecemeal or unthinking. Inservice education needs to look outside of the school to the research literature and local communities, while at the same time highlighting immediate and practical concerns and strategies. Gillborn (1995) emphasizes the critical role that the headteacher or principal plays in this process. He cautions that some members of the school community can be easily threatened by antiracism talk and practice. Schools need to take a flexible approach to antiracism, one that doesn't alienate people and acknowledges that people do make mistakes, a topic I return to in Chapter 9.

CHAPTER 6

PROMOTING INCLUSIVE SCHOOL-COMMUNITY RELATIONSHIPS

The previous two chapters addressed racism. In particular, they described principals' perceptions of this significant impediment to inclusion and documented what they did about it. This chapter examines another dimension of inclusion – school-community relationships. It documents the measures that principals take to include the wider community in school activities. Efforts to include communities in school activities have figured prominently in many of the reforms in education over the past two decades. Among other inclusive initiatives, educational reformers have sought to include the parents of students, and the communities to which they belong, in the process of schooling in a meaningful way. Rejecting past practices that endorsed the separation of schools and the communities that they served, both progressive and conservative proponents of school reform have sponsored changes that have paved the way for parents and community members to take up roles and responsibilities that were formerly assumed exclusively by educational professionals. Not only have parents been encouraged to venture into their children's schools and classrooms, they have also been asked to participate in policy and decision-making processes. In various parts of the Western world, new policies and organizational arrangements have made it possible for parents to routinely come into classrooms to assist teachers, communicate with educators on a regular basis, and raise money for various school enterprises. They have also cleared the way for parents to sit on committees, boards and councils that make decisions about such key matters as the hiring of teachers and principals, the nature and use of curricular materials and various organizational and policy matters.

Reformers have opted to include parents and community members in school activities for a number of reasons (see for example, Leithwood et al., 1999 and Epstein, 1997). Of these, two stand out. The first revolves around student achievement. Reformers have sought inclusive arrangements because they believe that they can enhance student learning. These reformers base their arguments on recent research that indicates that parent involvement in their children's education can improve academic performance (Epstein, 1997). The other reason concerns matters of justice. Advocates argue that it is only right that parents have a say in the education of their own children because of the stake that they have in the outcomes.

These cases for inclusion become acutely relevant in situations where children's home and community culture differ from the culture of the school. In these situations, parents have, in the past, had little control over the content, delivery and organization of the curriculum; they have had little choice but to accept what schools and school systems have prescribed for their children. Children have had to cope with subject matter that was often outside the realm of their experience, and parents have had to deal with institutions that were foreign to them. Unfortunately, both parents and children have not always been successful at overcoming these barriers; parents tended to stay away from schools, students struggled with the curriculum and both failed to comprehend a variety of other school practices. Inclusive school policies and practices are designed to prevent these very situations. Reformers believe that welcoming parents, establishing cooperative relationships with them and giving them power in decision-making processes will help to make schools places where all students can succeed.

Those concerned with school-community relationships can no longer ignore the challenges that accompany diversity. Diversity continues to spread through virtually all aspects of contemporary life, including schools and their communities (see for example, Statistics Canada, 1993, 2001; Ryan, 1999). While reforms have in varying degrees outlined various kinds of community and parental involvement in schools throughout the Western world, it remains to be seen just how school leaders put into practice these policies in diverse contexts. It also remains to be seen what school leaders are doing to encourage community involvement in these schools. Research to date indicates that principals have an important role in school-community relationships, whether it involves activities that are enabling (Davis, 1995) or empowering (Leithwood et al., 1999; Malen & Ogawa, 1990). This chapter explores how school leaders promote inclusive community involvement in diverse contexts.

INCLUSION AND SCHOOL-COMMUNITY RELATIONSHIPS

Those concerned with the education of students from marginalized groups have looked upon the idea of inclusion with favour. They have done so because they recognize the harm that past and enduring exclusionary practices have done, and continue to do, to these groups. Such practices were, and in some cases continue to be, both blatant and subtle. Perhaps some of the most obvious exclusionary practices occurred in the United States during the so-called ante-bellum period (Lightfoot, 1978). In the South, slaves were expressly forbidden from pursuing any kind of education, while Northern Whites sought to explicitly prohibit Black children from attending White schools. This latter tactic endured well into the 20th century throughout the United States.

Canada's past has also been riddled with exclusionary practices. The case of Canada's Native people stands out in this regard. Even though authorities strongly encouraged Native people to attend educational institutions, missionaries and secular educators believed that they were the ones who should determine the form and substance of this education. The curriculum was exclusively European in content and input was seldom, if ever, sought from local communities, and their participation and presence was actively discouraged (see for example, Barman et al., 1986).

More recently, attempts have been made to include the community in the education of the young as local communities have assumed greater control. Nevertheless, exclusionary practices continue not only in Native schools, but in other public schools, often in more subtle ways, through for example, the knowledge favored in schools, the teaching and management practices that predominate, and the manner in which some schools and school systems make decisions.

More recently the discourse on inclusion has found its way into the area of school-community relationships. As mentioned above, reformers, academics and practitioners have sought to include parents and their respective communities in the operation of schools. These efforts have taken two forms, what Lewis and Nakagawa (1995) refer to as *empowerment* and *enablement*. Strategies associated with the former target what its advocates see as the main problem – the lack of power that various individuals and communities have over educational institutions (see for example, Carmichael & Hamilton, 1967; Levin, 1970; Fine, 1993). Proponents believe that the main culprits in this scenario are self-absorbed educational bureaucracies. They reason that these entities by their very nature seek to retain power for themselves, and in the process, exclude already powerless parents, particularly those who are poor and those who belong to particular ethnic groups. Ensuring meaningful inclusion requires the empowerment of these powerless parents. Advocates of this view believe that empowerment of this sort can only be accomplished if and when school systems display alternate structural arrangements that give parents a voice in the governance of educational institutions. They are convinced that parental empowerment will help make schools work for their children because these parents would facilitate school efforts geared to meeting the goals of those being served. With a greater say in the education of their children, parents would be more satisfied with their children's schools and thus be more committed to the educational enterprise generally. The end result would be increased student achievement (Lewis & Nakagawa, 1995).

The other approach to community inclusion is enablement. Advocates of the enablement option do not believe that the cause of exclusion is powerful, professionally staffed, self-absorbed bureaucracies (see for example, Comer, 1987; Epstein, 1997, Lightfoot, 1978). They do, however, acknowledge that in certain situations some people can have too much power, and others too little, and that power can sometimes be abused. They also admit that bureaucracies can be unresponsive and sometimes dysfunctional. But these people also believe that these power differentials and bureaucratic shortcomings can be resolved from within the system. So their emphasis is not on power *per se*, but on commitment to schools in a rapidly changing social environment. They believe that it is up to educational professionals to change themselves and the organizations in which they work in ways that will reach out to the community and draw it into the school enterprise. These educators are encouraged to provide incentives for parents to become involved in their children's education. Proponents value parental participation for educational rather than political ends. They believe that inviting parents to work as educational resources in their children's education, eliciting their commitment toward the educational enterprise, and working out more collaborative arrangements among the school, parents and the community will ultimately enhance student achievement (Lewis & Nakagawa, 1995).

Not all inclusive school-community proposals or practices turn out to be exclusively of the empowerment or enablement variety. Some include elements of both, and so-called enablement programs sometimes value empowerment. Perhaps the reforms that resemble most closely the empowerment model occurred in large urban American centers in the 1980s and 1990s. Looking for alternatives to systems that had failed the largely Black populations of these areas, various groups in such cities as Philadelphia, Baltimore, New York, Detroit and Chicago banded together to make changes to what were once large bureaucratic systems (Fine, 1993; Lewis & Nakagawa, 1995). Variations among districts notwithstanding, new legislation paved the way for massive decentralization that allowed local parents a voice in the governance of their children's schools.

Some urban American centers, however, followed another path. Lewis and Nakagawa (1995) maintain that educational reforms in Miami and Los Angeles followed more closely an enablement model. In these cities "insiders" rather than "outsiders" controlled the decentralization process, and as a result, they were able to make changes administratively and control the inclusionary process. Many inclusive school-community reforms in the Western world have been the result of a combination of these two models. In some areas, like Ontario, for example, although parental roles have been legislated, parents still remain relatively powerless. In the United Kingdom, on the other hand, legislation has provided parents with more power than what they had previously and undoubtedly more power than Ontario parents currently have. In both cases, though, a strengthening of central powers has rendered any gains parents have made relatively meaningless (see for example, Hatcher et al., 1996, Leithwood et al., 1999; Apple, 2000).

Despite such policies, however, schools and school leaders are often in positions to exercise considerable discretion in community-school relationships. For example, there are many different ways in which parents can be invited into schools and encouraged to become committed. And even in "enablement" jurisdictions, school professionals and community members can find ways for parents to become genuinely empowered (Leithwood et al. 1999). This chapter explores the efforts of schools and administrators to include, that is, to enable or empower, members of their diverse communities in school life.

ENABLEMENT STRATEGIES

Much of what has been written and legislated in the area of school–community relationships over the past two decades has favored an enablement approach. Some of the legislation that has been initiated outside education bureaucracies and geared to empower parents and community members has turned out to be mere window dressing. In Ontario, for example, recent legislation designed to find a place for local school councils has left parents with little real power – they are simply advisory in nature. Aside from well-intentioned empowering efforts, legislators, academics and educational practitioners have also looked to other inclusive strategies. Instead of approaching matters of inclusion from "outside" the system, they have worked within the current system to find approaches to get parents and the larger community involved in children's education. The nature of this involvement has largely revolved around efforts at communicating and collaborating with the community. This was true in the cases of the school administrators in this study. Given their limited knowledge of many of the communities that they served, it was all most of them could do to simply make contact with parents and community members, understand them, and to communicate with them. One principal, for example, maintained that she was frequently forced to make decisions in these areas, by the "seat of the pants," because of her limited knowledge of diverse community groups.

Administrators in this study talked almost exclusively of partnerships, collaborations and cooperation when speaking about including their diverse communities in school enterprises. Little thought was given to empowerment. These principals conceptualized these efforts in a number of ways. Generally speaking, though, the metaphors that they used to describe school-community relationships reflected the importance they attached to them. A number of principals spoke of these relationships as partnerships. Many saw this partnership as an equal one, not so much in terms of rights, but of responsibilities. In this regard, they believed that each partner had a responsibility in the relationship, based on what Wilbur, an elementary principal, saw as a "division of labour." Jake, on the other hand, felt that there were not two, but three partners – educators, parents, and children – and all three had an obligation to "pull their own weight." While these principals may have thought of these partnerships as equal, it was generally the school that initiated these sorts of partnerships, and it was the school people who set down the terms for them. Administrators recognized the need for the school not to wait for the community to come to it, but to be proactive in establishing relationships. Riley saw the necessity of "outreach and connection." He said

> One of the things that you can do to break the barrier [between school and community] down, and also move things forward, is to develop allegiances and alliances with people in the community... You know we recognize that there's give on their part too and that they're probably struggling more than we are because they are a minority and they are new here. It makes getting through that a whole lot easier.

Principals spoke of the importance of getting to know the other partners in these relationships. This, however, was not always easy within these diverse communities; educators sometimes knew less than they should about community groups, and many of these groups did not know how schools in this part of the world operated. Getting to know one another then required that the school, parents and the community share information. For many of the principals in this study, information-sharing was a key element in their interaction with parents and communities. They saw it as a two-way process; they provided the community with information about the school, seeking out information about the community. Most principals had more to say about getting information from the school to the community. Jerod, for example, maintained that "you must know what you are doing in a school and you must be able to articulate it to others." Others saw the need for "parent education." Tom believed that "parents have to be informed of the gaps that exist with their children when they enter a system such as this one." He went on to say that "as much as we require education in terms of learning about some of these differences within the school setting, they too have a lot of learning to do when it comes to understanding the norms, the values, the expectations of a North American culture and, specifically, of a North American school setting."

Administrators stressed the need to get to know the community; so the information sharing also moved in the other way – from the community to the school. In this regard, a number of administrators felt that listening skills were all-important. Janice, for example, believed that it was crucial for a principal to be "a good listener and talk to all the partners in the system. Talk to kids, talk to parents, talk to teachers, the other support staff in the building you work with. In education we may be good observers, but we're not good listeners." Although sympathetic to an inclusive ideal, the statements of many of these principals also demonstrated a certain ambivalence. On the one hand, as Janet's statement reveals, administrators proclaimed that schools needed to value their respective community's cultures, including them in the operation of the school. On the other hand, however, many administrators also took for granted that many of these groups would have to acknowledge and accept the values embedded in a "North American school culture." It is this latter culture that would inevitably prevail, excluding by necessity, often implicitly, the culture of other groups.

As described above, getting to know one another requires the exchange of information. This next section outlines the manner in which administrators sent out and acquired information from their diverse communities.

Sending Out and Acquiring Information

Administrators had a number of strategies for sending out and acquiring information. Much of this sharing involved personal interactions with members of the community. These kinds of transactions will be outlined later. For now, I want to describe three more-or-less technical or impersonal means – the use of newsletters, handbooks and surveys.

A number of principals who we interviewed used school handbooks and newsletters to convey information about the school, the community, and other matters to parents and community. School handbooks generally contained information about such things as school personnel, school programs, schedules, rules and regulations. They were often sent home with students at the beginning of the school year. High schools tended to employ handbooks, more so than newsletters. But they also produced student-generated school newspapers, and although primarily directed at the student body, they were also a useful source of information for the community. Generally speaking, school newsletters were more common at the elementary level. Many principals of these schools believed that newsletters played an important part in conveying information about the school and community to parents. For some, these newsletters were used to increase awareness of parents about the school and other relevant matters. Janice, for example, said that "what I have tried to do, through my newsletters ... [is] to heighten awareness." In cases where portions of the community were new to the country, principals judged that they needed to be made aware of things that most Canadian-born parents would take for granted, like dressing for the cold weather. Tom, for example, maintained:

> In this school we have to notify the community through newsletters and little posters [about] how to dress your child for the winter... I remember we sent home [information about the need for] gloves and a little girl came in the next day with gardening gloves on. Probably they were quite inexpensive, at the dollar shop or something. But we have children all the time who are not dressed for the weather. Parents call in concerned that we let them outside because their cheeks went red and they've never seen that.

Some of these newsletters go home in English, while others, or parts of them, are in a second, and sometimes a third, language. While many administrators recognized the value of second language newsletters, not all had the resources to employ a language other than English. One principal found a way around this obstacle. She would have teachers read the newsletter with students before they took it home, so that children would be able to explain or translate it for their parents. In some cases, she would have someone call home and explain what was in the newsletter.

Principals also employed various methods to gather information about the community. One technique that proved useful to some of the participants was the employment of questionnaires or surveys. These techniques allowed the principals to acquire information from a large number of people and to capture it in a concise fashion. They relied upon surveys to gather information on a specific issue or on more general things. Ronda, for example, found surveys useful in finding out what the community wanted in terms of religious celebrations. Most pressing for her was to try and capture a sense of what her school community expected of the school at the end of December.

Principals also used these surveys for other ends. Bob, for example, used a questionnaire to create a school vision. In this two-year endeavor, he solicited information from parents, students and members of the business community. Besides the surveys, he had the parents' group and teachers phone parents to come in for an information meeting where parents voiced their preferences about what they wanted to see at the school. At times, principals may get information from these techniques that they had not anticipated. Janice, for example, found that one of her questionnaires revealed that there were several groups in her community that she had not known about. She said that "There were a couple of Ba'hai families that I didn't know existed. They were very quiet, low-key about the whole thing, and I didn't know too much about the religion." So in order to learn more about them, she invited one of their church elders to come to the school.

Connecting with Individuals

Sending out and acquiring information through impersonal means like surveys proved to be an efficient means of getting to know the community. Most administrators realized, however, that they had to find other avenues to exchange information and develop relationships. One strategy that they adapted was to attempt as much as possible to interact on a personal basis with parents and community members. Administrators believed that "making connections" with individual parents and community members was a superior way to get to know the community and to have the community know them. As a result, many administrators spent considerable time interacting with individuals.

Some administrators believed that achieving good relationships with communities of people required that they get to know certain individuals within those communities. Heather felt that "you have to make connections with those key people or else you continue to make mistakes." She learned over time, and after some errors, that certain protocols helped her communicate with the Somali community in her school area. She discovered that it helped if she learned who the "men in charge" were or which people were willing to be spokespeople. She found out that communications were facilitated if she connected with these people or with others who had been in the country for longer periods of time. Edward, on the other hand, discovered that developing a good relationship with the nearby Native community required that he connect not only with the parents of students, but also with the elders. He came to recognize the importance of elders in Native culture, and as a result, found ways to convey this respect in his overtures to the community.

Principals also emphasized that they needed to spend time interacting directly with parents. They felt it was important to make themselves available and accessible. Janice said that "one thing we need to do here is spend a lot of time in direct contact with parents." She said that she spends a lot of time on the phone and in person. Other studies have indicated that much can be accomplished on the phone. Davis (1995), for example, said that he placed 23,000 positive calls to parents over 15 years, most of these outside of school hours. Walter also felt that it was important that he make himself available to parents and community members. As principal of a large high school, he claimed to make every effort to see that parents got through to him when they felt the need. He said:

> One of the most positive things about this school was that if you wanted to talk to the principal you always got to talk to him, and if you didn't talk to him right away, he always called back, which is part of my commitment to parents. If you need me, I'm going to find you. I'll get back to you. And most calls are returned the same day or the following day. It's rare that I have a parent phone call that I don't return within a matter of hours. And the community very, very much appreciates that and wants that to happen.

But principals also said that they cannot just wait for parents to approach them in order to begin to establish relationships. Administrators had a number of strategies for being the one to initiate contacts. Heather, for example, an elementary principal, kept an "eye out" for parents before and after school (see also Davis, 1995). She watched for parents because she knew that there was generally somebody walking the children home. Heather said, "I'm always on the lookout for so-and-so's dad or so-and-so's uncle. I stop them and say 'Do you know that this happened or that happened?' or 'We're having this at the school.'" Besides her after- and pre-school vigilance, Heather took other measures to make sure that she became acquainted with parents. She made sure that she was always around the reception area, took children home when they were ill, and generally kept up "that constant communication."

Other principals attempted to get "out into the community." This involved meeting parents on their home turf, approaching community organizations and speaking to community groups. Malcolm was one of many principals who believed that it was important for principals to move out beyond the school walls. One of the first things that he did after being appointed principal was to go out and learn about his diverse community. He remembered telling his vice principal, "I'm going to take three months. I'm going to visit classes; I'm going to talk to parents; I'm going to learn about the community, drive the community." He went to a few community meetings, just as a visitor and a listener. He also made himself visible and let people know who he was. Malcolm did much of this on his own time, mostly in the evenings. He wanted to meet parents "on an equal basis" and to be able to put "a name to a face, and a face to a name."

Roberta's strategies for linking with parents and community members saw her sitting down with members of a particular community and having coffee with them. On one occasion when problems arose, she remembered calling up a particular parent, and asking if she could come over to talk. The parent agreed, and when she arrived, was offered a cup of coffee. Roberta said that she had learned never to refuse anything that is offered, even if the offering wasn't to her liking. Refusal would be considered bad manners and could potentially impair dialogue and even disrupt relationships.

While administrators acknowledged that it was important for them to make contact with parents and community members, some also recognized the importance of encouraging teachers to do the same. Clarence, for example, maintained that "We actively encourage our teachers to establish ongoing dialogue with the parents if there is an issue. They're strongly encouraged to call home, talk with the parent." Clarence and others recognized, though, that these dialogues should not begin only after problems arise, but be an ongoing thing. Tom encouraged this type of contact in his school. He said that "Every teacher on this staff is in communication with parents, not just over difficulties with the youngster, but also over the good things the youngsters contribute to school life. And they're on the phone constantly. So parents know, when they hear from the school, it's not just because there's a problem." Davis (1995) also maintains that it is important to have something positive to say to parents during these sorts of interchanges. To do this, he devised a weekly award system that provided him with a reason for phoning home with positive news about students.

Connecting with Community Organizations

While many principals saw value in getting to know parents and members of the community on an individual basis, they also felt that it was important to connect with community organizations. Many of these administrators attempted to establish connections with religious, cultural, social service and business groups because they believed that these relationships had much to offer the school and community. These kinds of connections can help the school and community get to know one another better, provide adjustment supports for new Canadians, supply various services, promote cultural celebrations, furnish resources for the school and community and provide assistance to educators.

Administrators liaised with many kinds of organizations in the community. Perhaps the ones that they sought out the most frequently were religious and cultural organizations. Many found that connections with groups that emphasized religious functions or heritage activities yielded ways for them to get to know the community and vice versa. Principals also found that dealing with social service agencies could also benefit the community and school, as could efforts to connect with local business organizations. One important reason for connecting with these community organizations is to help both school and community become familiar with one another. Barry found that the local Catholic Community Services group was helpful in this regard in a number of ways. One of its projects was to provide venues where new Canadians could learn about their new country, including the education system. Others looked to organizations like the West Indies Caribbean Association, the Spanish Multicultural Council and the Christian Alliance Church to facilitate relationships with their respective diverse communities, and to help new families adjust to their new country, and in some instances to provide them with resources. Tom, for example, remembered the time that one of these groups provided much needed resources for one family. He said:

> We had a little boy from Vietnam that came, a Vietnamese boy that [couldn't speak] a word of English. His mum was working a [distance from the home] and was riding a bicycle to get there. He had an invalid father. They were living in a basement apartment in one of these homes and every day she would put this little boy on her bicycle handlebars and ride him to the school – just a tiny little guy with no [English] language, no understanding, had never seen a setting like this with buildings and people. And I remember once it was winter and even snowing [and] that lady was on that bicycle, conscientious in coming and getting the child, but inappropriately dressed herself. The child was inappropriately dressed. She had a pair of socks on her hands as mittens. And finally the church intervened. The next thing you know the child was getting dental care, and was clothed.

Principals also found that community organizations could provide them with other sorts of assistance. Janet, for example, made contact with a Hong Kong-based film company and worked out an arrangement with it that has helped out some of her students. Heather, on the other hand, discovered that the local cross-cultural centre was of considerable use in helping her interact with people who had customs with which she was not familiar. Referring to a person from the centre, she said

> He would mirror for me right then in a meeting – like the parents would leave the room to go and do something and he would turn to me and say "Try this, say this." Just as an example, [he would tell me] that as normal practice when people come in offer them a cup of coffee or they will think you are very angry at them.

In recent years a number of initiatives have attempted to integrate a range of social services and community organizations with the school (Smrekar & Mawhinney, 1999). Although laudable in their intent, many of these efforts have fallen short of their goals. Furman and Metz (1996) maintain that they do not strengthen weak links between schools and communities. Despite the fact that these collaborations are designed to empower families, their bureaucratic structures do little to ensure the empowerment. While the principals in this study did mention the difficulties that they had with trying to elicit cooperation with and between government agencies, they also indicated that they found good success when they approached agencies on their own, as principals of individual schools and not necessary as agents of larger (bureaucratic) entities.

School Contact Processes

While principals discerned that establishing relationships with individuals and community organizations was important, they also employed other methods to connect with the community. In this regard, most of them described processes that they or their predecessors had set up for bringing the community into the school.

These frequently involved mechanisms for arranging various meeting situations, assistance scenarios and learning opportunities.

The most obvious contact situation was the traditional parent-teacher night. These events do not always attract parents in diverse communities, however. Delgato-Gaitin (1991), in a study conducted in a diverse school community, noted that conventional events such as parent-teacher nights, were not successful in attracting many parents. Most administrators in our study also admitted that these events had mixed results. Some attempted to make adjustments in the ways in which these occasions were conducted. Stephanie changed the form that these parent-teacher conferences took. She instituted a plan that attempted as much as possible to include the student in these interchanges. The student would take a leading role in the process, a move Stephanie believed would benefit all the parties.

Many administrators attempted to introduce other sorts of events that were designed to attract parents who would normally tend to stay away from the school. Roberta was one of a number of principals who spoke of orientation activities. She was particularly fond of her school's grade nine barbecue. Administrators may also hold periodic meetings through the year to inform parents about what the school is doing. Tom, for example, said that he organizes these events to "educate" parents about such concerns as the school curriculum, mediation services and other special services and resources that are available. He also offered opportunities for parents to learn about other kinds of things not directly related to school matters. He stated:

> As much as we require education in terms of learning about some [cultural] differences with the school, they [the parents] too have a lot of learning when it comes to understanding the norms, the values, the expectations of a North American culture and, specifically, of a North American school setting. And child-rearing practices. We had a meeting last night in school with support services, and the psychologist who was at that meeting offered parenting courses for any parents interested in attending those in this community. Now of the fifty people who were present last night, there was a sign-up sheet drafted and there were twelve or thirteen names put on the list.

While a number of parents, in this case, indicated an interest in this type of "education," it remains to be seen how effective it is. Other more nontraditional methods may prove to be more successful. Delgato-Gaitin (1991) described two successful strategies. In one preschool, teachers worked to make parents co-teachers. They did this by using the parents' native language, culture, concepts and practices in their instruction. Delgato-Gaitin (1991) also describes a situation where parents organized their own instruction. Weary of waiting for school officials to do something constructive, Spanish-speaking parents came together, on their own, to learn about the school. They looked to those among them who had both knowledge and skill. In doing so, they sought to understand the school system and their rights and responsibilities as parents. Among a number of learning exercises, this group of parents rehearsed communicating with educators in order to learn how their children were doing in school and to advocate for them.

A number of administrators attempted to find possibilities to inject levels of comfort into these school-community interchanges. They found that providing translation services not only in the advertising bulletins, but also in the meeting itself encourages more parents to attend. Other principals talked about arrangements that they believed helped to attract parents and community members to the school. Juanita started a "drop-in centre for multicultural folks." She did so to entice grandparents and parents who walked their kids to school to come to the resource centre, to have a cup of coffee or tea, and to read a magazine in their first language while they waited. Heather, on the other hand, introduced what she referred to as an "ESL coffee hour."

Principals also sought to include members of the community and parents by inviting them into the school to help out with various activities. They made it possible for parents to help out in routine ways or on special occasions. Many schools provided opportunities for parents to help out in classrooms or libraries or on fieldtrips. Heather, for instance, maintained that her "Middle East Mums" particularly enjoyed checking out books in the library. Cathy, on the other hand, told us that in her school parents came in to help with the school's "publishing house," typing manuscripts and binding the final products. Others mentioned that parents of elementary school children were happy to come in and help teachers in the classroom, while others helped patrol hallways, lunchrooms and schoolyards at various times during the day. Administrators also involved parents in less routine ways. For example, they arranged for parents and community members to come in for "cultural" displays or days. Principals also made use of parents for their expertise in other areas. Jake, for example, had one parent come in to talk to students about racism.

Several principals also noted that parents came to school by virtue of their status as students. Indeed, some schools offered ESL courses that were attended by parents of the regular day-stream students. In these situations, parents could either work toward a diploma or simply learn the English language. One school had three generations of a family that were in one way or another associated with school programs. A grandmother and her daughter took language lessons, while the grandson was enrolled in a regular day program. A number of principals, however, found that shrinking budgets made it difficult to offer programs for adults, despite their recognition of these programs' value. Noreen was one of these principals. She noted that there was a need for these programs, but this need had not been acknowledged by other community organizations.

EMPOWERMENT STRATEGIES

The other side of school-community inclusion is empowerment. As alluded to previously, there is no definitive way of distinguishing empowerment practices from enabling practices. This is because empowerment is a relative term. Some might see helping out in the classroom or supervising in the schoolyard as empowering; others might not. The latter would probably view substantive input into decisions regarding personnel, finances and curriculum as genuinely empowering. Anything less would be superficial, at best. In Ontario, parents or school councils do not have legislative authority in these areas, except in an advisory capacity. Leithwood et al. (1999) go so far as to say that these school councils do not actually empower parents. They state, however, that schools, like one in their study, can extend to parents and school councils some "unofficial" decision-making powers. While most of the principals in this study spoke of enabling measures, some did allude to measures that they took to extend to parents a role in policy decisions. At the same time, however, more than a few indicated that they did not wish to see parents or school councils with power over such things as personnel. Robert, for example, maintained that his school community wouldn't go along with a council that made decisions in this area. He held that "in terms of hiring and firing of teachers and so forth, we [as a school council] certainly don't do that, nor would we as a community, support that sort of thing."

Principals spoke of a number of routes through which they extended a measure of power to parents and community members. Perhaps the most cited strategy involved getting information from parents and then acting on it. One way of gathering information, as previously mentioned, was by means of surveys. Another means of giving parents and community members input into school decisions involved giving them the opportunity to participate in large group discussions on policy issues. Ron spoke of doing this sort of activity when he first took up his position at his high school. He noted that at the time, the school had many problems, and believed that his administration needed to get input from the community in order to address them. He advertised a meeting and many parents came and voiced their opinions on, for example, the general treatment of students, issues of racism, behaviour codes and so on. Over the course of the next few weeks, Ron worked with a representative committee to work out new school policies in some of these areas. Other principals did this sort of pursuit on a more ongoing basis. Edward said that he runs what he refers to as a "bear-pit session for parents to come out and talk about whatever." He noted that he runs sessions of this sort every term so that "people could come out and air their beefs."

At the time of this research, Parent Councils were in their infancies. Many principals already had experience with parent teacher associations of various sorts, some initiated on their own. Stephanie, for example, began with a couple of parents and expanded from there. With the help of these parents, she canvassed the community about their needs, asked for volunteers and approached people. Others simply sent home notices with students and asked for volunteers. Other principals said that they still had difficulty filling all the seats on their school councils, and they sometimes found themselves encouraging people to put their names forward.

Another inclusion issue here involves the identity of the participants on school councils. Other jurisdictions have reported that not only do certain parents tend not to serve on local school councils (Hatcher et al., 1996), but that when they do their voices are dominated by others (Malen & Ogawa, 1990; Fine, 1993; Lewis & Nakagawa, 1995). These patterns also surfaced in this study. While principals tried to ensure that their school councils were diverse, many admitted failure. Some, however, were successful in this regard. Gail, for example, said that she was fortunate in that her school council had "members of visible minority groups." She confessed that this didn't happen by design, "it was just the way it happened and that was good." As it turned out, there were many "minority" parents in the community who were "very interested" in the school, and, as a consequence, made efforts to become involved. For most principals, however, this was not the case. In most cases, principals said that "visible minority" groups were generally underrepresented on these councils. This was particularly the case when it came to Chinese parents. Clarence was just one of many principals who maintained that "Caucasian parents are much more involved in the school than non-Caucasian parents generally." He also found that "Black and Indian parents will still be more ready to involve themselves in the school than the Chinese will."

Principals had various explanations for why Chinese parents are not involved in school councils and schools generally. Pat felt that it may be uncomfortable for Chinese parents to approach the school, given some of the differences in language and culture. Some, he believed, may be intimidated by the school and its practices. Others have different theories. Donald maintained that language insecurity plays a part in Chinese parents' reluctance to get involved in school organization. He also felt that parents believe that it is the school's responsibility to educate their children, and as a consequence, prefer to leave educational matters to professional educators. In this regard, Edward thought that some parents feel shame when they have to approach the school. Other principals also noted that it is not just Chinese parents who are reluctant to get involved in school organizations and activities. Many groups of immigrants, particularly those from Asia and Africa, are also not always anxious to approach the school (Hatcher et al., 1996; Wang, 1995).

The functions of school councils vary from school to school, even though their mandates are inscribed in legislation. Some administrators noted that many of these organizations are still involved in fund-raising activities and other issues in which they were involved before school councils were legislated. Others are more concerned with program matters. Sometimes the suggestion that school councils concern themselves with matters other than fundraising can come from the principal. Ronda said that she actively discouraged her school council from exclusively pursuing fundraising, something that members wanted to do. On the other hand, councils may insist that they do not become preoccupied with fund raising. Bill maintained that the council at his high school maintained that they had enough of this kind of thing at the elementary level. This council used its time to provide feedback on board policies.

> If ... they want input on board policies or things that are going to the board, I'll send out copies to them to make input on those, like the homework policy for the school. I sent them copies of that – the draft – for them to make input... So it's not just a token thing. We would like them to be involved in some of the things that affect their children.

INCLUSIVE COMMUNITY PRACTICE

Most, if not all, principals in this study favored practices that included parents and community members in the operation of their respective schools. The ways in which they followed through on these beliefs varied, and so did the extent to which parents became involved. Most principals said that they were preoccupied with strategies that enabled rather than empowered parents and community members. They were more concerned with simply making contact with individuals and groups, understanding them, and encouraging them to become involved in their children's education in whatever way they could. Given the situation of many of the groups in these diverse communities and the structure of education in the province that extends to parents little more than an advisory role, principals were less concerned with extending to parents a role in governance matters.

Principals concentrated mostly on enabling parents and community members to participate in their children's education. They did so because of the gulf they saw between school culture and the culture of many community groups. These mostly Anglo principals found that they frequently knew very little of the sometimes upward of sixty different groups in their communities. Language, values, cultural practices, religious beliefs, and attitudes toward education were frequently sources of puzzlement for them. On the other hand, these principals also found that parents and community members did not understand how schooling in this part of the world worked. Parents regularly struggled with the English language, understanding both the content and processes of school, and their roles in the education of their children. For these principals, then, closing the gap between the school and parents in these diverse communities required that they establish a dialogue with them. A dialogue, many believed, would allow the respective parties to get to know one another better, help parents and educators learn about each other, and in doing so make it possible for parents to become involved in the education of their children.

Principals did many things to establish dialogues, to learn about the community and to educate the community about the school. Establishing these dialogues required that principals first forge relationships with individuals and groups. To do so, they placed themselves in positions that would bring them into contact with members of the community. Spending time on the phone for positive reasons, making themselves available at all times, hanging around areas that parents frequent, going out into the community for meetings and for seeing parents in their homes, were just some of the strategies that principals in this study employed to get to know their respective school communities. They also employed strategies for exchanging information. They used surveys to acquire information about the groups in the community and to discover how they felt about selected school matters, newsletters, school newspapers and meetings organized to channel information out into the community. Many principals also made efforts to persuade parents and community groups to come into the schools to meet teachers and to help out in various roles. Unfortunately, the more traditional of these events, like parent-teacher nights, were not terribly successful in attracting parents. Principals in this study and in other situations (Delgato-Gaitin, 1991; Davis, 1995) found that more parents came to non-traditional activities.

While enabling tactics and events are important in getting parents – particularly those who are reluctant – involved in school activities (Dehli, 1994), they only constitute part of inclusive practice. Inclusion goes beyond bake sales, cultural events, parent nights and the like. Enabling strategies of this sort are designed almost exclusively to help diverse groups adjust to what will be new and very different environments. The educators who use them generally take for granted that it will be these families and not the school that must change; diverse community groups are expected to acclimatize themselves to practices that do not include their routines. In other words, educators endorse these enabling practices because they acknowledge – often implicitly – that the formal education that goes on in their schools is exclusive. And while some schools may make valiant efforts to include the languages, cultures, values and knowledge of the respective community groups in the content and process of schooling, given current circumstances, there is no guarantee that any of this will occur. So if school knowledge is to be consistently inclusive in a way that empowerment advocates would recommend, power relationships cannot exclusively favour an (Anglo-European based) school system. Rather, these power relationships must make it possible for community groups to make decisions that will allow school knowledge to be inclusive. If schools are to pay more than lip service to the idea of inclusion, then these groups need to be genuinely empowered. But can the participation of parents in governance at the school level ensure this sort of inclusion, and can it ensure that traditionally marginalized students will succeed at school?

For some time now, a number of scholars and politicians have believed that local- and community-managed schools represented a solution to the problems that many "minority" students faced in schools. They were convinced that the input of parents and community members would unhinge schools from their bureaucratic and impersonal tendencies, make them more responsive to local needs, and in doing so, boost student achievement. Inevitably these beliefs were put into practice, although the configuration of these structures varied considerably. And so did the potency of local parent input – from weaker forms in Ontario to stronger forms in places like Chicago. Recent research on school councils in Ontario (Leithwood et al. 1999), Chicago (Lewis & Nakagawa, 1995) and in the United Kingdom (Hatcher et al., 1996), however, indicates that these local school councils have not fulfilled their mandate. It seems that even in situations where parent councils have power over finances, school programs and personnel, relationships between community and schools have not changed all that much (Lewis & Nakagawa, 1995) and student achievement gains are inconsistent at best (Hess, 1999; Shipps et al., 1999). In this regard local community management generally has floundered in three areas – participation on school councils, power on the school councils and the relationship of governance to teaching and learning.

The principals in this study noted that their school councils tended to be populated by Anglo and middle class parents, and even when "minority" parents did participate, they tended to have difficulty with group interactions. These findings are consistent with the findings from other studies (Hatcher et al. 1996; Dehli, 1994; Delgato-Gaitin, 1991; Chambers, 2001). These studies indicate that "minority" parents are often under-represented on governance councils. Hatcher et al. (1996), for example, contend that in the United Kingdom this happens because "minority" parents are not part of the influential informal parent, business, political and educational networks that generally place individuals on the councils. They also maintain that Asian parents do not participate on school councils because they lack confidence in their language abilities and in their ability to interact in the White-dominated formal environment of the school. Work commitments and the reluctance of women to go to meetings on their own also account for this low turnout. But even when "minority" parents do show up, they often find that they are unable to penetrate the forms of language and interaction that councils generally adopt.

Those with little experience of formal meetings, like many of the "minority" and immigrant parents to which principals in this study referred, have difficulty with the formalities of chaired meetings (Hatcher et al. 1996; Dehli, (1994), with "middle class proceduralism" (Lewis & Nakagawa, 1995). Not only do many of these parents have to struggle with language barriers, but they also have difficulty with the peculiar type of interaction that this setting engenders and with the informal ways of talking that goes on. These incongruities routinely obstruct the voices of parents and block or filter issues of race (Hatcher et al., 1996). One Philadelphia council member expresses his frustration with the process by saying that

> Due to the fact that the participants of the Governance Council are from a very specific situation – all are teachers/administrators, are from the same school, and have been oriented through the years to a particular system and culture – the language, thinking and dialogue left me always playing catch-up ball with such important subjects as meaning of words and concepts, philosophy of education, and contextual questions that relate [to this high school]. This promotes a high level of frustration (Fine, 1993, p. 468).

While parents – particularly some "minority" and working class parents – generally do not have the resources or skills to influence governance situations, principals do. Leithwood et al. (1999) maintain that principals have demonstrated a remarkable capacity to either derail community-dominated councils (Dehli, 1994) in order to retain decision-making control for themselves (Malen & Ogawa, 1990) or ensure council effectiveness (Hess, 1995). On the positive side, they can help create participatory decision-making structures and foster collaborative work among council members (Odden & Wohlsletter, 1995), clearly defining goals and roles for parents and for the council, and act as an information provider, motivator, and friend of the council (Odden, 1995). On the other hand, the principal's unique access to information, their positional power, their ability to use abstract language to talk about educational issues, and to set meeting agendas makes it possible for them to stifle or exclude individuals and initiatives that do not meet with their approval. Of course, in situations where councils have the power to dismiss principals, the relationship between council and principal may be different, even though principals still have access to resources that council members do not.

With these power imbalances, what possibilities do these forms of inclusion offer for the resolution of issues of diversity and "race"? Lewis and Nakagawa (1995) are decidedly pessimistic about the prospects of urban decentralization for rectifying racial inequalities in the United States. They maintain that decentralization has masked rather than resolved issues of "race" and class in inclusionary policies. It has done so by using the ideology of inclusion to give the appearance of change without much resource redistribution; Whites maintain their hegemony, while Blacks maintain their "control" of the public schools. Lewis and Nakagawa (1995) argue that, despite all the changes, the relationship between educational institutions and parents has not changed, and this made it difficult for parents to assume a role (in governance), that they neither wanted nor were prepared for. In addition, decentralization has not had a noticeable impact on student achievement; changes in student marks have been inconsistent at best (Hess, 1999; Shipps et al., 1999).

Changes in the relationship between schools and communities will require changes in society generally. Parents need to organize; school and communities need to be restructured to work toward democracies of difference (Fine, 1993); and everyone needs to work to develop conditions of life that facilitate these inclusive practices. But in order to achieve this end, parents, community members and educators have to work together. Parents should not be saddled with running schools, nor should they be subordinated to the existing structure. Lewis and

Nakagawa (1995) contend instead that a model needs to be developed that allows for parents and educators to collaborate in certain parts of children's education. But this involvement should not be mandated; rather, policy should merely set the stage for parents and schools to work together. Most critically, this collaboration needs to prioritize children's learning. In this regard, it needs to acknowledge the necessity of finding a way to accommodate both professional and "nonprofessional" commitment and expertise.

Long-term improvement in student achievement will require the development of the capacities of professional educators (Shipps et al., 1999). This is because constraints on the exercise of these capacities will inevitably limit the improvement in student learning opportunities. So management or organizational changes and administrative practices must be geared toward improving the professional expertise and commitment of educators. But these practices cannot be exclusive, as they have traditionally tended to be. Rather, professional teaching practice needs to be inclusive, that is, it must incorporate a range of diverse community knowledge, practices and values. And in order to ensure that this happens, aside from their many other potential roles, parents and community members also need to play some part in collaborative governance arrangements. Only in this way can parents, community members and educators expect to improve student learning for all students, and to address and alleviate the racial inequalities that have plagued educational institutions and the conditions of life generally.

In order to enhance school-community relationships in diverse contexts, principals also have to find ways to meet the challenges that accompany the differences that they see between and among themselves and the various groups that are a part of their communities. The next two chapters explore these efforts.

CHAPTER 7

ADMINISTRATOR PERCEPTIONS OF AND
RESPONSES TO DIFFERENCE

As I have emphasized in the previous chapters, administrators of diverse schools face many challenges in promoting inclusive education. A number of these challenges can be traced to the mismatch of school culture and the culture of students and their families. Administrators and teachers frequently find themselves in the position of having to provide for the education of young people who may speak different languages, adhere to different religious beliefs and practices, subscribe to different ideas about schooling, and favour different ways of interacting. This diversity, however, is not always restricted to a few groups. Many schools, including a number in this study, cater to upwards of sixty distinct groups. In these situations, administrators scramble not only to acknowledge, understand and include some of the various groups in school activities, but also to identify the very presence of groups. This is no small task. But it is one which administrators need to address, for their ability to understand and react appropriately to these differences will affect the kind of education that their students will receive. This chapter describes how administrators understand the various differences associated with religious beliefs and expectations of schooling and what they do to meet the challenges associated with including these beliefs and expectations in process of schooling.

THE QUALITY OF DIVERSITY

Diversity has always been a part of public education, even though it has not always been acknowledged or emphasized in the way it is today. In 19th century Ontario (Upper Canada), for example, school promoters acknowledged the diversity of the communities that schools sought to serve (Prentice, 1977). Difference in this day and age was calculated in terms of how others compared to the mostly English and Scottish majority. The group that was labeled as different at that time was the Irish immigrants. Real or imagined, those who ran public schools were readily able to identify a number of differences between themselves and the less favored Irish. Among other things, they saw these immigrants as "harbingers of a worse pestilence of social insubordination and disorder" (Prentice, 1977, p. 56). The function of public schools, the school promoters asserted, was to provide the means through which the Irish could be taught such values as Christian love, order, the sanctity of property and correct social behaviour. It was these qualities that the school promoters and believed distinguished their kind from the Irish.

Looking back from a contemporary perspective, these differences seem trivial, at best. In keeping with the current awareness of diversity, differences between

111

English or Scottish and Irish people or their contemporary descendents would appear to be barely worth mentioning. In hindsight, some would probably cite racist motivations at the time for the identification of these differences and the diminution that accompanied this identification. On the other hand, the conditions of life in 21st century Ontario are considerably different from life in the 19th century. It would be more difficult today to distinguish those of Irish heritage from those of English or Scottish heritage. More than likely though, many with English, Scottish and Irish heritage would now also boast mixed heritages. So someone with an Irish heritage would likely also have either Scottish or English "blood" or come from a range of other, often European, lines. Many people of my generation in Ontario (born in the 1950s), which include many current school administrators, are of Anglo or mixed European ancestry. My grandparents, for example, were of German, French, Scottish and Irish ancestry. Only my German grandmother was born in Europe. My point here is that the comparatively trivial differences between various European traditions blended over the years to form a culture that was articulated within the dominant Anglo tradition. It has continued to provide the framework for the conditions of life in Ontario and in the school system. This is not to say that there were no non-European groups or groups that resisted this culture. There were, of course, but their numbers were not sufficient to draw significant attention to them or the diversity that they represented. This all changed, however, with the changes in the levels and quality of diversity that began in the late 1960s (see Chapter 1).

The most recent wave of immigration has prompted a new awareness of diversity on the part of the mostly Anglo/European educators who work in Canadian schools. There are at least two reasons for this changing awareness. The first is the quality of diversity that these immigrants represent. Educators routinely notice that the differences between themselves and these new Canadians are sometimes significant, and those who have been around for a time admit that these differences are greater now than they ever were. Many find that they often know little about many of these groups, and have even more difficulty trying to understand some of the customs or practices that they do observe. But beyond these changing qualities, educators also find that they have to deal with the quantity of diversity. Many Anglo/European administrators and teachers are faced with many novel situations, and in order to solve them they must "fly by the seat of their pants." Donald, an administrator in one of these diverse schools, worried about the implications of his ignorance.

> Suddenly I have someone in who wants to pray on a carpet and I haven't a clue what this means, and so I'm reticent to ask a lot of questions because I don't want to embarrass the person or the parties and I don't want to demonstrate my ignorance either. Lack of knowledge is an issue. It's an issue for students and it's an issue for parents, and it's an issue for staff. The Board is trying but our staff is top-heavy White Anglo Protestant and we don't have a lot of different cultures represented on staff anywhere.

The differences that pose the biggest challenges for administrators often involve the discontinuities between "non-Western" and "Western" views and practices. Although useful, this Western/non-Western dichotomy can also be misleading. This is because it is an oversimplification of the similarities and differences between and among groups who are considered Western and non-Western (Reagan, 2000). Just as there are similarities between Western traditions, considerable differences also loom among them. This also holds true for non-Western traditions. There are similarities between Western and non-Western traditions; people of Western heritage may hold stereotypical non-Western beliefs, and vice versa. We also should keep in mind that the two traditions have had considerable influence on each other's development. For example, the bedrock of Western civilization, ancient Greece, owes much to African traditions (Said, 1978).

Perhaps the most significant marker of Western/non-Western distinctions is the value attached to the respective traditions. Many of European heritage who live in North America, Europe and Australia regard, often implicitly, their own Western traditions as superior to other, non-Western, ones. This is a phenomenon we have come to know as ethnocentrism. Reagan (2000) identifies two related kinds of ethnocentrism. The first is cultural. It refers to our sociocultural context as inevitably shaping how we view other societies and practices. The norms, concepts and practices in which we are immersed filter the ways in which we come to know the world about us and those in distant lands. As mentioned above, these views are not always positive. The second kind of ethnocentrism that Reagan (2000) identifies is epistemological. It refers to the kind of knowledge that is valued. In Western societies, the most valued form of knowledge is scientific. It is considered to be more legitimate than, say, "softer" or more personal ways of knowing that are often characteristic of non-Western traditions. Both of these forms of ethnocentrism combine to filter how Westerners have come to understand non-Western traditions and people. The scientific framework selectively generates knowledge about those things that it can measure and disseminates it to an audience that scans it through its already biased cultural lens.

Epistemological and cultural ethnocentrism finds expression in a number of areas of study. Among the most telling are explorations of the impressive accomplishments of non-Western cultures. Reagan (2000) maintains that these achievements have often been either rejected altogether, diminished in importance or attributed to other civilizations and sources. He cites the example of the ruins and ancient mineshafts of Great Zimbabwe in southern Africa. Instead of attributing them to a local people, some scholars have claimed that these accomplishments were the work of some mysterious civilization. They believed the architects to be related to the Carthaginians, some other ancient people, or even extraterrestrials. Other "New Age" rhetoric has attempted to explain Mesoamerican and other non-Western civilizations by proposing ties to Atlantis, ancient Egypt, Stonehenge and to various extraterrestrial sources. Reagan (2000, p. 13) concludes that these views

are all based on the idea that various aspects of human civilizations (almost always non-Western civilizations, interestingly enough) cannot be explained by "normal" human history, sociocultural development, and so on. Instead they all posit some sort of *deus ex machina* who, it is asserted, must have been responsible for the emergence of the great non-Western civilizations. The problem with such explanations ... is that they also serve to support and reinforce beliefs and ideologies that are demonstrably racist in both origin and nature. In short, to assume that the indigenous peoples of Mesoamerica, for instance, needed help from escaping Atlanteans, planet-hopping extraterrestrials, or whomever, would inevitably seem to suggest that they were not themselves capable of creating the civilizations whose ruins and remnants remain so impressive even today.

Like most other people of Western heritage, administrators and teachers are not immune from the ethnocentrism that pervades their social milieu. Most will only have a partial view of other lands and people, and will, often implicitly, evaluate them negatively. The challenge for administrators then, if they are to make education an equitable and inclusive enterprise, is not just to include elements of these different cultures in the content and structure of schools, but also to recognize, understand and ultimately confront the ethnocentrism that shapes their own and other's views of these non-Western traditions. Only in this way can they see through the harmful filters that shape their views of non-Western students and their communities, and take appropriate steps to make sure that all students receive a good education. Two of the areas that administrators struggle with are non-Western religions and views of education.

RELIGION

Principals in this study acknowledged that religion was one of the many things about their diverse communities of which they knew little. Many went on to confess that they found a number of religious practices puzzling, even though most administrators, as best they could, attempted to accommodate them. The religions that they perceived as the most different, and as a consequence the most unsettling, were the non-Western ones, i.e., Hindu, Buddhist, Islamic and North American Indigenous beliefs and practices. It was not always easy for these administrators to understand or reconcile many of these associated beliefs with their own Christian doctrines. Not only do these religions differ from Christianity, they also differ from one another in significant ways. Among other things, they vary with respect to their beliefs, organization and the relationship with people's lives.

Most of these non-Western religions, like Christianity, revolve around a supreme being. Members of the respective religions seek to honour the supreme being by living their lives in ways that respect the supreme being's wishes and teachings. With the exception of indigenous oral traditions, and similar to Christianity, these teachings are readily available in scriptures. These scriptures have been passed down in various ways. In Islam, for example, the Angel Gabriel passed on the literal words of God to its most important and last prophet, Muhammad, and these words were subsequently preserved in Islam's sacred text, the *Qur'an*. Because the principles on which Islam based have been Divinely revealed, they are constant, unalterable and universal. However, the details may be adjusted as necessary within an Islamic framework to fit existing needs and circumstances. Core beliefs remain the same but the ways in which they will be interpreted and manifested in practice may differ in various social and cultural contexts. On the other hand, while Hinduism also has ancient scriptures that provide guidance for Hindus, it does not have a fixed doctrine. In fact identification of oneself as Hindu depends less on doctrinal agreement than on self-definition and acceptance by the Hindu community (Reagan, 2000).

Buddhism, the only non-Western religion that does not revolve around a supreme being, is a religion without a god. Based on the teachings of a man, Buddha, who lived in what is now Nepal around 500 B.C.E., it is less concerned with metaphysical and theological matters than with psychological ones. It is first and foremost concerned with human suffering and the means to alleviate this suffering. This is not to say that Buddha denied the existence of a god. Rather, he believed that speculations concerning the origins of the universe were immaterial. Not only were they a waste of time, but they also postponed deliverance from suffering by engendering ill-will in oneself and others. Unlike other religions, like Islam for example, Buddhism displays no clear boundaries that separate insiders from outsiders. As a result, it exists easily alongside other religions.

Christian and Jewish beliefs differ from these non-Western religious beliefs in varieties of ways. However, they differ from Buddhism and Hinduism more so than they do from Islam. This is because Islam is part of a Judeo-Christian-Islamic tradition (Reagan, 2000). It shares with Christianity and Judaism many core ideas, beliefs and values. For example, Islam accepts both the Torah and the Gospel as revealed scriptures. Aside from God, it also recognizes as prophets, Adam, Abraham, Moses, Noah, and Jesus, and it believes in an afterlife, a final judgement and an eternal paradise. So Islam is not really non-Western in the way other religions are. Despite its connections to Judaism and Christianity, however, it has traditionally been seen – not always accurately – as alien and different. A view of Islam as "other" is as strong today as it ever was. A lack of knowledge coupled with fear and an active dislike has led many people to see Islam as a non-Western religion, even though this view is contested.

One of the reasons that principals quickly become aware of other religions is the role that they play in the respective practitioners' lives. Religion is frequently a more significant influence in non-Western people's lives than it is in many Westerners'. Put another way, Western life is, in many ways, secular. While many people of European heritage may practice a religion, they will often see it as a distinct sphere of life. Moreover, many Westerners look to explanations of life and moral codes that are not divinely inspired. This attitude stands in marked contrast to those who practice Hinduism and Islam. Hindus, for example, have a broader understanding of Hinduism as a religion than say, many Christians do of the respective Christian denominations. For them, Hinduism has more encompassing conception of the duties of the individual. It involves a total disciplinary approach to training the will, rather than simply attending to the rightness or wrongs of single acts. Islam also involves a comprehensive approach to life. It is not simply a body of religious beliefs, but a unified, consistent way of life for both the individual and the community. Islam provides far more than a framework for social organization; it is a total way of life in which religion is integral to economics, politics, law and society. In this regard, Sarwar (1989, p. 166-167) maintains that

> Islam is a complete way of life. It is the guidance provided by Allah, the Creator of the Universe, for all mankind. It covers all the things people do in their lifetime. Islam tells us the purpose of our creation, our final destiny and our place among other creatures. It shows us the best way to conduct our private, social, political, economic, moral and spiritual affairs.

Because Islam pervades the lives of its practitioners, it routinely shows itself in schools. Muslim students frequently practice their faith, when required, in these settings. They have little choice in the matter for their Islamic faith demands that they engage in certain mandatory practices. Two of the pillars of their religion involve praying and fasting. Muslims pray five times a day – at daybreak, noon, mid-afternoon, sunset and evening. Prayer is preceded by ritual absolution, usually done by water. When Muslims pray, they face Mecca and recite a series of prayers and passages from the *Qur'an*. While administrators in this study admitted that they did not always understand the significance of the associated prayer practices, virtually all we talked with attempted to find ways to help students engage in their prayer activities. Providing them with rooms and times for devotion was the most common accommodation mentioned.

Principals also said that they made efforts to accommodate students during Ramadan. During the month of Ramadan, all adult Muslims are required to fast from sunrise to sunset. They must abstain from eating, drinking, smoking and having sex during daylight hours. It is a time for reflection and self-discipline. During Ramadan Muslims thank God for His blessings, repent for their sins, discipline the body, strengthen their moral character, respond to the needs of the poor and hungry, and remember their ultimate dependence on God. Abstaining from food can be a challenge for some students during this time. To help Muslim students during this time of the year, administrators tried different approaches. Some acknowledged the difficulties associated with fasting, and made it a point to keep in close contact with parents during this time. Bryan, for example, believed that this was particularly important in cases where students appear to be struggling with their fasting. He maintained:

> During Ramadan when many of the older children are fasting from sun up to sunset, it's very difficult for them. They're weak, they're dizzy, it's hard to learn. And that lasts a month. So with some of the parents, if I call and say, "Your child's dizzy, they have a headache." And they'll say, "Oh, they're just beginning to fast, it's their first year and I told them that they don't have to fast every day, so I'm glad you gave me this feedback because I think I should send something for them to eat." They're not letting down the side if they do this.

Other administrators consulted with students on these matters.   Diane, for example, talked with one of her Muslim students before acting. She said

> Last year we talked about it. He said, "I'd like to try to stay in the classroom at lunch time, but if I can't handle it, can I do something else?" So I said, "Fine. Do you feel comfortable if I leave it up to you?" And he said, "Yep. Absolutely." Well it lasted about a week and then he said, "I can't handle this. I look at the walls and try not to smell the foods." And you know he was finding it really hard. So we left it open. And the same thing happened this year. He wanted to stay in the classroom, and then one day he really lost it. And I talked to him and I said, "Mohammad, you didn't mention it this year. Is there any possibility that you might be feeling hungry? Your nerves may not be the same as they are the rest of the time." And he said, "Yes." So he comes down and helps me [in the office] at lunchtime and he thinks it's great.

Others find other things that they can do to ease the food challenges for Muslim students. Jerry said that he thought that it would be a good idea to reschedule things like pizza lunches to make things easier for the significant Muslim student population in his school. He also said that it was possible to make other kinds of scheduling changes.

> It's difficult if you're fasting. I make my staff aware of that. So if you're doing gymnastics or something, maybe don't do it that month. You're not changing the whole program for them; you're just shifting it. There are times when you can do health lessons; instead of three periods of gym, you might do two of health that week.

Administrators may also need assistance in identifying special religious days. Some school districts help with these matters. Wesley's board, for example, issues a calendar that identifies all the significant religious days. It also encourages schools to avoid scheduling events on these days. Some administrators may also take steps to celebrate these days. A number of administrators pointed out that they organized committees to oversee these celebrations. Julie organized a committee that was principally populated by members of her parents' group. Jane had a similar "celebrations committee." It was composed of "six or eight" people from different faiths and backgrounds. It decided on matters like what celebrations would take place, what would be involved, and where they would be held. Pat's school took this kind of information and circulated it to the community. He said

> We send out flyers. We have what we call the "pink memo" or "Friday memo." And we'll put things in it like, "Next week is Rosh Hashanah and here's what it means. Would you talk to your class next week?" because a kid from Hong Kong had probably never heard of Rosh Hashanah, doesn't know what the celebration is, the purpose of it – so a one page flyer that talks about celebrating that.

Beside Rosh Hashanah, administrators also referred to other celebrations. Two that were frequently mentioned were Divali and Christmas. Divali, a Hindu festival that runs for five days, is celebrated throughout India and the world by devout Hindus. Divali or Deepavali means "festival of lights" or "row of lights." Among the legends connected with the origin of Divali, are the marriage of the Goddess Lakshmi and Lord Vishnu, Lord Krishna's triumph over the demon Narakasura, and Lord Rama's triumphant return to Ayodya after defeating Ravana. Many also believe that Lakshmi, the Goddess of wealth and good fortune, visits the homes of devotees during this time. A number of administrators talked about the ways in which they attempted to celebrate Divali in their schools. Barry said that in his school community

> The Hindu community got together and they put on, from 3:30 to 5:30 at the school, a show for the school and for the community, whoever was available. They had dances in Hindi; they had cultural dances; they had a fashion parade; they had singing; and they had all East Indian foods. And we had about 200 to 300 people here.

Throughout the year, Barry's school community celebrates in turn the various days that are set aside by the Chinese, Muslim, Hindu and Christian groups. Barry reported that there was little or no controversy over these celebrations. At other schools, however, celebrating selected religious days is not always so unproblematic. Ironically the controversies that do arise, do not generally concern non-Western religious celebrations but Christian ones, and in particular, Christmas. A number of administrators said that they had experienced problems when it came to celebrating Christmas in their schools. Janice, for example, maintained that problems often arose in her school around the belief that "you're not supposed to celebrate Christmas." She felt that this belief came from the questionable way in which people interpreted Ontario Ministry of Education edicts.[1] On the other hand,

---

[1] In response to court challenges (e.g., Zylberberg et al. v. Sudbury Board of Education, 1988; Canadian Civil Liberties Association v. Ontario, 1990; Islamic Schools Federation of Ontario v. Ottawa Board of Education, 1994) the Ontario Ministry of Education and the various school districts across the province

Larry spoke of the "great Christmas concert debate" in his school board. People took sides on the issues of whether there should be an event called a Christmas Concert. He said that at one point the central office issued a directive telling schools that they needed to be "very aware of how they presented things." Principals also reported, however, that resistance to Christian celebrations rarely came from non-Christians. Janice told us that some of the biggest resistors to Christmas celebrations were her teachers. She said that last Christmas she had some

> difficulty with the staff; it wasn't the parents at all. It was some of the staff who were resisting having anything to do with Christmas, the real Christmas at the school. It was fine to have Santa Claus and it was fine to have snowflakes and all the stuff from winter, but they were having great difficulty with anything to do with the real meaning of Christmas.

Some administrators acknowledged that a perceived commitment to honour non-Christian practices at what some believed to be at the expense of Christian practices has led to a backlash. Some administrators have heard from Christian parents who complain that they don't always have the opportunity to celebrate their traditions and faith to the extent that other non-Christian groups do. Larry reflected that

> There's something surfacing that is interesting and I don't know whether you'd call it a backlash or certain folks saying, "Everybody's identity has been taken care of but mine. And in this focus of making sure that the rights or the customs of other groups have been taken care of, we're feeling that ours are not important." – ours being the White folk, the WASPs. And I notice it here occasionally. So here, where nobody kicks up a fuss if we sing Christmas carols, when we went to more neutral type of concert, we got a few comments about, "Well, how come we're not celebrating our customs? Why is it that we cannot have Christmas carols? Why is it that we cannot have Christmas plays?"

Administrators also talked of their responses to these complaints. Some pointed out to parents that they didn't have any control over these sorts of approaches because they were in the board's hands. When parents complained to him about moving "away from Christmas," he said to them, "Okay, we were just trying to follow some Board directives, but thank you for that comment and I'll pass it along to someone else." Other administrators took a more proactive approach in planning Christmas activities. Some said that they gathered information about the wishes of their respective communities and encouraged dialogue among the various concerned groups. Jerry attempted to have such dialogue occur in committees or groups that included members of the community. What most administrators have discovered in these dialogues is that most non-Christian groups have no objections whatsoever to the celebration of Christian feasts in the school. Julie remembered the outcome of a meeting of parents that she organized to deal with religious celebrations. She said:

> In one of the groups, one of the Jewish moms said, "I have no difficulty with Christmas carols. In fact I'd really like my kids to be involved in the Christmas carols." And of course it was interesting watching the dynamics of the table because we had the traditional (Christian) parents who said "You don't sing Christmas carols," [while the other, non-Christian parents said], "Oh yes, we sing some of the traditional (Christian) songs. You know just because it's not part of our heritage we still recognize that it is part of Canada and so we would be just as adamantly opposed to not having any kind of traditional [Christian] thing."

---

have issued policies regarding formerly taken for granted Christian religious practices in schools. One of these cases (Zylberberg et al. v. Sudbury Board of Education, 1988) successfully challenged the reading of the Lord's Prayer. See also Dickinson & Dolmage (1996).

Other administrators attempted to resolve Christmas dilemmas in other ways. Ronda, for example, has sent out questionnaires into the community for the last three years. This questionnaire asks parents what they want the school to do at Christmas time. She said

> We sent a questionnaire home and we had a 96% return, which I thought was absolutely phenomenal. And the questionnaire addressed everything from the format, like (a), Do you want some kind of celebration? It doesn't matter what it is at that time of the year, or is that even necessary? If you did, do you want it to have any kind of overtones, particularly related to Christmas or Hanukkah or whatever. The next year when we asked again and the reply was overwhelming that the community wanted a Christmas activity, a Christmas pageant.

A number of administrators admitted that they were surprised at the willingness of non-Christians to accept Christian customs, particularly those that involve Christmas. Diane was surprised at the willingness of the non-Christian parents to have her children participate in Christmas celebrations. At one point, she had children volunteer to read passages from one of her favorite Christmas stories in front of an audience. After the readings, she discovered, much to her horror, that two of the readers, who incidentally loved the story, were Jewish. She remembered that

> As soon as I found out, I think I had heart palpitations. I got worried. You know, "What have I done wrong?" So anyhow, I called the mother and explained what happened. She said, "I'm fully aware of it," and she chuckled.

While the outcomes of these kinds of deliberations and surveys indicated that most people were in favour of celebrating Christmas, they also revealed that most people would like to see some recognition of other events around that time and at other times. The Celebrations Committee in Janice's school decided that the school "should recognize all and diminish none" of the various religious celebrations. The result was that at Christmas time, they had a "nice mixture of Hanukkah and Christmas."

ATTITUDES TOWARD EDUCATION

Not all parents, or students for that matter, have the same kinds of ideas about education as teachers or administrators. This difference is perhaps more pronounced between educators and those who come from Eastern or non-Western traditions. Many of the latter have had different kinds of educational experiences than those that are available in Western schools. One of the consequences of this is that those from non-Western traditions may have different expectations than educators about the kind of schooling that their children should receive. These parents may take issue with both the purposes and means of education. They may not agree with what teachers are trying to achieve and they may not approve of the strategies that they employ to meet these ends. Their children, on the other hand, may also experience difficulties adapting to expectations that are part of a system for which they are ill-prepared. The fallout from some of these differences inevitably falls into the lap of administrators, who must deal with it.

The educational experiences and expectations that parents and their children bring with them from a wide variety of traditions have their roots in long-standing historical traditions, Western colonialism, and more recent institutional practices. While some of the traditions are no longer practiced in ways that they once were and Western colonialism operates in different ways, they nevertheless continue to exert influence on individuals. For example, traditional North American and African indigenous and Hindu educational practices provide a background for the way in which many who belong to these traditions think about and would prefer to practice education. On the other hand, educational practices introduced during colonial periods still influence the way schools are organized and subjects are taught.

One of the key differences between these traditions and contemporary Western practices revolves around the nature of knowledge and its relationship to life. Western formal education tends to break down knowledge into distinct pieces and section it off from other parts of life. Native North American, African and Hindu traditions, on the other hand, approach education in a more holistic manner. Education and the knowledge associated with it had, and still has, a close relationship with life. In this regard the young were instructed as they went about their everyday lives. They learned everywhere and all the time, as opposed to learning in predetermined times and places, as occurs in most Western schools. These young people followed a more holistic life curriculum that was designed to assist them, not just to be knowledgeable, but also to be moral.

These holistic approaches to education may also be closely associated with moral or religious aspects of these traditions. In contrast to Western traditions in which knowledge is, at least in some ways, divorced from morality, some non-Western educational traditions revolve around religion or spirituality. Some Native North American traditions stress the importance of spirituality in the education of the young, for without a spiritual core, knowledge may be used in inappropriate ways (Ryan, 1988). The focus of traditional Hindu education, on the other hand, is on the spiritual growth of the individual. Islamic education also revolves around Islamic principles. Indeed education from an Islamic point of view makes little sense if it is removed from a religious context, that is, if it doesn't acknowledge the *Qur'an*. This is because the *Qur'an* lays down the foundations and principles for education. As such, Islamic education is characterized by a deep spirituality as well as common sense; knowledge is acquired through human reason and from the light of God.

Administrators in this study spoke of these and other views of education that they encountered in their respective school communities. They also noted that parents did not always agree with the ways in which they perceived that their children were educated. Some of these parents took issue with the lessons that students were learning, while others expressed dissatisfaction with teaching methods. Many of the views that they had the most difficulty understanding were associated with Asian students and their parents. The principals to whom we spoke found that they had to justify the school's approach to education to parents who appeared to take issue with the apparent lack of emphasis on math and science, experiential as opposed to rote forms of learning, and the lack of discipline that they perceived in schools. Instead of attempting to accommodate these beliefs, as they would have done in the case of religious beliefs, administrators tended to defend their preferred way of conducting education.

Administrators told us that they sometimes had to field concerns from Asian parents who assumed teachers did not always emphasize or spend enough time on math and science activities. Tom, for example, was challenged on curriculum night by parents who were upset that younger children are permitted to play rather than work with math materials. He said

> If you have curriculum night, there are umpteen questions around this whole area of pedagogy. "Why do you let the children play at that table so much with the math materials? Why doesn't my child know the five-times table in grade two?"

Research would seem to confirm Tom's perceptions. Stevenson et al. (1990) in their study of Chinese, Japanese and American parents and children, contend that the former two tend to have different expectations of education than the latter. They maintain that Chinese and Japanese mothers tend to be more concerned with academic achievement than their American counterparts. While American mothers were preoccupied with their children's education, they were more concerned with their general cognitive development; they favored activities that fostered this sort of growth over those that produced academic excellence. As such, American parents were happy to have their children engaged in activities that make them into what they perceived to be well-rounded individuals. Play activities in school suited many of these parents, because such activities were oriented towards producing this more rounded child. Japanese and Chinese parents, on the other hand, were less satisfied with such activities. They saw this unstructured time as time away from activities that directly influenced the child's academic achievement.

The interest in math and science among (many, it seems) Asian students and their parents has a long history. It may explain why many – but not all – Asian students do well in these areas and why, in contrast to American students, they consider themselves "bright" if they do well in math (Stevenson et al., 1990). The scientific and technological heritage of the Chinese, for example, is every bit as impressive as their contributions in other areas. Many Chinese scientific discoveries occurred before those of the Greeks, and according to Reagan (2000), they were more elaborately articulated and practically applied. Reagan goes on to say that the Chinese were much more effective than Europeans in exploring nature and in using natural knowledge for the benefit of humankind for fourteen centuries or so before the scientific revolution.

This interest in science and technology is not restricted to the Chinese, however. Nor can it be explained exclusively in "cultural" terms. The interest in science also extends to other Southeast Asian countries and can be attributed as well to the influence of Western colonialism on the subsequent institutional priorities of the region (Macias, 1993; Spring, 2001). The influence of colonialism extends as far back as the 19th century to Germany and as recently to post World War II efforts on the part of the United States. While colonizers established themselves in the region for the usual reasons, like territorial expansion, the extraction of resources and so on, they also sought to expand Western cultural and intellectual influence. They did so, in part, by emphasizing the importance of science and technology in the modern economic development of the region. The Asian countries accepted this fact and in their efforts to ensure this development, adopted Western-style educational institutions that emphasized science and technology. In time and with the direct assistance of former colonizers or wartime enemies, these nations developed educational institutions of superior quality, particularly in the areas of science and technology.   But the value of science did not remain exclusively within these institutions. Rather, this "scientific temperament" has been disseminated throughout these societies. Not only has it been enshrined in policy, it has also infiltrated individual, familial and societal values and motivations throughout the region.

The emphasis that has been placed on science-related areas and the Western-based educational institutions that foster these ideals have made it possible for many immigrant Asian students to do well, particularly in the areas of math and science, in the schools of Western countries. Of course, science-related subjects do not demand the same level of language proficiency as say, arts-based subjects, and this may also account for many of these students performing well in these particular subjects. However, it is not the case, despite the common impression, that most Asian immigrants fare well in Western schools (Macias, 1993; Lee, 1995; Ryan, 1999). Many of these young people struggle with their studies, for not all who emigrate from Asia have had the benefit of the superior quality of education in their home countries. Indeed, the cultural and economic diversity among these students often goes unrecognized.   For example, the first Vietnamese who traveled to the West were educated, familiar with Western culture, and possessed English language skills, and generally their children did well in school.   However, those who left their country after 1978 displayed considerable more variety in ethnicities and skills. Another subsequent wave of refugees that included Chinese from Vietnam, and Hmong and Mien from Loas and other areas, also displayed similar kinds of diversity. Today in the United States Vietnamese attend community colleges and other less selective institutions, and some struggle academically (Macias, 1993). So administrators and teachers should not always expect Asian students to be gifted and compliant students, and they should not expect all parents to have the same expectations and experiences as those who attended the best Western-style schools in Asia.

Administrators also maintained that they had to defend what some called an "experiential" or individualized approach to education. From time to time, they encountered parents from the East who favored the rote learning approach that they experienced in their own schooling. Tom noted that some parents had

> ... experiences [that] were different. The experience in their culture was oftentimes a rote form of learning; it was a memorized fact learning. It wasn't an experiential learning. And what we do in elementary schools in this country is more towards the experiential, experiential learning, where the child in fact understands concepts as opposed to just simply memorizing a lot of facts. The child understands the concept of two times three, not just is able to repeat "two times three equals six," and that's a concept that's hard sometimes to get into parents' minds. And sometimes you don't.

Other administrators spoke of a related difference between the interactive learning that Western schools favored and the teacher-directed learning that some parents favored. Roger observed that some students who came from Eastern countries experienced interactive learning for the first time.

> There's all sorts of literature out there extolling direct teaching methods that are used in Japan and China. I find it marvelous when those kids come here and don't by and large get the same kinds of teaching methodology. Instead of sitting in rows and getting rote learning, all of a

sudden they're working in groups and they're getting interactive learning. They're getting their first experience with student-centred learning.

Group rote learning is common in a number of Eastern traditions. The purposes of this kind of learning, however, extend beyond a mere ability to automatically recite isolated details. In Japan, for example, the practice of drill and repetition in classrooms has been passed down from ancient traditions; it is common practice for Japanese students to read in chorus and answer in unison (Hess & Azuma, 1991). These methods, however, are designed not merely for memorization, but as a prerequisite for analytical understanding. This repetition is believed to clear the way for students to acquire a deeper understanding of the meaning of the things that they are repeating. Hess and Asuma (1991) also note that this custom of learning through repetition is common not just in Japan. It is a powerful socializing technique designed to transmit adult norms unchanged in relatively closed societies that are resistant to change. It is featured in environments that have clear notions of hierarchy, favor structured forms of order, and employ particular kinds of socializing techniques.

A number of Eastern cultures have strong traditions of respect for hierarchy and order that make this form of rote learning possible. Confucianism is one of these traditions. Still one of the defining characteristics of Chinese mentality (Spring, 2001), Confucian moral thought is grounded in hierarchical relationships (Reagan, 2000). Whether it be husband and wife, ruler and subject, or father and son, each individual is expected to abide by his or her station in life. Everyone is tied to others, obliged to act in keeping with the specified nature of the relationships that they have with them. In this view of life, everyone has a responsibility to fulfil the duties that accompany his or her respective roles. This reciprocity is, however, not equal. It is based on enduring inequalities. Like other similar societies, this highly stratified social order is inherently conservative.

Respect for hierarchy and particular forms of social order make it possible for teachers to use rote learning and teacher-directed teaching techniques. In turn, respect for hierarchy is fostered in child-rearing attitudes and techniques. These techniques are evident in both Confucian and Japanese traditions. In the Confucian tradition, children were brought up to be affable, gentle and obedient (Reagan, 2000). They were taught to be content with their lot in life, to prize self-restraint and to value politeness. Children learned respect for elders and betters, not to answer back when their parents spoke to them, and not to sit when elders spoke to them. Many Japanese mothers, on the other hand, attempt to foster in their children first and foremost the characteristics of compliance and patience, as opposed to American mothers who favor such qualities as independence and tolerance (Hess & Azuma, 1991). For these Japanese mothers, a good child is one who is obedient, mild, gentle and self-controlled. They favor skills that promote group cooperation and compliance with authority. These views contrast with those of many American mothers who tend to believe that a good child is assertive, independent and socially competent.

Japanese parents, however, do not tend to use their own authority to socialize their children. In contrast to Western parenting strategies that rely on reward-based techniques, many Japanese parents do not resort to using resources and sanctions

(Holloway, 1988). Instead they rely on more unobtrusive control strategies. Among other things, they may encourage obedience by appealing to a child's understanding of the situation and their emotional commitment. In contrast to many American parents, Japanese parents tend to build on the child's desire to please, to create an understanding of, and commitment to, the adult's goals, and to diminish the salience of adult authority through the use of peers as socializing agents (Holloway, 1988). In this way, they do not jeopardize the intense bond that they have with their children. By not relying on external sanctions, they engender in the children a self-imposed or internalized sense of discipline. This carries over to school settings where Japanese teachers rely on the adaptive capacities of children rather than modifications in classroom environments for ensuring that students remain on-task. So Japanese teachers would be more likely to dwell on problems or themes for greater periods of time than would most American teachers who feel that they have to constantly modify the curriculum and teaching strategies to hold students' interest (Holloway, 1988). Japanese teachers can adopt such strategies because they are able to rely on students' internalized sense of patience and respect for authority.

Besides fielding parent questions about, and objections to, experiential and individualized learning strategies, administrators may also have to deal with problems related to different approaches to authority and advocacy. Pat noted that in contrast to some other students, Chinese students do not always have the skills to advocate for themselves. This, he believes, can lead to abuses on the part of administrators or teachers. He said:

> The Chinese kids are not advocates for themselves. So you call on a kid, you sit them down, you say, "You swore at your teacher." They'll hang their head and say, "Yes." "Well why did you do it?" "I'm sorry." "No I didn't ask you to apologize. I asked you why you did it." And without going into the whole thing, the Chinese kids don't defy authority, don't speak back, and therefore can become victims of an administration that's bully-ish or teachers that are bully-ish. And they don't fight back.... You've got to be really careful. You can't treat them [like students who advocate for themselves]. You have to be very gentle and very slow and take a lot of time if they're going to get fair treatment.

Administrators also spoke of other unexpected dilemmas that they encountered with students who had their own assumptions about authority relations. Paul remembered a time when a group of mostly Asian students were attempting to put together a student council. When it came time to figure out a method of selecting members, they felt that it would be best if they left it to teachers to choose. Their rationale was that teachers knew the students well and because they did, they could select the best members. They had difficulty accepting the idea, when Paul explained it to them, that they and not the teachers or the administration should be the ones to figure out how members should be chosen and that they should also be the ones who made the decisions. Paul suggested a compromise that the students eventually accepted.

DIFFERENCE AND INCLUSION

Administrators face many challenges in their quests to provide inclusive education for their students. These challenges become particularly obvious in contexts where there is considerably diversity. Administrators admit that they routinely struggle in their attempts to understand the various forms of diversity that they encounter and in their efforts to figure how to deal with them. These mostly Anglo administrators also acknowledge that they struggle most with non-Western traditions. Even so, administrators in this study talked about the various ways in which they attempted to include or accommodate these traditions in school activities. They made it possible for students to practice individual forms of religious worship. They also looked for ways to acknowledge and honour the various rituals and religious feasts that were celebrated in their respective communities. Principals adopted various strategies for figuring out what feasts they should recognize and how they should celebrate them. These included surveying community preferences and forming committees that represented many segments of the community.

Aside from religious diversity, administrators in this study also struggled with philosophies and conceptions of education that were different from their own. A number of administrators in this study said that they had to defend more "experiential" forms of education to parents who favored more structured approaches. They found that this was the case with parents and students who came from Eastern traditions. Some of these parents favored rote forms of learning, teacher-centered instruction and rigid forms of hierarchy; their children were frequently more comfortable in these kinds of learning situations, at least initially. In contrast to their efforts to accommodate religious beliefs, administrators resisted the wishes of those parents who wanted to see more structured approaches. Rather, they spent their time defending what they believed to be more sensible learning and teaching strategies. Administrators, however, did acknowledge that they did have an obligation to advocate for those students whose respect for authority did not permit them to advocate for themselves.

While including elements of various religious beliefs, attitudes towards education, and other elements of various cultural traditions in school activities is an important part of inclusive education and leadership, it only constitutes part of what administrators will have to do. Administrators will also need to adopt an appropriately critical framework for recognizing, understanding and doing something about differences that frequently do not work in the interests of groups whose culture differs from that of the school. This is because many school administrators, like others in the Western world, are trapped within a Eurocentric view. This Eurocentrism sometimes makes it difficult to recognize and understand the full significance and value of, say, non-Western cultural practices. So it is up to administrators to critically reflect on their own and others' taken for granted views of different others, to understand them in ways that both honour and work in the latter's interests, and to take action that is based on this orientation.

The next chapter extends this examination of differences. In doing so, it focuses on two particular cases.

CHAPTER 8

DEALING WITH DILEMMAS OF DIFFERENCE: TWO CASES

In this chapter, I continue to pursue issues of difference, but in a slightly different way. This time, I focus on two particular dilemmas that two administrators face. One attempts to come to terms with a gender-related issue and the other explores experiences with knowledge and interaction. The two administrators attempt to resolve their respective dilemmas by focusing on the concept of understanding. For both, the key to solving the problem rests with their ability to grasp the "culture" of the people involved in the dilemma. This understanding, they believe, will enable them to comprehend what is going on in the respective situations and to devise strategies that will result in solutions that will satisfy all parties. Unfortunately, their attempts at understanding fall short of what they need for ideal solutions. While one of the administrators is reasonably successful in satisfying the participants, her understanding of the situation is a narrow one that fails to tackle some of its complexities. The other administrator finds herself unable to understand the situation at all. The experiences of both of these administrators speak to the limitations of attempts to comprehend the worlds of different others. It also addresses the complexities involved in attempts at inclusion. On the one hand, a failure to understand different others may defeat efforts to include them in school activities. On the other hand, however, understanding may also increase efforts to resist inclusion.

UNDERSTANDING AND DIFFERENCE

The concept of understanding is featured prominently in particular approaches to multicultural education. The theory is that educators and others in the school community need to understand different others because this reckoning will engender acceptance and reduce racism. So, for example, Gibson (1976, p. 9), citing this variation of multicultural education, maintains that "multicultural education programs will provide [for the cultural enrichment of all students] by fostering understanding and acceptance of cultural differences and that these programs will in turn decrease racism and prejudice and increase social justice." These differences that educators may need to understand include conceptions of, beliefs in, and practices associated with: patterns of language and communication (Corson, 1992; Erickson & Mohatt, 1982; Philips, 1983); teaching and learning styles (Appleton, 1983; Cazden &, Leggett, 1981; Ramirez, 1989; Ryan, 1992a); testing (Deyhle, 1983, 1986); cognitive processing (Cole & Scribner, 1974; Das, Kirby, & Jarman, 1979; Gay & Cole, 1967; Tharp, 1989); self-concept (Clifton, 1975); family traditions and commitments (Divoky, 1988; Gibson, 1987; Olson, 1988); locus of control (Tyler & Holsinger, 1975; Zenter, 1971); attitudes toward cooperation and competition (Clifton, 1975; Goldman & McDermott, 1987; Ryan, 1992b); aspirations (Gue, 1975; Grygier, 1977); and space and time (Clifton, 1977; Ryan, 1991). While educators and social scientists may disagree over the precise ways in which differences between the dominant Western-based tradition and other traditions play themselves out in schools and classrooms (see for example, Erickson, 1987; Ogbu, 1987; Trueba, 1988), most agree that these differences contribute to problems for both students and the educators responsible for their education.

This theory of multiculturalism is based on at least two key assumptions. The first one is that it is possible to understand different others "the way that they really are." This theory posits that if administrators take the time then they presumably would be able to ferret out an accurate picture of the group in which they were interested. Unfortunately, this view ignores the manner in which meaning is constructed. People make sense of the world within the confines of sense-making frameworks or discourses with which they are familiar (Ryan, 1999). Since these discourses are culturally specific, then the meanings that administrators attribute to the actions of particular groups of people will inevitably be filtered through lenses that have been nurtured within this (Anglo/European) cultural framework. So when they attempt to understand different others they will inevitably place the latter's actions, words and values into their own culturally conditioned frameworks. Because frameworks for understanding are nurtured in very different contexts, the chances are that Western educators will not always interpret life in ways that non-Western students and parents will. Given this, accuracy, that is, an isomorphism between peoples' interpretations and "the way things really are," is a state that never can be attained. The best that administrators can do is to understand episodes in the same way that different others in their school communities do. But since they routinely bring different interpretive frameworks to bear than members of their school communities, then the chances are that administrators will not always see situations in the same way as the latter. In other words, they will not always be able to "understand" some of the groups in their communities.

The other assumption upon which this view of understanding rests is that once understanding is achieved – something that in itself is problematic – then fair treatment will automatically follow. In this view, racism will disappear and social justice will prevail if and when people understand other people. This position overlooks two key elements. The first is that racism extends beyond individual and group differences and runs deeper than people's conscious understandings. It is this system of racism that makes it possible for people to notice certain differences and to evaluate them in a variety of ways. Antiracism advocates like Tryona (1993) maintain that "cultural understanding" will do little to reduce racism because it fails to address the wider structural realities in which it is entangled.

Others also contend that understanding will not necessarily reduce racism. McCarthy (1990) maintains that there is no guarantee that "understanding" will produce this result. It is just as likely to increase negative feelings toward different others. There is also a danger that focusing on differences will "pathologize" them (Brah & Minhas, 1985). This means that people will tend not to look at different cultural attributes in a neutral manner, but will evaluate them in a negative way. Seen through their own Western lenses, educators will see these cultural proclivities as inferior to their own or as just plain "bad." In one of the cases described here, the administrator interprets particular and different internal family and gender relationships that she encounters as undesirable.

Inclusive approaches to education will inevitably involve efforts to understand others. However, administrators and other educators need to realize that there are limitations to understanding. Comprehending these limitations represents a step toward the provision of inclusion. This chapter illustrates these limitations.

TWO DILEMMAS

In the day-to-day management of schools with diverse ethnocultural populations, administrators are likely to encounter situations that perplex them. Barbara and Joan are administrators who face such dilemmas. Their quandaries are typical of the predicaments described by administrators interviewed in the course of this research. As these and other administrators grapple with their dilemmas, they are limited by their own life histories and ideological frameworks. Their attempts to understand the meaning of these situations are caught within their own limited culturally-imposed worldviews. The following section presents details of two selected dilemmas.

Barbara's Predicament

Barbara stood as her five guests were ushered into her office. She had expected four of them and was somewhat surprised to see the fifth. Barbara recognized this additional guest, in spite of a black veil partially hiding her face, as the teenage daughter of one of the couples. Barbara was quite surprised to see the girl, because she had been told that the young woman had returned to Asia last week to care for her ailing grandmother. In her third month as an administrator in South Haven School, Barbara was already accustomed to these sorts of surprises. Even so, she realized that she had much to learn about, and from, the many non-Western groups that were represented at this suburban secondary school. Barbara knew immediately that this encounter was about to serve up one of those learning occasions.

The group hesitated as they entered the office, apparently a little uncomfortable with what was to come. Barbara tried to put them at ease, offering them seats and coffee. They seated themselves quickly, but respectfully declined the beverage, as Barbara knew they would. As Barbara was to discover, the two families were from strict religious communities. Both of these communities had, by Canadian standards, rigid codes of behavior for their teenage daughters. Community norms dictated that young women not consort with members of the opposite sex. Among other things, they were forbidden to touch potential husbands or to make any sort of eye contact with them. Dating was out of the question, and marriages were always arranged by the parents.

One of the fathers spoke first. Barbara could tell by the strain in his voice that he regarded this matter as extremely serious. In hesitant tones he explained to Barbara that, over the past week, his family had received four phone calls from a young man who claimed that his daughter had been dating young men, skipping classes, and "doing this and doing that." The other family had received two similar phone calls. Despite vigorous denials from the two young women, both families viewed their problem as extremely serious. In fact, the young women's denials were quite beside the point. Apparently, if news of their daughters' indiscretions spread – whether it be fact or fiction – the young women would be seen as unmarriageable in the community. So concerned were the parents about confidentiality in the matter that they insisted that no translators be present at the meeting and that the matter not be discussed beyond the office walls. They believed such talk could sabotage their daughters' chances at marriage and they wanted it stopped at once. In the end, the father of one young woman, who sat silently with her head bowed, threatened to take the matter to the board if Barbara could not solve the problem herself. This was no simple or straightforward problem for Barbara, particularly because she did not approve of gender-related beliefs that she believed dominated relationships among this group.

Joan's Quandary

Across town, Joan was experiencing another kind of dilemma. Although the specific details were substantially different from Barbara's experience, the situation also involved an encounter with a group who did not share the beliefs and understandings of many Canadian educators. Not long ago, Joan was appointed principal of a new school. In the first few weeks she was delighted with the warm welcome that the community extended to her and her colleagues. One of the many community members who stopped in to greet her was the father of a First Nation student at the school. He brought with him a gift of sweetgrass. While Joan sincerely appreciated the gesture, she did not completely understand the significance of the gift and so she asked the man about it. He responded to her first question by telling her that, if hung on the inside of the school wall facing east and blessed by an elder, the sweetgrass would protect the school from evil spirits and bring good fortune. Wanting to know more, Joan then inquired into the history of the tradition. Her visitor's response to this second question, however, took her completely by surprise. Instead of answering he became, in Joan's words, "agitated, very agitated." She confessed that, at the time, she was completely bewildered by his behavior. The man left a short time later, leaving Joan uneasy about the encounter, and particularly disappointed because the man had come in good faith but had left in anger. Joan was most uncomfortable, however, because she had no idea why he had left in such a state.

Unwilling to let things hang, Joan pursued the matter further. She contacted the man and he agreed to meet again with her. At the meeting, he explained to her that he had perceived her inquiries as a questioning of his gesture, and he told her, "In my culture you do not question gifts." Joan explained that her intent was not to question the gift but rather to understand the custom. "My intent was genuinely one of wanting to understand the custom. I always have this need of knowing why, it doesn't matter whether it's technology or culture or whatever." When the man left the second time, Joan felt that she still was not much wiser, even though she now understood that, in his culture, gifts were not to be questioned. She now faced a perplexing dilemma. She wanted to learn more about aboriginal beliefs so that in the future she would be able to respond in appropriate ways. However, if she attempted to learn more, she believed that she also risked offending the gentleman once again. Joan continued to wonder: "When is it okay to ask something? How do you know it's okay to ask?" But even as she asked, Joan was bewildered about how she could go about finding answers to her questions.

THE PROBLEM-SOLVING CONTEXT

The above dilemmas are by no means unique to administrators in Ontario, Canada. What's more, many administrators in North America, the United Kingdom and Australia who are experiencing diversity in their school communities are likely to face similar situations. One response to the difficulties associated with this diversity has been the initiation of antiracist education. The Province of Ontario, for example, where both Barbara and Joan administer schools, declared some years ago that all school districts must develop antiracist and ethnocultural equity policies for their schools (The Ontario Ministry of Education and Training, 1993). By 1995, all districts were expected to have policies and practices in place that addressed leadership, school-community relationships, language, curriculum, assessment, counseling, harassment, and staff development issues. These moves were based on a recognition that "Ontario's education system has been primarily Western European in content and perspective, reflecting the original patterns of settlement in the province" (The Ontario Ministry of Education and Training, 1992. p. 2). The antiracism program outlined here was to begin by acknowledging that some "existing policies, procedures, and practices in the school system are racist in their impact, if not their intention" (The Ontario Ministry of Education and Training, 1993. p. 5). Such education sought to correct past biases at the system, school, and classroom level. From this perspective, educators were encouraged to "recognize how discrimination, distortions and omissions occur . . . [and take steps] to correct distortions and remedy omissions and discriminatory conditions" (The Ontario Ministry of Education and Training, 1992, p.2).

Although this province-wide antiracism policy has since been dropped, both Barbara's and Joan's school districts have adopted antiracist education, developing antiracist and ethnocultural equity policies well before most other districts in the province. Quite beyond this institutional assurance, both Barbara and Joan are personally committed to a philosophy of equity. Both believe schools have an obligation to accommodate the various cultural practices and beliefs of the schools' client groups and eliminate subject matter or schooling practices that denigrate, devalue, or discriminate against particular groups of students and their families. Barbara, for example, explains that "we are a multicultural nation. It's not a melting pot. We're a mosaic and we have to accommodate as much as we possibly can." Joan also actively promotes diversity in her school. She goes out of her way to include the community in school activities, to sensitize teachers to the complexities of diversity, to encourage teachers to critically scrutinize curriculum and reading materials, and generally to make life in school more comfortable for all students. Such initiatives, however, can be complex, even paradoxical. Indeed, there are situations, as we will see, where ethnocultural equity may conflict with other deeply held beliefs about other kinds of equity, or where attempts to achieve an understanding may be frustrated by the very efforts made to attain it.

DEALING WITH ADMINISTRATIVE DILEMMAS

How do administrators handle these diversity-related challenges? What initiatives can they take to promote equity and inclusion in their schools? In the cases at hand, how did Barbara and Joan deal with their own dilemmas? Let us first consider Barbara's experience. Asked what she does in situations like the one described above, she replied: "You fly by the seat of your pants, you really do. And you . . . get information." Improvisation is not something unique to Barbara. In fact, many of the administrators we interviewed approached these kinds of situations in much the same way. They did so because, with few exceptions, they had little experience in similar situations. They were generally unable to rely either on their personal experience or on conventional wisdom in administration to work their way through the challenge. This is because they were often confronted by understandings and beliefs that they did not totally comprehend. Therefore, in many of these cases, a first step in addressing the situation was to understand the situation at hand. To do so, administrators needed to acquire information about the particular group in question and the circumstances surrounding the situation in question.

Gender Equity

Barbara conducted what she described as her research both before and after her meeting with the parents. Because she had a general sense of the issue in advance, she was able to consult a number of sources and use the information as she prepared for the meeting. Barbara approached several teachers and students and spoke with a board consultant. From the students and teachers, she learned details of the specific situation and developed a general overview of the religious sect in question. The consultant, on the other hand, supplied her with further details about the practices of this group. On the basis of this information, Barbara was able to establish that the callers were in all probability young suitors who had been rejected by the daughters of the two families. The calls were, in her estimation, acts of retribution. These young men apparently knew "how to press the fathers' buttons" and did so with the intention of retaliating against the girls. Barbara also learned more about the particular religious groups, and this knowledge was subsequently confirmed in her meeting with the parents. While the parents were obviously concerned with the actual behavior of their daughters, they were apparently even more concerned about the impression that might be left within their communities. If word spread about their daughters' alleged indiscretions, these parents would have little or no chance of arranging marriages for them. In other words, the parents' priority was to save face in their communities. When it came time to meet the parents, Barbara felt she knew exactly what the parents were talking and thinking about. In her own words, Barbara recalls her efforts to understand the situation: "I hastened to understand their perspective. And I did. I did understand that it had little to do with the girl, that it had a lot to do with her reputation. So now we know what we're talking about. And if these boys do not stop these phone calls, these girls could have to go back to Asia because there is a chance that the community will know."

Barbara's research was at least partly successful in enabling her to understand the particular Islamic group with whom she was dealing. That is, her interpretations of some – but not all – of the practices that had a bearing on the situation at hand coincided with those of the people involved. Barbara and the parents would have both understood the expectations that the Islamic community had for relationships between adolescent boys and girls. These relationships are part of the conditions necessary for successful marriages to take place. Marriage has existed as a sacred and central Islamic tradition. It is vitally important because it is seen as the foundation for family and community – institutions that represent the essential structure of the Islamic way of life (Haw, 1998). Because marriage is so important in the continuation of Islamic tradition, members of the community put much effort into safeguarding it. Parents, in particular, take on the responsibility of seeing that their children are married within an Islamic tradition. Not only do they want to avoid the stigma that accompanies spinsterhood for a daughter, but they also are anxious to avoid the inevitable humiliation that accompanies the conditions for marriage ineligibility. In doing so, they come prepared to ward off threats that jeopardize this process.

Islamic parents generally see a number of threats in the mixed-sex schools that their children attend in the Western world (Haw, 1998). The biggest threat comes in the form of their daughters' actions or perceived actions. In the eyes of their parents, these young women can jeopardize their chances for marriage if they violate accepted forms of behaviour. Unacceptable behaviour in these cases usually involves familiar or close contact with members of the opposite sex. So parents and the community, notwithstanding variations in community standards, will have strict boundaries for contact between the two groups – dating is simply out of the question. In this patriarchal context, it is generally the young women who are at risk when community norms are violated or perceived to be violated. Presumably the parents of prospective husbands, and the ones who normally choose spouses for their children, would see young women who consorted in inappropriate ways with the opposite sex as unsuitable partners for their sons. Given the importance of marriage in Islam, and a wish to avoid humiliation and stigma, parents of young women take pains to ensure that their daughters continue to be seen as eligible for marriage by containing their activities. Perceptions are particularly important here. It really doesn't matter if young women are abiding by cultural rules if the perception in the community is that they are not. So parents will go to considerable lengths to ensure that community perceptions of their daughters are ones that do not jeopardize their eligibility for marriage.

Barbara's understanding helped her resolve this dilemma, at least on a temporary basis. The resolution, however, allowed her to avoid what she believed to be a central issue in this dilemma – conflicting equity prerogatives. On the one hand, Barbara, her school, and her school district are committed to ethnocultural and gender equity. On the other hand, however, Barbara perceived that particular groups – like the one with which she was currently dealing – hold strong patriarchal values and beliefs. To fully accommodate the wishes and beliefs of these religious groups, Barbara and her school would have to violate their commitment to gender equity, or so it appeared. Barbara herself is a strong advocate of gender equity, and while she makes every effort to acknowledge and respect beliefs of all cultural groups, she readily admits that she finds these gender-related practices personally offensive. In this case, the actions of the parents, in particular the father, made her "sad" and "enraged." She had particular difficulty with what she perceived to be the relationships of the fathers to the mothers and daughters and the kinds of restrictions that were placed on the women. Indeed, Barbara was upset by the way that one mother apparently deferred to the father instead of standing up for the daughter, and by the father's lack of trust in the young woman. She freely admitted wanting, at one point, to "crunch this little man." Barbara also objected that these young women were not permitted to mix freely with other students in the way that most other students were. Referring to one of the girls, she maintained that "this is a 14-year-old girl. She just turned 14. She's just a kid." In the end, however, Barbara felt that it was her responsibility to emphasize the commitment to gender equity to the parents. She explained: "I think my responsibility is to reiterate to the parents what Ontario public schools are all about and to let them know we believe in gender equity and let them know we encourage boys and girls in different cultures to mix." Barbara bluntly admits that she sometimes takes a stand against particular ethnocultural values that contradict the ones that she favors, however difficult taking such a stand may be. She explains directly that:

> When you're not accommodating you feel somehow you've failed, because we are a multicultural nation .... We're a mosaic and we have to accommodate as much as we can. It really does hurt not to be able to do that. And in some cases you want to take a stand. [But] I can't accommodate that kind of abuse of young women. It would be the same thing if I found out a young girl was to undergo circumcision .... I couldn't stand it. I wouldn't give a damn about their culture or what they believe is important. There comes a point where you have to say: "This is wrong, you're in Canada now."

How, then, does Barbara reconcile her personal beliefs with the wishes of the parents in her office? Is it possible for her to satisfy the parents without compromising her deeply held beliefs? To achieve her goal, Barbara took two separate tacts. First, she reiterated her philosophy about gender-related freedoms to the parents in their meeting. "Our major concern in school," she maintained, "is the academic progress of your daughter, as well as her physical growth and well-being. And we encourage girls and boys to talk together." Anticipating pleas from the parents to isolate their daughters, she went on to tell them she "could not make false promises. There [are] 2,000 kids in the school and I certainly can't walk around after their daughters and make sure they don't talk to anybody." The parents claimed they understood, but they still wanted to ensure that their daughters acted appropriately and to prevent any talk about their alleged indiscretions.

Barbara also took other measures for her own peace of mind. First, she kept from the parents much of what she knew of their daughters' activities at school. These young women, like many others in their situation, according to Barbara, take advantage of their new-found freedom. She maintained that "What I perceive when I walk around the halls are these girls who are absolutely going wild as a result of the strict behavior they have to maintain at home. And they're flirting like crazy with these boys and they're kissing each other and throwing snow at each other and rolling on the ground. And I know if their fathers saw them, they'd be flogged. I know that. And here I was sitting there with [this] knowledge ... And you know, it's a terrible thing to know."

Barbara chose not to reveal these details to the parents. Doing so, she obviously felt, would compromise her personal belief that these young women had the right to partake in certain interactions, not to mention the harsh punishment she felt would be forthcoming were their habits discovered. Barbara was also engaged in what she referred to as "a conspiracy" with the two girls in question, albeit after the fact. In the course of a conversation with one of the multicultural assessment officers in the school district, the woman offered to consult with the young women. Desperately wanting someone to talk to about their situations, both jumped at the chance. Barbara was well aware that their parents would not approve, but felt it was the least she could do to assist these young women with the injustices she believed were being perpetrated against them.

How did Barbara placate the parents? For her, a key was in her understanding that the parents were first and foremost concerned with stifling rumors about their daughters. Because she was aware of this, Barbara concentrated on issues associated with the circulation and curtailment of information rather than on the behavior of the young women. In the meeting she told the parents about what she believed to be the origin and reason for the phone calls. She also took care to attribute the improprieties to the boys and not to their daughters. Barbara stated: "I did suggest ... to the parents that their buttons were being pushed [and that] perhaps they could consider changing their phone numbers, [or] perhaps they could consider hanging up. But I let it be known that I was much more annoyed with the activities of these boys than I was with what the girls were doing."

She did not, however, ignore policing measures. Acknowledging that she could not ensure conformity to the parents' rules, Barbara suggested that one of the mothers, who had a master's degree in mathematics, could tutor in the learning center at the school. In this way, she would be able to supervise her daughter during the lunch hour. The woman seemed very interested but ultimately declined because she had to care for her four year-old at home. In the end, Barbara believed that the parents left the meeting "happy," apparently satisfied that she was doing all she could to help them out. The parents seemed now to understand more about the disturbing calls they were getting, and they appeared to accept that it wasn't necessarily their daughters' indiscretions that were prompting them. Most importantly, they seemed to believe that the calls did not necessarily mean that they would lose face in their communities or that they would have to send their daughters back to India to ensure their marriagability.

Barbara had at least two key objectives in her dealings with the parents and their children. The first was to placate the parents. So in this respect, her understanding about marriage and relationships between adolescents helped her out. She was able to use this knowledge to successfully allay the concerns of the parents. But Barbara was also concerned about the daughters. She was quite frank about her distaste for the gender related practices that she perceived to exist among this group, and she vowed that she would go behind the parents' back to give the young women the help that she felt they needed. While Barbara's interpretation of the relationship-related practices appeared to coincide with that of the parents, her take on the nature and place of gender related practices within this culture did not. In fact, her view of these practices was a narrow one. Among other things, she failed to comprehend the complexity of these gender practices within the context of Islamic families and communities.

Gender practices are an integral part of the fabric of Islamic family and community life. As mentioned previously, family and community life is the bedrock of Islamic society. Despite the many local and cultural variations in the Islamic world, the family and community remain constant. This communal orientation differs from the individualism that characterizes life in much of the Western world (See, for example, Ryan, 1992a). Maintenance of these integral institutions requires that men, women and children honour the specific rights, duties and obligations that accompany family and community membership. While the roles of men and women differ within the family, they are nevertheless meant to be complementary; ideally the fulfillment of these mutual obligations will enrich family life. Together these two roles, if carried out in appropriate ways, will ensure the integrity of the family, and in turn, the community (Haw, 1998; Reagan, 2000).

Much has been made of the patriarchy in the Islamic world. Barbara is only one of many who carry the stereotypical views of what they believe to be sexist Islamic traditions. Now there is little doubt that, variations notwithstanding, Islamic societies, like Western societies, are patriarchal. This patriarchy, however, is not something that can be attributed to Islam. In fact, Islam commends plurality, diversity and equality (Haw, 1998). The *Qur'an* does not recognize distinctions in status between men and women. Rather, it enjoins both equally to acquire knowledge and seek God through religion. The status of women, moreover, was improved markedly by Islam in the time of the prophet Mohammad. Islam gives women important rights and privileges. They have the right to enter into contracts, to earn money and to possess goods in their own right. They are also equal to men in the pursuit of knowledge (Haw, 1998). Thus the patriarchy that we find in Islamic societies ought not to be attributed to Islamic teachings but to the patriarchal societies in which the religion operates. Among other things, these secular patriarchal patterns have, over the years, penetrated interpretations of the *Qur'an* and have come to relegate women to inferior positions in a number of Islamic communities.

In their attempts to get to the heart of "cultural dilemmas" like the one described here, educators like Barbara tend to pathologize the Asian family (Brah & Minhas, 1985). In other words, they believe that the cause of the problem lies with the family. Their superficial understanding of family relationships leads them to portray it, and in particular its perceived gender relationships, as dysfunctional. To understand the situation at hand, Barbara reaches for the popular discourse that represents Islam as a faith imposing intellectual slavery, female oppression and terrorism, and Muslim women as exoticized and ruthlessly oppressed and in need of liberation, as guardian and guarded, and as victim/emblem of religious fundamentalism (Haw, 1998). This lens, however, does not do justice to the complexity of the gender (and "race" and class) relationships operating not only within the family, but also outside of it, in the school and world in which these young women interact. In fact, this particular form of Western liberalism has little to offer many Muslim women (Haw, 1998).

The Western liberal framework that Barbara employs to understand and do something about the "cultural dilemma" is simplistic on two counts (Haw, 1998). The first concerns her understanding of what the central problem is for these young women. Like other educators in her situation, Barbara believes that it revolves around the warring generations in the young women's families. She is under the impression that the primary cause of the young women's anxiety is the differences that they have with their parents, and the actions she takes are designed to relieve this anxiety. Unfortunately these understandings and actions do not account for or address the underlying social problems of poverty, inequality, male honour and power relationships which maintain female oppression. It also does not account for or address the racism and sexism that they experience in school and outside of school (Brah & Minhas, 1985). While there is little doubt that the intergenerational conflict that they experience may be stressful for them, they also have to deal with "Western" sexism and racism on a daily basis. Focusing on intergenerational conflict merely deflects attention away from this more global issue.

The other limitation of this view is that it presents a narrow view of Islamic families. The two generations are depicted as warring against each other. The father is frequently seen as authoritarian, uncompromising, and oppressive. Contrary to these stereotypes, Brah and Minhas (1985) maintain that the majority of Asian girls have strong, positive, and mutually supportive relationships with their parents. Furthermore, the intergenerational conflict among Asian families is not any higher than among "White families." Because Barbara understood little about the private sphere of Asian family life and its dynamic and vibrant female cultures, she jumped to conclusions about what she perceived to be injustices and acted accordingly. Beyond that, her actions ran the risk of alienating these young women from their families and the communities upon which they depend for support.

Knowledge and Interaction

Like Barbara, Joan placed a high value on understanding other cultural perspectives. She believed that understanding can prevent the type of stereotyping that can be so harmful to many individuals and groups. Joan said: "I think that a lot of the stereotypes come about because we don't understand. And it's that fear or that ignorance that creates negative stereotypes." She also believed that the key to understanding involves the collection of information. For her, understanding is very much an empirical enterprise. Joan has initiated a number of strategies to gather information, including sending out questionnaires and highlighting different cultural heritages within the school. She elaborated:

> Other cultures were brought in. Information was brought in through that. We initially celebrated things like, you know, let's find out where we're from. "Where did you come from? What school did you come from?" And now let's take it a step further. "Where were you born? Were you born in Canada? If not in Canada, let's find it on the globe, let's locate it on the map. What language

do you speak?" Some of the typical things that probably a lot of schools do. Beyond that, through our "emergency" form that goes home at the beginning of the year, we also made parents aware that if they had any information that they wanted to share with us about their family life, about customs, to please feel free and come in.

Joan's data collection strategy, however, as we have seen in this particular case, proved to be insufficient to cope with the situation. Ironically, the strategy itself proved to be part of the problem. Indeed, Joan admitted that her previous knowledge of First Nations people – obtained largely through university courses – left her with the faulty impression that she had an adequate grasp of First Nations issues and cultural practices. But as she subsequently recognized, "a little knowledge can be a dangerous thing." Thus, when the man made his initial exit, Joan was completely bewildered. While she learned a little more during his second visit, she was then unsure how to learn more, as was her customary strategy in these cases. Certainly, direct questioning of the man was simply out of the question. At this point she called on the race relations officer at the central office and discussed the issue with another consultant as well. These discussions proved to be helpful, and through them Joan began gradually to understand some of the conventions surrounding the prerogatives of individual men and women and intrusive behavior among this particular group of First Nations people (see, for example, Ryan, 1992b).

Groups of First Nations people in Canada and the United States have in the past subscribed to communication styles that were markedly different than those practiced by non-Native people. While these practices are not as prevalent as they once were, and may vary considerably from group to group, they nevertheless provide the framework for ways in which some Native people continue to interact with others. These conventions are closely associated with practices of social control that are alien to Western forms of social organization. Many Northern nomadic hunting societies, for example, displayed uniquely egalitarian characters (Riddington, 1988). These nomadic people lived without the formal hierarchical structures that pervaded Western social organization. First and foremost they valued personal autonomy and the right to make decisions about those things that mattered most in their lives. They were quite content having others make their own decisions because they had a deep abiding trust in them. Riddington, (1988, p. 107), for example, maintains that

> The individualism of the Northern Indian people is based on a fundamental social compact, a trust in the individual's social responsibility and informed intelligence. Northern hunting people trust the individual to be responsible, not only to him or herself, but to all other humans and trans-human persons.

Thus, the control one has over another in these societies was limited. Efforts to directly influence another or to penetrate another's space were simply not tolerated. Philips (1983) provides a comparatively recent example of this practice. She illustrates how these values influence the communication practices of the Warm Springs Native people. The issue of control, Philips claims, plays a central role in the ways Warm Springs people interact with one another. Unlike most Anglos, Warm Springs people who find themselves in the role of listener do not attempt to control the length of the speaker's discourse, nor when they speak, do they seek to influence who speaks next. In fact, in most cases, the address of the speaker is so general that a response, immediate or otherwise, is not required. People speak when they are ready to do so. Intrusive actions such as gazing at one another, demanding a reply to a query, or asking what may be perceived as personal questions constitute inappropriate acts of control. They are insulting to those to whom these acts are directed because they violate the fundamental trust that the people have in one another.

These First Nation conventions conflict with common Western conventions, and in particular, those interactions or communicative practices that involve the acquisition of knowledge. Acquiring knowledge in the Western world, whether it is part of medical practice (Foucault, 1973), science (Foucault, 1970, 1979) or simply part of personal daily routines, commonly involves inquisition tactics. People interrogate, scrutinize and observe that which they wish to understand. Some actually slip into scientific discourses when describing their efforts to find out about something. Joan, for example, speaks about conducting "research" to acquire "data." While some of these methods are benign, others can be intrusive. This is particularly true for cases that involve people. Information seekers in these cases may resort to forms of interrogation when seeking knowledge about a subject. For those who value highly personal autonomy, like the gentleman in Joan's scenario, such actions can be troubling. They can be troubling for some Native people because they undermine the trust and respect that these people extend to and expect from others. Asking penetrating and repetitive questions about motives, for example, may give the impression that the person in question is incapable of acting in a responsible manner.

Despite Joan's "research," she admitted that she was still far from a thorough understanding of the situation. Fortunately for her, the father was also dissatisfied with the current state of their relationship and decided to do something about it. As Joan tells it: "The gentleman must have thought about it as well, because he came back a long time later with two pieces of photocopied material on sweetgrass. Because the other things learned from that is that it's never written down, that the only person who could tell me that would be an elder. Well, he went and spoke to an elder, and explained to him and I guess they said it was okay to give us some information." In the end, Joan felt that she had made some progress. She understood a little more about her intrusive behavior, and her relationship with the man had improved to a point. However, Joan admitted she still had no answer to her central problem – how to learn more about such practices so that she could understand them and, thus, act in more appropriate ways when she was apparently not permitted to ask questions. She still had no answer to her question, a question she posed to the parent a number of times in their last meeting. Joan recounts: "I said to him, you know, 'Tell me, then' –I guess I said that 41 times – 'Tell me, how can I understand and how can I ensure that I treat someone the way they would like to be treated when I now feel that I can't ask any questions?'"

THE LIMITS OF UNDERSTANDING

Despite the apparent move away from a model that highlights understanding other cultural practices and beliefs, school administrators like Barbara and Joan may find themselves devoting considerable effort in their attempts to understand ways of life that differ from their own. Routine activities such as accommodating the wishes of parents, satisfying their concerns or demands, or solving a problem unique to a particular group, demand that administrators grasp the situation and, therefore, understand the perspectives of various participants. What does understanding entail? What, for example, do Barbara and Joan mean when they refer to understanding? Does this differ from the processes of understanding in which each of us engages in our day-to-day activities? Schutz (1967) provides us with insight here. For Schutz, understanding occurs in the course of making sense of our own experience. As we "get on" with our lives, we routinely attribute meaning to our daily experiences. In other words, understanding is a matter of interpreting the world we experience in order to decide on future courses of action. Doing so often requires that we come to terms with the meanings that others attribute to situations. This does not mean, Schutz contends, that we interpret the experiences of others. Rather, we simply reinterpret our own experiences. We appeal to our own experience and knowledge and not to the minds of others, integrating what we perceive into our own pre-existing frames of reference and the particular life patterns with which we are familiar. As part of this process, we attempt to come to terms with what Schutz (1967) refers to as the "because" and the "in order to" motives of others.

Understanding in this sense involves knowing why people are doing what they do – determining what caused them to act in certain ways and what they intended to do in the circumstances. For both Barbara and Joan, understanding involves making sense of the motives of others. They are able to do so, however, only within their own frames of reference. Sense is acquired when their perceptions correspond to, or are integrated into, familiar patterns of interaction. This is not to say that understanding is exclusively a personal or individual process. Rather, it always takes place in a social and cultural context that generates constraints and possibilities for the ways in which particular situations can be understood. In other words, men and women draw on resources that are provided by such phenomena as discourses and institutional arrangements, for example, to make sense of what they perceive (Ryan, 1999). In the final analysis, Barbara and Joan can be said to understand a situation or a way of life if and when they are in a position to make predictions about the future behavior of individual men and women. They are only able to do so, however, by appealing to their own cultural frames of reference.

This process, of course, is not unique to Barbara and Joan. All human beings are engaged in interpretative work of one sort or another. Every situation encountered demands interpretation. Men and women in administrative positions draw upon their experience and their current knowledge as they attempt to make sense of what they encounter. Thus, novel and well-known experiences are integrated into familiar patterns and acted on accordingly. Well-known experiences, naturally, are less demanding than the novel ones. Here people fit familiar patterns easily into well-established typifications or categories. The process breaks down, however, when elements of new experiences cannot be integrated into these patterns. Such was the case with Joan's encounter. She simply could not make sense of the man's actions or his attitude toward questioning. Her usual tactic of gathering data was not possible in this case because she was unable to ask the man himself. In fact, her attempt at data gathering proved to be part of the problem. In the end, Joan was unable to understand the man's motives. She could not comprehend what propelled him to do certain things – and perhaps, more importantly, she could not predict how he would respond to her conciliatory gestures.

Barbara, on the other hand, was somewhat more successful in making sense of her guests' motives. Her research proved to be helpful in this regard. It unearthed key details that enabled her to connect their motives to one with which she was most familiar – saving face. This connection made it possible for Barbara to anticipate their reactions to her tactics, and in the end the parents left her office happy. However, understanding in this case did not engender acceptance of the practice, as one model of multicultural education would have us believe. On the contrary, Barbara's understanding of the group's religious beliefs, in particular those concerning saving face and marriage, repulsed her. She was particularly offended with what she regarded as the parents' apparent lack of regard for their daughters, displayed by their exclusive concern with reputation in the community, their unwillingness to accept their daughters' word, and the obsessive restrictions that they placed on the daughters' behavior. But because she believed she understood where they were coming from, she was able to satisfy their concerns without sacrificing her own beliefs about gender equity. There is also evidence, however, that Barbara, like Joan, did not completely understand the situation at hand. In particular, it appears she may not have understood the gender relationships among and between the mother, father, and daughter. Like everyone else, Barbara's perceptions were constrained by her Western cultural frame of reference that, according to Brah and Minhas (1985), is often guilty of propagating erroneous stereotypes about Asian girls and their relationship with their parents and the school. Barbara appeared not to understand the complexity of the family and gender relationships operating here; that is, she did not appear to believe that the majority of Asian girls have strong, positive, and mutually supportive relationships with their parents (Brah & Minhas, 1985). Because Barbara understood little about the private sphere of Asian family life and its dynamic and vibrant female cultures, she jumped to conclusions about what she perceived to be injustices, and acted accordingly.

INCLUSION AND UNDERSTANDING

Providing inclusive education will require that members of diverse school communities make attempts to understand one another. Inclusive processes, particularly when they involve issues of understanding, however, can be complex. They do not always involve simply recognizing or understanding different values and practices and unproblematically including or accommodating them. There are at least four obstacles that get in the way of this sort of this straightforward scenario. The first is the difficulty in understanding different perspectives. As the above cases have illustrated, understanding different others is not always easy or possible. Despite valiant efforts, educators may never totally comprehend perspectives that differ radically from their own. The second problem with the recognition/inclusion scenario is that understanding will not always lead people to embrace what they have understood. In fact, quite the opposite may occur, as we saw in Barbara's case.

Her understanding of the group's beliefs only reinforced her own different beliefs, prompting her to reject the community perspective, and to engage in covert activity. The third complexity revolves around conflicting inclusive priorities. In Barbara's case, accommodating ethnocultural values required that certain gender-related rights be ignored. The inclusion of one meant the exclusion of the other. While in this case, Barbara managed to appease the parents, she had to make a choice between the two conflicting priorities. Finally, administrators may be so preoccupied with appeasing the parties in conflict situations that promoting inclusion may take a back seat to this appeasement. Getting through the day may take priority over promoting inclusion. While Barbara did hold inclusionary principles, she nevertheless gave priority to satisfying the complaining parents.

Administrators of diverse schools will likely have to devote substantial efforts to understanding different perspectives, particularly in schools that serve a wide range of diverse groups. Many of their basic tasks, such as communicating with parents, community members, and students, require at least a rudimentary understanding of other perspectives. Although their efforts at understanding may do little to address the structural inequalities that find expression in our education system, they will continue to be an important part of the administrator's role. But the sooner that administrators acknowledge the limits of understanding others and the complexities of inclusion, the sooner they will be able to get on with the work of providing inclusive education for their students.

Administrators freely admitted that they needed help in understanding differences in their school communities. They also indicated that they and others could stand to be educated about these matters. The next chapter explores these educative efforts.

CHAPTER 9

EDUCATIVE LEADERSHIP IN DIVERSE CONTEXTS

One thing that has become clear so far is that administrators of diverse schools have much to learn. Many admitted to "flying by the seats of their pants." They found themselves in these positions because they often knew little about some of the groups that they encountered, and had to scramble to acquire the information that they needed to make good decisions. As we have seen in the previous chapters, administrators knew too little about such things as the gender-related values or privacy concerns of certain groups, and as a result, had to do research on them before they acted. And despite this research, they may never completely understand the respective group's proclivities or arrive at acceptable solutions for all concerned parties. Administrators may also not know enough about diversity-related processes. For example, as we have seen, many of them have a parochial view of racism. But administrators are not the only ones in diverse communities who need to know more about the situations that they encounter. As previously illustrated, parents and their children, particularly those new to the country, often know little about the school system and the community generally. Teachers also find themselves knowing little about different groups and diversity related situations. Like administrators, the majority group Anglo teachers have relatively little experience with the wide variety of cultures that they meet in their schools and as a result may not always know what to do about the novel situations that inevitably arise.

The learning needs of diverse school communities have consequences for administrators. This is because administrators will need to assume responsibility for much of this learning. Not only will they have to find ways to engage themselves in this learning process, they will also need to help others learn. In other words, administrators will have to become teachers as well as learners. Unfortunately, administrators have few places that they can turn to for inspiration in these matters. One place where they might look for help, the scholarly branch of educational administration, has traditionally not seen fit to explore the educational side of administration. In fact, some scholars (Greenfield & Ribbins, 1993; Evans, 1999; Smyth, 1989; Codd, 1989) claim that education and administration have traditionally had very little to do with one another. As Evans (1999) suggests, educational administration consists of "two solitudes." Scholars in administration have often assumed that administering education is fundamentally different than educating. Moreover, they have tended to favour the former over the latter. Importing discourses, theories and assumptions from the discipline of management studies over the years, scholars in the field have developed their own concepts, methods and language for understanding administration that have very little to do with the idea of education. More often than not, managing, administering and leading have taken

143

precedence over teaching and learning. Yet scholars have not ignored completely the educational aspect of administration. In fact, in recent times they have directed more efforts to this aspect of administration.

Over the past couple of decades scholars in the field of educational administration have attempted, in more concerted ways, to address the gulf between education and administration. They have approached this task in a variety of ways. First, they have explored the administrator's role in classroom instruction. Subsequently labeled instructional leadership, this approach sought to examine administrative efforts that directly affected the growth of students (Leithwood & Duke, 1996; Duke, 1987; Smith & Andrews, 1989; Hallinger & Murphy, 1985). A second group of scholars explored learning from the administrator's perspective. They looked at this phenomenon in the terms of leaders' capacity to reflect upon their practice (Schon, 1983; Codd, 1989; Hodgkinson, 1978, 1991; Coombs, 2000). Another position focused on the administrator as educator. Drawing on critical traditions, scholars in this area encouraged leaders to make those they worked with aware of the deep-seated patterns of disadvantage that worked against some groups of students, and to do something about them (Smyth, 1989). Finally, the most recent efforts have involved organizational learning. Supporters of this position believe that applying a learning metaphor to organizations will help them devise ways to help schools cope with the current rapidly changing and unpredictable world in which they exist (Leithwood & Louis, 1998; Leithwood, 2000).

Each of these educative approaches to administration has something to offer leaders in the quest for inclusive education. Each perspective by itself, however, has its limitations. The approach that is most consistent with the type of inclusive leadership promoted here is the critical approach. This is because it acknowledges the deeper and more subtle issues that accompany diversity. So, for example, proponents of this perspective maintain that efforts to provide inclusive education must go beyond simply providing information to and about groups of students and their communities. They contend that solutions to challenges associated with diversity must acknowledge the wider social, cultural and institutional mechanisms that shape what counts as difference and the value attached to these differences (Young & Liable, 2000). In this view, achieving inclusion must also involve not just learning about different groups, but must also include efforts to help people understand and take action to resist systemic racism. According to Young and Liable (2000), racism is the main cause of the underachievement of students of colour, and so it is vital that administrators understand how it works so that they can do something about it. Young and Laible (2000, p. 389) maintain that

> We can[not] ... realize the widely touted goal of providing equal educational opportunities and outcomes for all students until we understand the system of White racism within which we all live and work. In particular, we Whites need to understand our participation in the system. Indeed, understanding our participation and then unlearning our patterns of thought and action that support racism are necessary steps for dismantling the system of White racism that now exists in our society and in our schools.

The other three approaches to educative leadership complement this critical approach. Reflective practice techniques, a focus on student learning and whole-school approaches to learning all have a part to play in educating the school

community. Reflective practice can help members of the school community to step
back from the press of daily life and to reconsider aspects of it that they have often
taken for granted. It can assist administrators, teachers, students and parents to see
things in different ways and to acquire new understandings. It is also important to
find ways to assist teachers with their instruction. This is the heart of the
educational enterprise and serious efforts are needed to assist teachers in their efforts
to provide more equitable education for all students. Finally, if principals are to
have any success in educating their school communities, they cannot be satisfied
with isolated or haphazard projects. Rather, they must promote organizational
learning; that is, find ways to ensure that systematic and coordinated learning is
occurring on a regular basis in their respective schools.

This chapter explores how administrators of diverse school communities
approached their own learning and how they provided for the learning of others. It
examines what administrators believed they need to know, how they felt they
learned best, what they believed others need to know and how others should learn.
The potential of these practices and beliefs to contribute to inclusive education is
also traced.

LEARNING

Most of the principals interviewed in this study acknowledged that they had much to
learn in the culturally diverse contexts in which they found themselves. Many also
contended that nobody is to blame for this lack of preparation. Murray maintained
that the reason for this has been the increase in diversity "in the last, say, three or
four years." Tom, on the other hand, said that much of what has been done in his
school district has been of the "trail and error variety." He believed that this was
unfortunate, and that there were certain things that administrators who were new to
schools could be made aware of, such as the "cultural groups you're dealing with ...
and some of the things that cultural groups expect." Tom also believed that
administrators should know about strategies that would help these groups feel as if
they were part of the school. In this regard, administrators typically talked about
needing to learn about how groups differ from their own culture and what the
implications of these differences are. Reg reflected the sentiments of a number of
principals when he said

> I could use some very basic training about what cultures are in this community, what they
> believe, what their religious orientation is. What is unique about their culture – or at least what's
> different than mine? What kinds of things are sore spots and cause problems? What elements
> are easy? What kind of things are easier with respect to achieving integration as opposed to
> others? What kinds of comments or philosophies will get me into trouble when I deal with
> them? What are they going to take exception to that I'm not used to? Those are all important
> things.

The view that Reg is expressing is consistent with a form of liberal
multiculturalism. It emphasizes the importance of learning about different others.
Among things, the acquisition of this sort of knowledge is believed to help educators
understand different others, smooth over the discontinuities between cultures and
project a more positive image of the groups. Now there is no question that
administrators need to learn about the groups that make up their school

communities.   But relying solely on one type of knowledge has its limitations.
Young and Laible (2000) identify three shortcomings.   First, it assumes, wrongly,
that educators and others have the resources, training and desire to fairly represent
such groups.   Second, it is based on the erroneous belief that people will passively
ingest this information and it will reduce whatever prejudices they possess.   Finally,
it ignores the economic, social and ideological structures that shape these
differences.   So while knowing about different others is important, there are other
key forms of knowledge that administrators need to acquire and circulate.

Administrators also need to know something about the underlying structures that
shape the ways in which they and others perceive differences.   Aside from
knowledge of the various groups with which they deal, administrators have to
acquire knowledge about the wider system that provides the basis for these
differences and the situations that arise from them.   This includes an awareness of
how the system of racism works and what can be done to counteract it.   Few of the
administrators interviewed, however, spoke of their need to understand these more
subtle processes.   This is understandable in view of administrators' difficulties in
recognizing the presence of racism.   Even so, not all of those interviewed avoided
references to racism or underlying structures; a few did acknowledge the need to
educate themselves and others about these issues.   They spoke, for example, of
getting in touch with their own biases and opening others' eyes to the not-so-visible
"underbelly."

Research about what administrators of diverse schools need to know is scarce.
One exception is Herrity and Glasman's (1999) survey of "expert" principals of
culturally- and linguistically-diverse schools.   Principal responses reflect much the
same sentiments as the administrators who we interviewed. Herrity and Glasman's
research indicates these principals (only 3 of the 27 were at the secondary level)
presumed that they needed to know something about bilingual education, second
language acquisition, bilingual instruction, organizational and scheduling models,
cultural norms and diversity issues and pragmatics related to diversity. With regard
to the last two areas, Herrity and Glasman (1999) contend that since differences in
language and culture are often subtle, principals must learn about those norms in
classroom and social situations, and know how to apply knowledge of this diversity
in real-life situations.   There is no mention here of racism or antiracism, the wider
structural processes that influence the conditions in these diverse schools, critical
appraisals of these structures or suggestions about how to change these structures.
This view stands in contrast to what Young and Laible (2000) believe school
administrators need to know about diversity. They contend that administrators need
to understand (a) the system of White racial dominance; (b) how White racial
dominance works through and on our society, our institutions, and ourselves in
reproducing relations of domination; and (c) how to take action that opposes the
system of White racism.   Young and Laible believe that knowledge in this case
should not be restricted to information.   In addition to broadening their information
base, administrators also need to extend empathy and to balance the emotional and
cognitive aspects of learning.

The administrators in this study indicated that they learned in two different kinds
of settings.   They made reference to informal and formal settings.   The former

included unstructured and unplanned learning opportunities, while the latter involved situations that were organized specifically for learning.

Informal Learning

The administrators interviewed had definite preferences about their learning. Not only did they believe that they learned most from informal settings, but they also preferred these learning situations over more structured ones. This held true for the survey. Respondents indicated that they learned the most from past experience (mean = 3.72) and on-the-job training (mean = 3.66), while they learned the least from university courses (mean = 2.15), central office specialists, and other experts (mean = 2.73). These findings, however, are not consistent with those of Herrity and Glasman (1999). They found that administrators felt that a university-based administrator preparation program would be the best way to prepare them to meet the needs of a multiethnic student population. Administrators in our study said that they learned the most from their past on-the-job experience. They learned from situations similar to their current ones, and from people – parents, experts, students, and colleagues. Some also said that they learned from reflection.

Many principals insisted that the best training for being an administrator came from experience. For many, "live" situations presented the most potential for learning. Robin, for example, said that these live situations were the best because they force administrators to learn. They have little choice in the matter – either learn or fail. Administrators also believe that this kind of learning is better because it provides more enduring lessons, unlike forms of book learning. On this issue, Wilbur said:

> I think I learned a great deal from experience. There are a lot of people who have the same experience time and time again. I've had a lot of different experiences because I learned from them and there's all kinds of research, there's all kinds of books you can read. And I know the people who read all the books and do all the research, but they don't internalize what happens. So consequently they read the book and go back to doing what they've always done.

While most admitted that personal experience is the best teacher, a few administrators were wary about it. Tom, for one, said that he knows of no better way of learning than experience on the job. However, he also admitted that this way of learning presents risks. He said:

> We learn too much by experience. And experience is great if you're learning how to chop a tree down and you screw up the first tree. But if you're learning from kids and you screw up the first time, you've screwed up the kid. You know, someone paid a price for it. So learning by experience is tougher, but I don't know how else you learn. Yeah, I learned by dealing with kids at this school.

Many administrators had little choice but to learn from on-the-job experience because they came to their position with little or no training in diversity-related areas. Janice said that she was "thrown in with absolutely no experience" and said you "learned as you walked." The best kind of training, administrators reiterated, was experience as an administrator in a diverse school. But they also said that similar kinds of experiences also helped. Being a teacher in a multiethnic school or an English-as-a-Second-Language teacher were mentioned as being useful. Others also said that life experiences outside of school also helped them in their learning. Edward insisted that

> Preparation comes through personal experiences and your own background... But my background includes having lived in a wide variety of socioeconomic areas, from well-to-do to run-down – just through my own family background of having come from a split home and going from really good times to really tough times and having to go out and put myself through university. In working and teaching, I have been in inner-city situations, and been, as I mentioned earlier, in well-to-do situations.

Learning on the job can take many forms and arise in many different situations. Administrators, though, talked most often about learning from others and learning from themselves. They spoke of learning from parents, students, so-called experts and their fellow administrators. The principals who responded to the survey indicated that after past experience, they learned the most from students (mean = 3.71) and parents (mean = 3.51). Wilbur maintained that "I learn more when I walk about school. So my advice would be to go and do that; keep your eyes open and your mouth shut, and you really get to know the place well." Mary Jo talked about how she learned from students and parents. She observed that this knowledge not only helped her do her job, but it also enriched her life. She spoke in one instance of learning much from a conversation she had with an Islamic woman who told her of the tensions between new and traditional expectations in her family life. Mary Jo also felt that

> It's really important to stress, in a community such as the one we have, that we have the opportunity to learn from our students and from our parents. They have such diverse backgrounds that it becomes very interesting, in terms of our own daily experiences, to learn from them, and it enriches all our experiences because of what we have learned.

Administrators can also learn about the community and their own school from members of the community who are not necessarily parents of students. Mack was one of those principals who has learned much from community members and from going to what he felt were key places. He said that this sort of strategy is particularly useful for new administrators. He stated that

> I'd find out who some of the key people in town are. I'd go over to the local variety store and sit in the local restaurant, and ask what goes on. That's what I would do if I were going into a new situation because it's a way to get acquainted really quickly. In one day you could find out a whole lot about your community just by sitting in some key places and listening. You want to know about my school? Go sit in the coffee shop across the street. Talk to the lady in the drugstore.

Administrators also indicated that they learned from "board experts." But the people that they preferred to contact when they needed advice were their colleagues – fellow administrators who worked in diverse contexts. Martha is one administrator who finds comfort in always being able to call on one of her more experienced colleagues. She said

> I'm not sure that we are always well prepared for the many, many surprises that come at us. But my sense in responding to these incidents in the past and now is that I know that there is someone a phone call away, either a more experienced principal, a principal who has said, "If you ever need help, give a call."

Principals can also learn from the administrators they work with in their own buildings. Fellow administrators can be particularly helpful in assisting administrators to see some of the more invisible or taken-for-granted aspects of their interactions with others. Gary, for example, believed that most administrators probably have some racist tendencies that they have never quite acknowledged or realized, and that it sometimes takes others to point these things out. He says that most people would say:

> "I'm not a racist. I'm very liberal and so I don't have a problem with all of these people coming in." You'd better take a step back because that's probably not true. We believe that there are all sorts of hidden things that we do in dealing with races different than us and we've got to be cognizant of them. And in admin we tell each other if it happens: "Hey, I saw you talking to that kid, your body language was such-and-such."... One of the vice-principals in a meeting said to me, "Have you noticed the difference in the way you talk to Hong Kong families as opposed to South African families?" I said "there's no difference. I treat every family the same." "No," he said, "when a Hong Kong family comes in, and there's the mother and father and about eight kids, an auntie who's going to speak for them because none of them speak English, ... you're not always as warm and wonderful as you should be and you're sometimes patronizing"... And my instincts say "No. That's not true. I don't do that." But I do. I believe I do and I believe everybody does. You don't need to be a racist to have small shifts in the way you act toward people. And so we can act as windows for each other and say, "Hey. Wait a minute. Here's what I saw."

Here Gary explicitly acknowledged a propensity that he would not have believed he had – a practice of treating different groups in different and sometimes demeaning ways. It was not likely, however, something that he would have been able to recognize on his own. Like many other administrators he believed, wrongly, that he would never engage in biased, demeaning or racist acts. It took one of his colleagues to point this out to him before he recognized it in himself. This interaction with his fellow administrator provided him with the opportunity to critically reflect on his practice in a way that illuminated that which was previously invisible or taken for granted. Other administrators also spoke of their willingness to be reflective. Pat said that "You need to examine yourself very carefully about what kind of experience and background you bring to the role." Pauline, on the other hand, believed that as a leader, she needs "to get in touch with her own biases." A number of administrators in this study, then, believed that reflection furnishes the means by which they can get in touch with what can often be taken for granted and invisible aspects of their interactions, aspects that may not always work in the interests of all students.

Formal Learning

Most administrators are, or have been, engaged in formal learning situations. In order to be considered for the principalship in Ontario, Canada, for example, candidates need to take a principal preparation course. To earn admission to the program, aspiring administrators must have already completed graduate courses or specialist qualifications, and have had five successful years of teaching experience. Of course, different jurisdictions throughout the Western world demand different formal qualifications of their administrators, and many of these are different from what happens in Ontario. Administrators also may have many opportunities to attend various workshops, conferences and in-service activities. These opportunities may vary considerably from district to district. Some regions may place demands on administrators regarding their own professional development. In Ontario, for example, administrators (and teachers) are now required to spend a specified number of hours in developmental activities.

Despite such requirements and opportunities, there is little evidence that administrators have any routine exposure to organized learning opportunities that specifically target diversity issues. The administrators in this study confirm this gap. They said that there were few formally organized programs that would have prepared them for what they are now facing in their schools. And if there are such programs or courses, they are not specifically required to take them. Paul is typical of many of these administrators. He said that he had "virtually no [formal] training," and although he did acknowledge that there were probably courses in diversity issues, he didn't know if they were available for administrators. The evidence in other jurisdictions also confirms the dearth of exposure and the lack of availability of such programs. Herrity and Glasman (1999) contend that in the United States little is done to train administrators to specifically prepare for culturally- and linguistically-diverse populations. They say that little is known about such programs, including how many of them exist. On the other hand, Young and Laible (2000) maintain that racism is not addressed in most university educational administration programs in the United States. They maintain that in the 505 institutions that offer programs in educational administration, most fail to address White racism in any meaningful way; courses do not focus on it, instructors do not talk about it, and textbooks do not acknowledge it.

Administrators in this study told us of the opportunities they had to attend workshops and conferences, even though a number who did continued to insist that there is no substitute for personal experience. Most of these professional development opportunities were mounted by their respective school boards. Several recalled that certain of these were useful, at least to a point. Roger recalled attending a workshop that featured a big name educator who talked about improving schools from within, while Gail remembers sessions on diversity that offered choices to attendees. Other administrators referred positively to conferences that they attended. They spoke most positively about conferences in other cities where they had a chance to visit schools and talk to administrators and others involved in local school systems.

Most of the administrators in this study expressed views on the kind of professional development that they believe would help them in their diverse settings. Not all of these people, however, had a clear idea of the kinds of things they would like to see in professional development sessions. Mary, for example, said that "Nothing jumps into my head." Paul, on the other hand, wasn't sure how workshops could have helped him out when he first arrived. He said that he would not have had any reference point, since it took him a while before understanding what he faced in this new setting. Like many others, Paul stated that he learned from experience in his position. Administrators who had definite preferences about the kind of professional development that they needed expressed a wish for activities that are directly linked to practice and for opportunities to dialogue with their colleagues.

Noreen felt that training needed to be related to practical or real-life situations. She said:

> I'm a believer in training on the job. I really am. Any time I've gone to a theoretical workshop, it isn't until I've come back and actually had to handle it that I figure my real learning takes place. I guess, if anything, I would like something that is not hit-and-miss. I don't like disconnected workshops on different topics. I would like someone to sit down and plan, perhaps a series of workshops that dealt with the various kinds of issues that gave me some background on different cultures – the things that I might encounter as the cultural groups in this community increase. So a little bit of background knowledge about the groups, which I might expect, the kinds of situations that other principals have had that have arisen from that and how they successfully dealt with it. I'd like role-playing. I'd like acting out. I'd like in-basket kinds of things. For me, that's very helpful. I'd like interactive kinds of workshops as opposed to watching a film kind of thing.

Other administrators maintained that they would like to have opportunities to talk about the problems they face with other administrators. Rita said that "what would be really nice would be a conference which could sort of pull administrators together and talk." Tom also felt that

> It would take a dialogue session with other administrators in the system to be able to share the needs and concerns, so that they can see what they may have to deal with and then feel there's a network of someone they can call up, in addition to the workshops and inviting cultural representatives to come in and talk about their cultures. But I think you'd get a more day-to-day hands-on experiential dialogue going: "This is what we have to do and this is how we reacted to it. This is what we have to put in place" would be far more helpful and advantageous to running the schools on a daily basis.

The learning in which many administrators have been engaged has had an impact on them. They have acquired new skills and new ways of looking at situations. With these new skills and understandings have come changes in the administrators themselves. Kevin maintained that the many years he spent in diverse school changed him. He said that he has taken on what amounts to a new identity.

> I'm a different person now than I was fifteen years ago. Fifteen years ago I was like a lot of people, let's say, who would be [in the less diverse northern region]. I knew very few people who were not WASPs. But in the last twenty years that's certainly changed. And I have become more sensitized, too, to other cultures that make up this country.

Many administrators in this study didn't value formally-organized learning activities as much as they did personal experience. So it comes as no surprise that the kind of in-service or preparatory activities that they preferred were those that were closely connected with practice; they had little use for workshops that were not practical, or the "one-shot deals" that cover a topic and leave it at that. The recent trend in development activities in education has actually been moving in this direction. Attempts have been made to find ways to connect these learning situations to the everyday lives of educators (Griffin, 1987; Robertson, 1998) and to conduct ongoing series of meetings and activities. There are also some university diversity courses and programs that attempt to make a link between theory and practice. Herrity and Glasman (1999) describe a program that features in-depth fieldwork, internships, and real-life simulations that link learners with a wide range of diverse settings. They also call for school districts to become involved in diversity training and for universities and school districts to collaborate on such projects.

TEACHING

Because they have an obligation to educate others who need to be informed, administrators also have a responsibility to teach. This is because they are not the only ones who may find that they know too little about diversity related situations. Parents and community members, particularly those who are new to the country, often find themselves in this uniformed position, and we have seen the kinds of things that principals do or endorse to increase their learning. Many teachers also find themselves wishing they knew more about the different groups of parents and students with whom they associate. This is due, in part, to the fact that the majority of teachers are of Anglo/European heritage, while many of their new students are not (Merchant, 2000). It also appears that this trend will continue, at least in the United States, where 92% of students entering teacher education are White (Noel, 1995). Although teacher education faculties are addressing diversity issues more than they did in the past (see for example, Herrity & Glasman, 1999; *Journal of Teacher Education*, 46 (5), 1995), many teachers are not prepared for the diversity that they may face in their classrooms. Administrators in this study acknowledged that teachers, most of who are White and are born in Canada, have much to learn about classroom situations and diverse communities. Pat believed that many teachers have not had much experience with diversity. He said:

> Most of us don't have a background to give us a criteria to deal with this. You know, a teacher who started teaching in Ontario didn't have Chinese students, didn't have any Black kids, would have one or two Indian kids in their class, maybe. And that's about it. Most of us who were born in Canada, many of us in small towns, have no experience dealing with those issues. So we don't have the tools, and it's very hard to develop them.

Given this trend, administrators recognized the need to help their teachers with these novel situations. Robin felt that "the biggest challenge is keeping people up-to-date." Steve also understood the need for "a fair amount of talking and discussion and an awful lot of professional development," while Mary Jo said that "my role is to PD (employ professional development with) my staff as much as possible." Administrators pointed to the value of both informal and formal learning for teachers. One of the informal techniques mentioned was modeling. Administrators believed that their actions could set the tone for an atmosphere or culture that raises awareness of diversity issues. School communities can learn much from the way administrators talk about these concerns and what they do about them. Wilbur believed that principals can send an important message to the rest of the school community through the things they say and do. He said:

> There's the old theory that teachers will treat students the way the principal treats them. And maybe that works. But I've had my staff say to me, "Well, the reason for the atmosphere in the school is what you set down from the office." It starts right here. And if it doesn't start here, it can't happen.

Administrators may also encourage people to accept their views and visions by modeling the ideals associated with them. Kevin felt that by "living it [his vision], by talking about it," people will come to see it as "something really good." He believed that by modeling what he believes to be correct behaviour, people accept his ideas. He felt that this approach works better than workshops.

I think the message delivered by me again and again, and then the growing respect that the staff developed for me, I think that rubbed off on them. So in a way I have done six years of informal racism awareness and sensitivity training in the staff. I don't line them all up in the staff meetings and say, "Okay today we're going to learn to deal with Sikhs," but I think just my attitude, my talking, my philosophy, I think it rubs off on everybody else. I think that's how I did it ... by example. I think that ... provides much better results than a half-day workshop on racism to a staff, because most people in a half-day workshop will sit there and listen to it and walk away and forget everything they heard after two or three days.

Administrators also referred to planned activities for teachers. These planned activities can take any number of forms. They may, for example, consist of conferences or workshops that may or may not be board-sponsored. More often, however, administrators stated that the responsibility for professional development rested more and more with individual schools or groups of schools. Noreen, as one example, said that most of her board's professional development days occurred in her school. In these instances, her staff was involved in planning and running sessions related to "race relations or multiculturalism." In her school, the teaching staff plans professional development days. Tom also provides opportunities for some of his teachers to offer in-service. He recalled that one of his English-as-a-Second-Language teachers offered noon-hour workshops on diversity. At Wilbur's school, groups of teachers and students run seminars and "lunches" that are designed to address issues of diversity and racism. Other administrators spoke of mobilizing staff who have been to conferences or workshops to share some of the ideas that they valued. Paul took the ideas expressed by a well know educator at a principals' conference and presented them to his staff on a school PD (professional development) day. The staff took this opportunity to discuss these ideas in depth. Paul felt that this strategy helped his teachers to engage in an ongoing dialogue. Some principals, like Diane use staff meetings for professional development. She said that her staff has chosen to have two staff meetings –one for routine matters and one devoted exclusively to professional development. Diane believed that if this was not done, development would "fall by the wayside." In these meetings the lead teachers from each division assist. At times they would also have teachers from outside the school come in. Almost always, the staff at Diane's school would look to small groups for discussion and conversation.

While many of these activities are locally managed, many administrators indicated that they have the option of using board experts and resources. They said that it is up to individual schools to take advantage of these resources. Administrators also claimed there were experts who were not necessarily designated as such. These included their teachers and also members of their communities. A number of these administrators sought to use their knowledge to educate teachers in organized sessions. Tom was one principal who recognized the value of having his staff talk with teachers who had experience in diverse settings.

Diane has used parents for teacher development in a format that teachers reportedly learned from. On one occasion she brought a group of Chinese parents to a development session, allowing staff and parents to break into smaller groups where the dialogue appeared to be more relaxed than it would have been in a larger setting. Diane said that these arrangements provided the support necessary for teachers to ask questions and for parents to answer them. She said that their teachers

learned much from this. Administrators also said that they have used parents'
connections to bring people in to talk with their teachers. Wilbur used a parent's
connections to bring in two people from the Royal Bank who did equity and racial
programs. His staff found this approach to systemic racism very useful. Some
administrators made use of other sources. One administrator explained that he used
student evaluations of teachers as part of his professional development for teachers.
Pat said that teachers hand out evaluation and feedback forms. The students fill
them in and hand them back to the teacher. The teacher then looks them over, and
teacher and students discuss the students' remarks. Pat believed that the process was
"not threatening" because everything was done in the classroom – nothing reached
the administration.

Professional development activities address areas both closely and remotely
associated with diversity. Administrators told us that their teachers attended
sessions that touched on racism, antiracism, conflict, cultural differences, cultural
sensitivity and so on. In response to requests from his teachers for developmental
sessions on understanding kids from different ethnic backgrounds, Wilbur organized
a number of sessions on conflict resolution. Cultural sensitivity was also a concern
for a number of principals. They believed that it would be useful for teachers to
become more sensitive to the "differences" that students brought to school, and so
attempted to organize developmental sessions that addressed this concern. Noreen
remembered one activity that she felt was particularly successful in heightening
teachers' awareness of diversity issues. She said:

> We had a workshop – it has a really funny name and I can't remember it – but what it does is it
> divides people up into different groups and they can only communicate in a specific way, which
> is not English. They learn a new language, and it gives you the feeling of what it's like to be
> someone new in a country where you can't understand the language and where you have to find
> ways of communicating other than language until you learn it. Its basic premise is to put you in
> a situation that is similar in some ways to what a refugee or new immigrant or whatever would
> feel when they came into another culture.

While many administrators mentioned sensitivity and understanding, fewer
referred to the need to raise teachers' awareness of some of the more invisible and
insidious patterns that find their way into schools, like racism. Elaine and Pauline
are two principals who attempted to sensitize teachers to these things. Elaine said
that "I see my role as being one of [raising] people's awareness. Before that, even
of making sure that they are aware of what policy and procedure is in terms of
multiculturalism.... what you're really trying to work is to develop that realization
and honest appreciation and understanding." Pauline preferred to see this function
as one that will "open their eyes to what is." She said that her role is to listen and
not bury those negative things that aren't nice to look at "and to look at ... the
underbelly and address the issues that are there." It was "also to open their eyes and
give them more knowledge so that they feel comfortable in reflecting to me the
negative aspects of how they feel and looking at ways of dealing with them."
Pauline maintained that many of the problems teachers, students and parents wrestle
with is the result of a lack of knowledge and "If you can give them that knowledge,
then things start to change." Noreen maintained that it was important for all to
"understand" their environment through awareness of it. But for her it was also a
"sensitivity issue," particularly for educators who needed to be immersed in the

issues that revolve around diversity. In this regard, Robin believed that his role was to have people "look at another side of a situation, not the other side, but another side of a situation." These administrators acknowledged that there are issues and patterns that may not always be apparent to members of their educational communities, and it is their job to open their eyes to some of these oppressive and invisible aspects of life in schools. They believed that providing them with knowledge about these things would help them reflect on what they do and provide the impetus for them to change, if necessary, theirs and others' practices.

Administrator efforts to educate teachers about diversity issues, whether they involve simply informing them about the community or delving into racism, are rarely straightforward. This is because the learning associated with these issues involves more than a simple transfer of information; it also entails changing values. Teachers may be expected to adopt new views and ways of being, and in the process change their values, attitudes and assumptions about a whole range of issues and ideas. Those who have written about teacher professional development and in-service have acknowledged this issue in recent years, and have recommended that those responsible for this sort of education incorporate this approach into the design of their respective approaches. They feel that professional development should no longer consist of the one way transfer of knowledge – from the experts to the supposed novices. Rather information needs to be presented in such a way that it can be manipulated, discussed and changed by participants (Sparks, 1994; Arnold, 1995). The hope is that if participants can meaningfully contribute developmental ideas, if they are given to freedom to engage in critique, if they feel that the activities have a practical application, and if they perceive that they have ownership over any changes to come, then they are more likely to change their beliefs or teaching practices (Griffin, 1987).

This doesn't mean that administrators will find immediate success if they employ these sorts of strategies, as some in this study found out. In fact, administrators perceived resistance to professional development initiatives on diversity. Some of this resistance was overt, but most took on more subtle forms, like foregoing sessions. Mary maintained:

> The board runs Black history TV. Some of our teachers have signed up for this and its PD. And this is vital, because we keep saying, "You have to infuse with perspectives other than Eurocentric perspectives." But these teachers have been through a Eurocentric education. They say, "What do I know? I don't know [anything], so you tell me." Well, you offer it to them and then half of them don't come. But you can't hog-tie them and take them there. There has to be a willingness for the teachers to learn.

These administrators are not the only ones who have experienced resistance to diversity-related professional development. Accounts of developmental activities of this sort show mixed results. For example, the two-year staff development program that Sleeter (1992) organized, had a limited impact on teachers' ability to deliver multicultural education. Program constraints, the demands of the profession generally and limited support from others, particularly administrators, made it difficult for even those who were committed to making changes in their respective schools. Finkel and Bolin (1996) report on a development initiative for eight members of a college staff that was a little more successful. Although participants initially were angry and in denial, the majority eventually indicated that they had a better understanding of diversity issues. A minority, though, did not believe that diversity was an important part of their development as a person. Robertson (1998) also reports mixed success in the equity development initiative that she studied. Although the majority of participants did change their views, those who held the most extreme (and negative) views proved to be the most resistant to change, and in some cases, engineered forms of backlash against the equity initiatives. Robertson (1998) also reported that certain areas of school life, like the curriculum, were resistant to change, while others, like school climate, were more amenable.

At least one administrator in this study felt that some of the in-service sessions for teachers that dealt with more critical areas like racism were too strident. He felt that teachers were not ready for the aggressive tone set in these sessions; it threatened people and made them defensive. According to Donald:

> I made a mistake a couple of years ago, bringing people in to talk about it (diversity/racism), because it was too soon and they weren't ready for it. We had a Black fellow come in and talk at a staff meeting about some of their cultural issues because we had a handful of Blacks in the school that were a bit tough to live with. So I think we brought him in for the wrong reason as well. And what happened was that the approach that the gentleman took was, "You know we have to change and you have to change and so the best approach for us is to understand each other and get on with it." Some of my staff said, "Nonsense! This is a melting pot. You know, I came in from Spain. I had to learn English and I had to become part of the culture and that's what I expect of everybody else." That was fine, okay twenty-five years ago, I suppose, but it's not okay now. But we were not ready for that at the time that that gentleman came in.

Recent initiatives in antiracism inservice in the United Kingdom are instructive here. They point to the need for less confrontational approaches to antiracism. These initiatives took root in the aftermath of the murder of an Asian student at a school in Manchester. This tragedy prompted those concerned with diversity to reassess approaches to antiracism, and in particular, the "hardline" taken by some proponents of antiracism. In his study of two schools, Gillborn (1995) observes that the in-service in these matters in the past was often confrontational. Participants at these sessions often felt that they were being told that "You are racist. You are this." The strong proponents of antiracism at the time felt that they were obliged to attack anything that could be construed as racism. They were unwilling to allow people to make mistakes and to think about what a mistake was. These tactics generated uncertainty and fear among many White teachers. Many felt that they had to think about everything they said and did because they believed that there was always a chance that it would be misinterpreted and that they would be accused of being a racist. MacDonald (cited in Gillborn, 1995) believes that this kind of approach reinforced the guilt of many well-meaning Whites, paralyzing them when any issues of race arose. Others simply buried their racism without changing their attitude. The end result was that it created resentment and anger and put an end to free discussion about related issues.

Educators in Gillborn's (1995) study took a more forgiving stance. One of these individuals maintained that simple confrontation was not going to work when dealing with racist views. While this teacher felt stereotypes and racist assumptions needed to be routinely challenged, she believed that this was done best within a relationship that was already built. She said, "You don't change people by criticizing them in the beginning. You need to make them think otherwise. And when they come back to you and say, 'Oh right, this is how we do it. Oh gosh when we first came how naïve I was.'" (Gillborn, 1995, p. 112). Gillborn goes on to say that schools need to find a balance that maintains the pressure to be reflective about current assumptions and practices, without moving into hostilities that merely reproduce and amplify existing conflicts. He favors a perspective that is positive without being comfortable, that is, one that prompts people to reflect on the state of things because they are uneasy with it, but also one that doesn't produce the fear and guilt that trigger further conflict. This view recognizes that people make mistakes, and these mistakes should be acknowledged and discussed in a constructive manner.

INCLUSION AND EDUCATIVE LEADERSHIP

Learning and teaching are key components of inclusive leadership in diverse contexts. This is because many educators, parents and students in these settings routinely know too little of the situations in which they find themselves. Administrators and teachers are often unfamiliar with groups of parents and students who differ from themselves, and they don't always know how to act in situations that involve them. On the other hand, students and parents who are not of European heritage may struggle with their understanding and/or acceptance of both school and community conventions. If all parties in the school community are to meet the challenges associated with diversity, then they will have to acquire new knowledge, understandings and attitudes. The responsibility for this learning rests first and foremost with principals. They are clearly the single most important individuals in the learning process, particularly in diverse contexts (Derkatz, 1996). Principals are in a position to set the tone for the school, engineer school-wide learning opportunities and provide support for a wide range of initiatives. Administrative support can mean the difference not only between the kind of learning that takes place, but also for ways in which the entire school community approaches diversity, equity and antiracism (Gillborn, 1995; Robertson, 1998). In this regard, administrators can make it possible for much needed whole-school approaches to learning and diversity generally, ensure that learning goes beyond acquiring supposedly factual information about different others, and provide approaches that are constructive rather than alienating.

Effective approaches to diversity require whole-school approaches (Nieto, 1992; May, 1994; Gillborn, 1995). So does the learning component associated with these diverse contexts (Robertson, 1998). Indeed well-meaning but individual attempts to learn about diversity, and to follow up on this learning, will often amount to very little if the efforts do not extend beyond the well-intentioned individuals who are its prime movers. If those committed to change do not receive support from those they work and interact with, change initiatives will probably not succeed (Sleeter, 1992). Teachers, students, parents and, particularly, administrators, all have to be involved in the learning enterprise. This learning enterprise also has to become a routine part of school life. It is best if the inquiry becomes part of the "culture" of the school. Administrators in this study spoke of some of the ways in which they played a part in influencing this kind of school atmosphere. Besides the things they did to overtly influence others and set processes in place, they also spoke some of the more subtle means of establishing a learning culture. These included modeling the behaviour that they wished to see in others and constantly talking about the things in which they believed.

Most principals in this study claimed that they learned best through experience, although they also valued other, more formally organized learning opportunities. Whether learning themselves or seeing to the learning of others, principals need to acknowledge that this learning must go beyond transferring information about groups thought to be different. Indeed, seeing so-called minority groups exclusively in terms of difference is limiting. Gillborn (1995) maintains that when such groups are seen in these terms, it is easy for educators to assume a position that is at best patronizing, and at worst disparaging and racist. Teachers and administrators need to realize that while they differ from students and parents, they also share many things with them. The challenge for educators, then, is to understand the processes that highlight particular differences among groups of people and the values and practices that are associated with these differences. This means taking a critical look at the system of racism that works in and beyond schools, for racism is intimately associated with the production and evaluation of differences. Administrators and teachers need to come to understand how this system of racism works, what its effects are, and how they can work to resist it.

Principals also need to provide appropriate educational strategies for their respective staffs. Given the current understandings and attitudes in their school communities, they need to take care not to overwhelm or alienate teachers, students or parents with too much information or with inflexible positions. This needs to be the case when presenting information about differences or about more controversial topics like racism and antiracism. These approaches should be designed to be constructive, and to avoid triggering fear, guilt and destructive reactions among teachers. It needs to be understood that people make mistakes, and they should have the opportunity to recognize these mistakes, understand them and talk about them in ways that will lead them not to repeat these. Teachers should not be made to feel too comfortable, however. A certain level of uneasiness provides the best atmosphere for reflective thought and positive action.

CHAPTER 10

THE BARRIERS TO INCLUSION

The previous nine chapters of this book have explored how principals include members of their ethnically diverse school communities in various schooling processes. I chose to explore diversity, administration and inclusion for a number of reasons. First of all, diversity is very much a contemporary issue. Among other things, the increasing levels of diversity – the product of changing immigration and local patterns and more intense media and consumption practices – present significant challenges for educators, students and members of the wider community. Contemporary diversity also challenges school administrators. Many principals find that they are not adequately prepared to deal with the novel situations that regularly arise in these diverse settings. They also do not always understand the processes associated with diversity, like racism, in helpful ways. Regrettably, however, little empirical research has been conducted in the area of administration and diversity. We know very little about what administrators do in these settings. This is unfortunate because principals are undoubtedly the most influential individuals at the school level. They, more than others, are in positions to make a difference in their respective schools. So presumably the more that we know about what these influential people do or should do, the more we will be able to do to augment conditions in schools that will favor all, and not just some students. The more administrators and concerned others know about leadership and diversity, the better prepared they will be to make decisions that will eliminate the difficulties that many non-Anglo/European students face in school and in life, ease the way for them to master the school curriculum, and increase their life chances.

This book does more than just describe how administrators do their jobs in diverse school settings. It also explores how they should do their jobs. In this regard I examine how they practice or fail to practice inclusion. Inclusion is seen as something for which administrators should strive. I favour inclusion because I believe that the practices associated with it represent the best way to resist or eliminate the exclusionary patterns that routinely place groups of non-Anglo/European students at a disadvantage in school and elsewhere. Inclusionary practices target those very things that are responsible for obstructing the academic and life opportunities of these particular groups of students. They are designed to put an end to exclusion by accommodating, for example, the knowledge, languages, religions, and values of non-Anglo/European groups, where possible, in the content and processes of the school. Where successful, these measures would allow students and their parents to feel that they are part of the school. In inclusionary settings students and parents identify with the school and they have a voice in decisions and policies that concern them.

Putting inclusion into practice, however, is never a simple or straightforward

159

matter. It involves much more than merely identifying exclusionary practices, eliminating or resisting them and substituting inclusive measures. To begin with, it is not always easy to identify exclusionary practices since many of them are taken for granted. Because exclusionary practices may be part of daily routines, they are sometimes difficult to recognize. They may, for example, easily masquerade as justifiable accountability measures or purportedly efficient organizational arrangements. Exclusion often operates on many levels, moreover, and so it is not always easy to recognize or identify the full extent of it. For example, while parents of different backgrounds may sit on a school council that has real power, they may not all have the personal resources to influence decisions. But even if administrators are able to recognize the full extent of exclusion, they may be reluctant to eliminate the practices associated with it. They may choose such a path because eliminating or resisting these practices may threaten their deeply-held values or the security and privilege that they currently enjoy. Such action may also conflict with other inclusionary principles that they or others hold, so including some aspect of community culture may negate another. Administrators may also surrender to the contingencies of daily pressures. They may, for example, opt to appease unhappy members of the school community rather than promote principles of inclusion if the former is able to get them through their day. Finally, administrators may simply not know enough about alternatives to exclusion to be able to confidently choose among them. In what follows, I elaborate on the difficulties involved in promoting inclusive practice and the measures that can be taken to overcome them.

BARRIERS TO INCLUSION

In this chapter I want to bring various threads together by describing the barriers to inclusion that administrators must overcome. I will follow up in the next chapter with strategies for overcoming these obstacles. To accomplish this task I will draw on my observations from the previous chapters.

Racism, the first obstacle to inclusion, is by its very nature exclusionary. Both the more obvious personal manifestations and the less apparent systemic forms routinely exclude students and their parents from opportunities that others enjoy. But it is not just racism itself that places certain students at a disadvantage. Administrator perceptions of, and attitudes toward, racism also contribute to this same end. Administrators' ambivalence toward racism and their tendency to see it in only prejudicial and individualistic terms limit the actions that they will inevitably take to resist or combat it. In this regard, administrators' propensity toward conservatism also limits the kinds of changes that they will be willing to make to the system in which they work.

Another obstacle to inclusion is knowledge – both the lack and nature of it. Administrators freely admit that they know too little about their diverse communities. This in itself presents problems for inclusion. Administrators who know little about their communities will not be aware of possible exclusions. The way in which administrators conceive of knowledge will also limit inclusion. Seeing knowledge exclusively in terms of facts or understandings rather than viewing it in critical ways will make it difficult for them to recognize and challenge the more systemic forms exclusion, like racism.

Finally, administrators' lack of attention to curriculum and pedagogy and the nature of school-community relationships will also limit what they can do about exclusion. Teaching and learning are at the heart of the education enterprise and administrators who do not direct their efforts here will ultimately not have much of an impact in their schools, regardless of their enthusiasm for inclusion.

Racism

Despite racism's undesirable exclusionary character, it is nevertheless present in schools, and generally more obvious in ethnically diverse schools. Most administrators who participated in the study grudgingly acknowledged this existence. But they also tended to downplay its presence, admitting to lower levels of racism in schools than have many researchers (see, for example, Dei et al., 1997). Most administrators identified individual and personal types of racism in their schools. The most common among these was harassment, although some administrators preferred not to classify such events as racist, even though they involved issues of "race." Other administrators identified forms of "school" racism, which included the actions of the occasional racist teacher. Most administrators, however, were more preoccupied with responding to charges from students and parents who claimed that the school was racist. Administrators also said that they had noticed racist symbols and graffiti, although some wondered whether students, particularly the younger ones, really understood their significance. They also acknowledged that members of their respective school communities employed common stereotypes. Administrators did not always equate stereotyping with racism, however, and they tended to see stereotypes as mistaken images of unfamiliar groups of people. Some believed that stereotyping would dissipate when people got to know one another a little better.

Acknowledging the presence of racism is an important first step in identifying and challenging exclusive practices. Unfortunately, not all administrators in this study readily admitted that racism had taken root in their schools. And when they did, they tended either to downplay it or see it as something perpetrated by misguided individuals. Administrators hold these views, out of an inability to see racism or issues of "race" – their ethnocentric lenses simply filter them out. It also may be possible that their desires to project positive images of their schools (and themselves) in an image-conscious and market-oriented world would prompt them either to minimize racism or to deny it. Seeing racism in individual rather than system terms also absolves them of any responsibility for racism that does exist in their organizations. In these scenarios, it is misguided individuals and not the school itself that is responsible for the racism. Unfortunately, failure to acknowledge racism, tendencies to minimize it, and views of it as an individual phenomenon, obstruct efforts to identify and resist it. Coupled together, these filters make it difficult to recognize and do something about the more subtle and systemic elements of racism.

Administrators' inability to see racism in systemic terms was perhaps best reflected in their favored antiracism measures. Many spoke of the measures that they and their respective schools took to prevent or punish individual acts of racism. The prevention of racism was a priority for a number of administrators. Administrators adopted these strategies to ward off potential racism. Toward this end, they sought to educate their school communities and to develop policies. The other strategy was reactive; it was taken after the fact. Its components included conversing with students and parents, and punishing offenders. As alluded to above, these measures were by and large, designed mostly to deal with only one kind of racism – individual prejudice. Both the preventative and reactionary strategies targeted, for the most part, individual acts of discrimination, while failing either to acknowledge or address racism as a systemic phenomenon. Now there is little question that schools need to discourage obvious prejudicial forms of racism. Like systemic forms, they isolate students, often at a more acutely emotional level, from the privileges that others enjoy. So the eradication of individual prejudice needs to be a priority for all schools. But administrators also need to acknowledge and do something about the more subtle and systemic dimensions of racism as well.

This failure to recognize or acknowledge systemic racism and administrators' reluctance to question, challenge and change the system that fosters it is associated with administrators' contradictory role as change agents in a conservative administrative context.

Administrative Conservatism and Change

Racism is a significant barrier to inclusion. But so is administrators' reluctance to acknowledge racism and its various forms. This reluctance is associated with administrators' contradictory roles as change agents. While administrators are increasingly seen as change agents (Leithwood et al., 1999), they may also find themselves resisting change. This is because many may identify strongly with the very system, or parts of it, that they are trying to change. Most administrators are conservative in their practice (Riehl, 2000; Rizvi, 1993b). They tend to orient their actions toward supporting and conserving the system in which they work and have difficulty when it comes to challenging or changing integral parts of it.[1] These tendencies are engendered by the context in which administrators work and the manner of their socialization.

Rizvi (1993b) maintains that most administrative work takes place in a context that is inherently conservative. Most schools and school systems foster uniformity rather than diversity (Solomon, 2001); they strive to find ways to get everyone to meet common goals and purposes. This preoccupation is perhaps best reflected in recent moves toward common curricula and standardized or criterion-referenced testing. Achieving these common ends requires that schools emphasize order, control and discipline. Indeed, the bureaucratic-like cultures that pervade

---

[1] This is not to say that conservatives always oppose change, but that the changes that they favour are inevitably ones that conserve rather than challenge the underlying elements or integral parts of the status quo.

contemporary school systems are seen by many as the best (and only) way to organize large groups of people to achieve these common goals, despite lip service to the contrary, particularly among conservative-minded groups that blame bureaucracies for many of society's ills. So in the pursuit of these ends, schools actually implant in students forms of compliant thinking and work to prevent expressions of social and cultural differences. Even though they may, on the surface, look to promote values of democracy, creativity, and diversity, schools actually operate under conditions that embody a competing set of values, like obedience, compliance, routine, conformity and homogeneity. Rizvi (1993b) emphasizes, however, that it is not just students who are the recipients (and messengers) of this ideology; administrators also work in this system and, like students, are subject to the pressures of this hidden curriculum. But administrators are implicated perhaps more deeply in this culture than students, for they are they ones who support, promote and monitor it.

It is this dominant and (superficially) homogeneous culture into which administrators are socialized (Marshall, 1993). This socialization process does not begin, however, with administrators' first appointment. It starts when they first enter educational institutions as students and continues as they take up positions as teachers. Indeed, by the time they are prepared to take up their roles as administrators, they are well socialized into a system that discourages social and cultural differences. If they had not been perceived as "company people" who are enthusiastic supporters of the systems in which they work, they would probably have never been offered administrative positions in the first place. Being chosen for an administrative track would normally require that potential candidates demonstrate higher levels of allegiance than their fellow teachers, who either do not seek out such appointments or who are unsuccessful in their efforts. Leithwood (2001) provides evidence that administrators demonstrate higher levels of system allegiance than teachers. In a series of studies where he asked similar questions of both administrators and teachers, administrators consistently scored significantly higher than teachers on those questions that implied support for the system.

The effects of this socialization process are also enhanced by the investment that administrators have in the system. Over the years they have benefited from the system, and they continue to benefit from it. Among other things, the system has bequeathed to them skills, attitudes and knowledge that have made it possible for them to acquire their current comparatively elite positions. It is this system and its procedures, practices and processes that garnered them their current identities and the means of making a good living. Moreover, any future ambitions within the system will depend, in part, on demonstrations of their allegiance to, and support for, the system. These demonstrations may take any number of forms. For example, principals may routinely find themselves in the position of having to defend integral parts of their school and school system – teachers, teaching practices, curriculum, organizational patterns, rules and policies – to parents, students, fellow educators and members of the public. These and other such tasks would be difficult, if not impossible, to carry out for people who do not identify with, or support, the system.

This identification and support for the system will influence, in many important ways, the manner in which administrators approach change. Many administrators in this study approached change in the way that Wolcott's (1973) research participant-principal, Ed Bell does. In his seemingly insignificant day-to-day activities, Ed works subtly to conserve, that is, to ensure the continuity of an organization that he supports. There is no sense that anything is wrong with the system of schooling over which he presides, and as a consequence, Ed does not entertain any considerations of substantive or radical change. Rather, he sees his primary task as doing what it takes to ensure the smooth running of his school. Likewise, many administrators in this study were not comfortable with fundamental challenges and changes to a system that they, like Ed Bell, support and in which they have an investment. To begin, it would be difficult to encourage them, as the data illustrate, to recognize that the system that gave, and continues to give them so much, could be fundamentally flawed. Most administrators were more likely to attribute problems to defective parts or technical malfunctions. They were comfortable attributing the cause of overtly racist acts to the individuals who committed them rather than to the system in which these actions occurred. Doing so did not seriously threaten their long-established values and worldviews or a system to which they owed their allegiance. Likewise, whatever changes that they did champion involved piecemeal, rather than fundamental alterations. They were, to use Henriques' (1984) metaphor, more comfortable extracting a few rotten apples than overturning the apple cart.

Guilt may also play a part in the way in which administrators approach change. Administrators (and teachers) who are the most susceptible to feelings of guilt are usually White and Anglo (Taylor, 1998), and they are the individuals who generally occupy these leadership positions (Bell & Chase, 1993). For example, only two of the administrators interviewed for this study were not White, despite student populations that were generally very diverse. Whites' guilt over the prospect that they are the beneficiaries of a system that systemically punishes non-Whites may engender considerable discomfort. It also may trigger subconscious mechanisms that work to protect individual psyches from this discomfort by filtering their perceptions of racism and their understandings of it.[2] Indeed, administrators would have an easier time attributing racism to ignorant or malicious individuals than they would to a system of which they are a part and from which they benefit. Most of these administrators, then, would be less threatened seeing things from a color-blind perspective (Taylor, 1998).

So administrators themselves can also impede inclusive school practices. The various conservative pressures that are exerted on their position can obstruct their view of racism and inhibit meaningful action. The state of their knowledge can also impede inclusion.

Knowledge

Knowledge is also a barrier to inclusion. In this instance, both what and how administrators know can obstruct inclusion. With respect to the former, it is administrators' lack of knowledge about the various groups in their communities and the processes of diversity, like racism, that hobble efforts at inclusion.

---

[2] For a description of how this general process works, see Real (1997).

Administrators in this study admitted that they frequently knew too little about their communities. Their knowledge was limited in this regard because of the degree of diversity in their respective communities and the differences between themselves and members of their communities. Administrators admitted that they had trouble keeping up with those who resided in their districts not only because there were so many, but also because of their transient nature – groups routinely came and went in short order. It was not uncommon for administrators to be surprised at who was or was not a member of their communities. Most administrators felt pushed not just in keeping track of the identities of community members but also trying to sort out the many different lifestyles and values of these respective groups.

Another reason that administrators knew little of their communities was because of the differences between them and community members. Virtually all of the administrators to whom we talked were White Anglos of European heritage. Most grew up in the general area and only recently had experienced different kinds of diversity. Many in their school communities, on the other hand, were of non-Western descent. They or their parents had emigrated from countries in Asia, Africa and South America. Of the many different aspects of these cultures, administrators struggled with the content and place of religions in the lives of non-Western students and parents and their attitudes toward education. They also were puzzled by some groups' gender practices and their views of knowledge. Administrators generally did their best to accommodate students' and parents' views on these issues. A number of administrators admitted, however, that they had trouble comprehending them, while others rejected such practices, even while claiming to understand them. Administrators' lack of knowledge of community groups and their cultures or lifestyles and values did not lend itself to inclusion. It would have been difficult, if not impossible, to include in the school aspects of community life that administrators knew little about.

The way in which administrators approached knowledge of groups and processes also impeded inclusion. Administrators in this study readily acknowledged that there was a great deal about diversity-related issues that they did not know. They also recognized that others in their school communities – teachers, students, parents – also lacked knowledge about these essentials. Given this situation, they took steps to educate themselves and others about diversity. In doing so they drew on three forms of knowledge. The dimensions that they didn't know and their efforts to learn and to teach others about them fell into three categories: (1) *factual* knowledge; (2) *interpretive* forms of knowledge, and in particular, intercultural understanding; and (3) *critical* forms of knowledge associated with taken for granted or invisible and systemic forms of life. These three categories bear a strong resemblance to Habermas' (1971) three forms of knowledge/interests – technical, practical and emancipatory. Unfortunately, administrators' inclination to see knowledge as either factual or interpretive did not put them in a position to recognize the full extent of exclusion, and, thus, impeded their efforts at inclusion. For them to be successful in this regard, they must also see teaching and learning in terms of critical or emancipatory knowledge.

The first kind of knowledge revolved around facts. In many cases, these facts were data that administrators or their communities simply had not encountered before, and administrators saw their task as one of receiving or supplying these unambiguous facts. So, for example, administrators believed that parents needed to be informed about certain background information about the school and school system that their children were attending. Since much of this information was straightforward or easily agreed upon, they felt that it was just a matter of finding ways to inform the communities about these things. Administrators believed, perhaps naively in some cases, that informing communities about such things as schedules, school policies, courses of study, or of the needs of adolescents or changing family dynamics was simply a matter of getting this information out to them. Little consideration was given to the possibility that there could be problems in understanding. This was the easiest of three forms of knowledge to deal with; administrators simply sought out resources or, people who knew about such things, or in the case where they felt they had to inform sectors of their communities, they mustered information through meetings, newsletters, and so on. For most administrators much of their learning and teaching revolved around the supply of information that went either from the people who were the experts to them, or from them to an unknowing community.

The second form of knowledge was interpretive in nature. In this case, the teaching and learning associated with this form of knowledge revolved around intercultural (mis)understandings. In identifying this form of teaching/learning as interpretive, I do not mean to imply that the previous so-called factual type of teaching/learning does not involve interpretation. It does, of course. The difference is that those involved in the above situations believed that meaning was not a problem in the transfer of information – both parties in the dialogue were thought to experience few problems in agreeing on the meaning of the so-called facts. This stands in contrast to the second form of knowledge/learning where meaning now becomes a problem. It does so when one of the two parties in the dialogue has difficulty making sense of the communication, at least in the same way that the other partner does, and, as a consequence, has to actively work at interpreting or making sense of what he or she encounters. These problems with meaning and understanding arose as some administrators found that mere access to information was not enough to enable them to comprehend what they encountered. This was particularly true when they came across situations that involved individuals or cultural groups with which they were not familiar. They found that they sometimes lacked the capacity to understand what was happening in these situations. Merely talking to people or consulting books, as most did, did little to facilitate their understanding.

There are at least two ways in which issues around intercultural (mis)understanding arise in these contexts. The first is when administrators interpret behaviors or words in different ways than the actors and speakers; the second involves not knowing why individuals did what they did or said what they said. One example of the former is the case where the administrator attempted to understand the actions of the parties by referring to what she believed were their unique, and offensive, gender practices (see Chapter 8). This administrator's parochial view of these practices did not coincide, however, with the group's more complex sense. The other case in Chapter 8 is an example of the latter issue in understanding – failing to comprehend the why's of the situation. In this instance, the administrator simply could not comprehend, from her unique Anglo/European perspective, the particular beliefs of a community group. She was completely bewildered, not having any idea how she might go about the process of understanding why a member of a community was saying and doing particular things. The bottom line here is that no matter how hard Anglo administrators of diverse schools may try, there will be times when they fail to comprehend the cultural practices of non-Anglo groups in their school communities.

Administrative teaching and learning also revolves around knowledge of some of the more invisible or taken-for-granted forms of life – forms of life that may systematically place some students at a disadvantage. This was the type of knowledge and learning referred to above as critical. While there are so-called factual and interpretive aspects to it, its identifying characteristic is its unobtrusive nature. This was perhaps the most difficult form of knowledge and associated teaching/learning for leaders to deal with. This was because the not-so-apparent forms of life that are the target of this kind of teaching and learning may not always be visible, and if they are, their (admitted) presence may threaten individuals, careers and communities. As a result, individuals may have been reluctant to admit to the presence of phenomena like racism, for example. As noted above, scholars have documented this tendency among school administrators. This may occur even in those instances where schools have adopted equity initiatives. In Lipman's (1998) study of educational reform, for example, the principal of one of the schools took pains to avoid any contentious issues, including, in particular, those that touched on racism. The result was that very little change occurred in the school that increased the opportunities of those students who persistently performed poorly. Understanding why administrators may or may not take these kinds of actions requires, as Anderson (1996) astutely points out, that we clarify who administrators actually work for. One might indeed seriously question the notion that many work for the marginalized. This is because, among other things, administrators are often more likely to respond to the wishes of politically-astute parents of Anglo students, wishes that may work against the former (Ryan & Tucker, 1997; Lipman, 1998). When faced with a choice, administrators may also simply favour their own Euro-centric practices, and yet at the same time, maintain that they are sensitive, supportive and sympathetic to diversity issues (Ryan & Wignall, 1996).

It is not surprising, then, in this study, that few administrators made reference to the more invisible and insidious practices that find their way into their schools – like racism, for example. For some, it was likely that their faith in the system and in humanity generally and their Anglo/European lenses would not permit them to acknowledge these patterns; for others, admitting that such things occurred in their schools would threaten the credibility of their organizations and, indeed, themselves personally. Ironically, however, this ability to both recognize and acknowledge these often taken for granted patterns is the first step in turning things around for those who are systematically disadvantaged in schools. Only when people acquire knowledge about these forms of disadvantage, can they work to counter them (Fay, 1987; Smyth, 1989; Ryan, 1998). Thus, for leaders to ensure that all students acquire the best possible education in their institutions, they must recognize, acknowledge, understand and learn about these forms of life, and they must also teach others about them. They must be open to hearing about these things and be willing to spread the word about them. As we have seen, however, not all administrators are willing to do this, and this impedes efforts at inclusion.

Community Relationships, Curriculum and the Nature of Administration

The ways in which administrators approach school-community relationships, the manner in which they involve themselves in curriculum matters and the nature of school administration can also have an impact on inclusion. Data from the study illustrate that administrators are generally very attentive to school-community relationships. Most, if not all, supported strategies for including the community in school activities, and many of these were of the enabling variety. Administrators spoke of their attempts to communicate with the community, to establish relationships with them. Towards this end, they spent much time sending out and acquiring information, connecting with individuals and with community organizations. Administrators also concentrated on developing contact processes that brought parents into the school. Unfortunately, activities like traditional parent nights were often less than successful. Administrators focused most of their efforts on enabling rather than empowering strategies because of the differences they perceived between themselves and community members and the lack of knowledge that both parties had of one another. Principals had their hands full simply getting to know the community and communicating with them. Most did not have the time or the inclination to attempt to motivate the community to become more involved in meaningful governance issues. The few who did found that only certain groups – generally the Anglo/Europeans – tended to participate. And even when other groups did become involved, they often did not have the resources at hand to influence decisions. For meaningful inclusion to occur, however, parents need to take on governance activities in ways that enable them to have a genuine voice. They need to occupy positions with which they are comfortable and that are able to affect the course of events in their school communities. School-community relationships that are merely enabling, will not, in the long run, ensure meaningful inclusion.

Administrators' agendas in curricular and instructional matters can also influence inclusive efforts. Unfortunately, the administrators in this study said little or nothing about pedagogy and curriculum, although they did make reference to teacher learning generally. When they did refer to student learning, they generally spoke of their efforts to purge racist or biased books from the library or from textbook lists. Those who did mention curriculum were generally from the elementary panel. Secondary school principals had many other things on their minds besides these sorts of issues, and as a consequence, rarely referred to instruction or student learning. This is unfortunate because no matter how much one favors inclusion, if one does not at some point target student learning then efforts towards this end will be for naught. Efforts at inclusion must ultimately find their way to the teaching/learning situation if they are to have any meaning or impact at all.

Finally, the nature of the job of school administration itself can also act as a barrier to inclusion. It would be an understatement to say that school administrators have difficult jobs. The administrators to whom we talked had days that were filled with crises. They regularly spent their time dealing with serious problems that demanded immediate attention and resolution. They also engaged in longer-term projects, like developing school improvement plans, sitting on too many committees, implementing a host of newly mandated programs, running the latest round of standardized testing, among many countless others. School administrators' days, and many of their nights, were filled with their work activities. Missing meals was a common occurrence for many of them. It is little wonder, then, that issues like inclusion can easily get lost in the press of the job and in administrators' often futile attempts to balance their personal lives with their professional ones. So, for example, satisfying complainers or seeing that conflict comes to an end may often take priority over ensuring inclusion. This was evident in one of the administrator's actions in this study. In Chapter 8, Barbara's primary goal was to placate the complaining parents, rather than to promote inclusion. She was more concerned with seeing that the parents' complaints went no further than her, than with respecting practices that she quite obviously opposed. Thus, the challenging nature of the job of school administration is as formidable a barrier to inclusion as any of the others previously mentioned.

CONCLUSION

Administrators encounter many barriers to inclusion. Some of these barriers are deeply entrenched in powerful global and systemic patterns and structures. Racism, for example, acts as a significant hindrance to inclusion. It also extends far beyond the individuals who act as its bearers. But these barriers also have a personal and local dimension. They show up in schools and in the ideas, values, knowledge and practices of educators and administrators. As we have seen, for example, administrators' conservative leanings can get in the way of inclusive efforts. Overcoming these barriers requires action that addresses both their global and local natures. Administrators can best play a part in resisting and changing these exclusive patterns if they first target their own backyards – their school communities, their teachers and themselves – for action. There are many things in their own realms that they can do to promote inclusion. The final chapter documents this action.

CHAPTER 11

LEADERSHIP AND INCLUSION

Principals are in ideal positions to promote inclusion in diverse school contexts. Moreso than perhaps any other individual, they have the power to shape leadership practices that are consistent with inclusion. To do so, they need to approach leadership not as sets of skills or activities associated with one individual, but as a communal process of people working together for just, democratic and inclusive schools and communities. There are many steps that they can take to set in motion and support this form of leadership. They can initiate and sustain dialogues between themselves and their various school constituencies. They can work to develop a critical consciousness in themselves and others. And they can introduce whole-school approaches to inclusion and learning, emphasize student learning, and advocate for communal and equitable policy making.

INITIATING AND SUSTAINING DIALOGUE

A key in establishing inclusive communities in schools is dialogue (Smyth, 1989; Lipman, 1998; Maxcy, 1998; May, 1994; Bogotch & Roy 1997; Tierney, 1993; Short & Greer, 1997; Robinson, 1996). For administrators to promote inclusive education, they need to initiate, foster, sustain, and reciprocate dialogues of respect and difference in ways that ensure that everyone has a voice. Principals in this study did many things to establish dialogues with other members of their school communities. They also provided conditions that enabled others to communicate with one another. Establishing these dialogues required that principals first forge connections and relationships with individuals and groups. To do so, they placed themselves in positions that brought them into contact with members of the community. Spending time on the phone for positive reasons, making themselves available at all times, hanging around areas that parents, students and parents frequent, going out into the community for meetings, and visiting parents in their homes, were just some of the strategies that principals in this study employed to establish dialogues. They also employed strategies for exchanging information. They used surveys to acquire knowledge about the groups in the community and to discover views about selected school matters[1], and they exploited newsletters, school newspapers and meetings to get information out into the community. Many

---

[1] Capper (1993) notes that surveys should also be used to uncover patterns of advantage and disadvantage in schools. She recommends that they be employed to uncover student representation in courses, disciplines, and student organizations, enrollment trends over time and student selection of, or assignment to, different courses. She also believes that data should also be collected on teacher/student interactions, including response opportunities, physical closeness, reproof techniques, listening/waiting time and high-level interactions.

also made efforts to beckon parents and community groups into the school to meet teachers and to help out in various capacities. Unfortunately, the more traditional of these events, like parent-teacher nights, did not prove terribly successful in attracting parents. Principals in this study and in other diverse settings (Delgato-Gaitin, 1991; Davis, 1995) found that more parents came to non-traditional activities.

Initiating these relationships is an important way to convey to parents that educators do care about students. It is also a way of cultivating the trust and respect that is necessary for dialogues to take place. Indeed, for dialogues to succeed, participants need to have emotional investments in them. Burbules (1993) insists that what draws participants into dialogical relationships are feelings towards others – the pleasures that communicants derive are not purely intellectual. Some of what is said in these situations, like statements of encouragement, are attempts to create and maintain bonds of mutual concern. Burbules (1993) contends that in dialogues we attempt to be fully with our partners, to engage them, because there is more at stake than just the topic at hand. A number of feelings are particularly important here, none more crucial than trust. Where there is an element of risk, participants need to know that they can rely on someone or something. They need to know that they can depend on another's good will. One way to inspire trust in others is to introduce certain sensitive and personal disclosures. Besides trust, other feelings enhance dialogues – respect, appreciation and affection for others. Hope can also play an important part in broadening and extending dialogues.

An important aspect of engaging in dialogue with various constituencies is a willingness to listen to individuals in the school community. At bottom, a key element in inclusive schooling and in dialogue is to ensure that all parties in dialogues have a voice. This does not mean, however, that everyone will always come to a consensus when dialoguing about various issues. Instead, it represents a starting point for grasping others' points of view. Advocates believe that dialogue allows participants to publicly identify institutional barriers that inhibit mutual understanding and consensus (Burbules, 1993). For this to happen, certain conditions must be present. For example, everyone must have an equal opportunity to speak, all members must respect other members' rights to speak out, all must feel safe to speak and all ideas must be tolerated and subjected to rational critical assessment (Ellsworth, 1989). Some scholars have spent considerable time and effort elaborating on complex schemes of this sort. Habermas (1987), for example, advocates what he refers to as an Ideal Speech Situation. For this to take place, he maintains that these settings must be characterized by the comprehensibility, truth, sincerity and rightness of the statements that constitute the dialogue. Each participant must have an equal opportunity to initiate and continue the conversation, to make assertions, recommendations and explanations and to explain his or her wishes, feelings and desires.

Many participants in the study recognized the importance of listening. However, most were not able to go in detail about the kinds of strategies that they used for listening. Whether or not they were aware of helpful techniques and employed them is open to question. There are a number of techniques that principals, as listeners, can use to make dialogue work. Listeners can establish eye contact, keeping in mind that eye contact will be inappropriate in certain situations, and depending upon the audience, take up a suitable distance from the speaker. Listeners may also want to avoid interrupting the speaker, comparing the speakers' experience to their own, and asking questions (Drake & Ryan, 1994). Levine-Rasky (1993) suggests that on occasions where dominant and non-dominant groups are engaged in dialogue, it is important for listeners from dominant groups to provide as much comfort as possible for the latter group to say what they have to say. In these circumstances, she contends that listeners need to abandon as far as possible any power or influence that they may have in the situation. Among other things, Levine-Rasky (1993) believes that listening involves: (1) a displacement of oneself as "knower" and "evaluator"; (2) abandoning the desire to assign relative worth to observations; (3) a degree of self-reflection on privilege; (4) a suspension of personal authority; and (5) a willingness to experience vulnerability, to admit one's ignorance. She also maintains that one may have to temporarily abandon one's identity. She uses the following citation from Delpit (1988, p. 297) to make her point.

> Listening requires not only open eyes and ears, but open hearts and minds ... to put our beliefs on hold is to cease to exist as ourselves for a moment and that is not easy. It is painful as well, because it means turning yourself inside out, giving up your own sense of who you are, and being willing to see yourself in the unflattering light of another's gaze.

Ideally, dialogue encourages the inclusion of those voices not normally heard and in doing so, acknowledges these perspectives. It would be naïve to think that dialogue in and of itself, however, can ensure that the marginalized can overturn the already entrenched power relationships, relationships that exclude them from many of the advantages others enjoy. Current and deeply entrenched unequal power relationships between raced, classed and gendered students and educators are difficult to overcome in the classroom and school community. But even skeptics like Ellsworth (1989) see merit in dialogue. While she believes that all participants will not always have equal opportunities to speak and be heard, she nevertheless sees dialogue as the means to build "coalitions among multiple shifting, intersecting and sometimes contradictory groups carrying unequal weights of legitimacy" (Ellsworth, 1989, p. 317). So one of the ways in which administrators can employ dialogue is for the purposes of building coalitions with others who support inclusion. They can also make it possible for other individuals and groups to build affinities with one another to ensure that their interests are fairly represented in the school community.

Establishing dialogues with members of the school community is important. But this task needs to be complemented by others. One of these is developing a critical consciousness.

DEVELOPING CRITICAL CONSCIOUSNESS

Critical consciousness is also a central element in developing inclusive school communities. Promoting and realizing inclusive communities requires that administrators develop in themselves and others critical ways of looking at the world. We have already seen how important the education of administrators and other members of the school community is in these diverse contexts. The mostly Anglo educators in this study often knew too little about the groups that attended their schools and generally did not understand the complexities associated with diversity processes like racism. They also recognized that they needed to acquire factual information and assistance in understanding forms of life different from their own.   But in order to promote inclusion they need to move beyond forms of knowledge that emphasize merely facts and understandings.   Members of diverse school communities must approach their learning in a critical manner.   This means that they have to develop a capacity to examine their own beliefs, practices, and taken-for-granted understandings. This includes being able to critically reflect on their own and other's situations, thoughts and actions and to acknowledge the impact of oppressive global, systemic and sometimes hard-to-detect forms of thought and practice.

For schools to become inclusive, administrators need to know something about the underlying and widespread structures that affect the ways in which they and others perceive and evaluate differences. Although educators, as well as everyone else, are implicated in their own beliefs and practices, these beliefs and practices do not originate exclusively with individuals. These practices and beliefs are social in nature; they have a history and are influenced, sustained and passed on by and through collective forces that operate within relationships of power.   So while individuals may be the bearers of particular beliefs and practices, they are not the exclusive creators of them.   Racism, for example, is not just an individual or personal phenomenon.   While individual men, women and children may commit racist acts, they do so within the context of a system of racism that also works in impersonal and silent ways; it is a collective force that works on and through individuals.   For administrators to have any success at promoting inclusion, then, they have to be aware of these systemic forms of life. They also need to know about their potentially oppressive nature. This includes an awareness of how the system of racism works and what can do done to counteract it.   Young and Liable (2000) believe school administrators need to understand (a) the system of White racial dominance, (b) how White racial dominance works through and on our society, our institutions, and ourselves in reproducing relations of domination, and (c) how to take action that opposes the system of White racism.   Young and Liable believe that knowledge in this case should not be restricted to information.   In addition to broadening their information base, administrators also need to extend empathy and to balance the emotional and cognitive aspects of learning.

One of the unique characteristics of these systemic forms of life is that they are often accepted as given.   Men and women have difficulty identifying them because these patterns are so ingrained in their daily lives that they rarely pause to take note of them.   The result is these powerful structures routinely become part of the woodwork of people's lives, rarely intruding in ways that cause people to notice them. In this regard, Shields (2002) refers to the phenomenon of "blindness."   She maintains that not only are educators and administrators susceptible to colour blindness, but they may also display class and spiritual blindness. It is not surprising then, in this study, that only some administrators made reference to the more invisible and insidious practices that find their way into their schools – like racism. As mentioned above, it was likely that their faith in the system and in humanity generally along with their conservative and Anglo/European lenses would not permit these principals to acknowledge these patterns; for others, admitting that such acts occurred in their schools would threaten the credibility of their organizations and, indeed, themselves personally. Ironically, however, this ability to both recognize and acknowledge these often taken-for-granted patterns is the first step in turning things around for those who are systematically disadvantaged in schools. Only when people acquire knowledge about forms of disadvantage, can they act to counter it (Fay, 1987; Smyth, 1989; Ryan, 1998). So, for leaders to ensure that all students acquire the best possible education in their institutions, they must recognize, acknowledge, understand and learn about these forms of life, and they must also teach others about them. They must be open to hearing about these things and be willing to spread the word about them.

While most administrators in this study spoke of other diversity issues, a few referred to the need to raise awareness of some of the more invisible and insidious patterns, such as racism, that find their way into schools. These administrators allowed that there were issues and patterns that were not always apparent to members of their educational communities, and it was their job to open their eyes to some of these oppressive and invisible aspects of life in schools. They believed that providing others with knowledge about these conditions would help them reflect on what they did and provide the impetus for them to change, if necessary, theirs and others' practices. These administrators spoke specifically of "raising people's awareness," "opening people's eyes," "not burying the negative things," "looking at the underbelly," "sensitizing," and "being open to other sides of situations." Administrators also spoke of other ways of raising awareness of these sometimes invisible structures. One strategy they mentioned was giving a chance for victims to talk about racism. One principal organized a theatrical production that made it possible for members of the audience to articulate their feelings. Other administrators arranged for speakers and "town hall meetings."

Developing a critical consciousness requires that administrators reflect on their ideas, practices and the situations that they face. It also requires that they help others to do the same. Engaging in critical reflection can be useful because it provides educators with an opportunity to penetrate the more insidious and presumed patterns that place some students at a disadvantage. Reflective practices can help people pause, step back from these ingrained patterns and problematize them. The practice itself involves the purposeful, deliberate act of inquiry into one's thoughts and actions (Coombs, 2000). When people reflect critically, they examine their own and others' thoughts, words and deeds and the assumptions upon which they are based. This can include questioning morals, ethical and other types of normative criteria, and existing ideas and patterns. Reflection usually occurs when something unexpected or unusual occurs (Schon, 1983). It does not generally take place when individuals are engaged in routine matters. When educators are engaged in routine activities they normally just go ahead with what they are doing without closely thinking about them. Unfortunately, the nature of administrators' work doesn't lend itself naturally to reflection and reorientation. The hurried pace of the day doesn't always allow time for reflection. The same also applies to the work of teachers. So if administrators want to ensure that they and their teaching staffs engage in the practice of reflection, then they have to find ways to build opportunities for it into their daily routines.

Coombs (2000) reviews a number of strategies that administrators can employ to ensure that they and their diverse school communities reflect on those issues that are often overlooked. These strategies include testing out platforms, modeling, cognitive apprenticeships, administrative portfolios, journals, case records and studies, two-column analyses, various scenario analyses and simulations and value audits. Coombs also cites a number of group activities that administrators and others can employ to critically reflect on issues. At least one administrator in this study also made reference to his use of group reflection. In one situation, his fellow administrators, after observing his behaviour, told him that he treated two groups of people in different ways. This statement prompted him to consider his behaviour and to question it and his assumed attitudes. Other administrators in this study also spoke of the need for reflection, but did not have concrete strategies for engaging in it. They nevertheless believed that reflection provided the means for them to get in touch with taken for granted and invisible aspects of their interactions, aspects that did not always work in the interests of all students.

Administrators can also employ two more strategies that will help them and their school communities reflect critically on their own and others' practices. The use of the arts and "jujitsu" techniques can help them see things in new and different ways. Shohat and Stam (1994) refer to the process of reversing ordinary ways of looking at things as "jujitsu." They cite the Australian short film, *Babakiueria* (1988) as an example. This film reverses the positions of Europeans and Aborigines; it is the Aborigines who colonize the "indigenous" White Europeans. In the process they unilaterally impose their values and practices on the unsuspecting and generally compliant Europeans. The film "makes strange" both the cultural practices of the Europeans (e.g., welfare, sports, recreation, work, religion) and the discourses employed to make sense of them (e.g., social science, progress). By forcing European viewers to identify with the "oppressed" in the film, it prompts them to take a critical, and perhaps different look at the process and effects of colonization. Other artistic forms can also prompt educators, including administrators, to step back from the press of daily life and look at it in new and different ways (Ryan, 1994). Literature and various representational forms of art can accomplish this in ways that social scientific studies cannot.

These and other strategies can provide administrators with the tools to explore their own cultures. Ideally, these strategies will be able to help administrators understand the ways in which their cultures have provided them and other members of their cultural groups with privileges that others do not have. Among other things, critical reflection can assist them in identifying how power is associated with their cultural and institutional positions and how it is exercised. Capper (1993) points out that all administrators have power over students and others by virtue of their positions. She also contends that this power is also a product not only of ethnicity, but also of social class, gender, sexual orientation and ability relationships. Critically reflecting on these privileged relationships can sensitize administrators to the consequences that these relationships have for their school communities and help them do something about the injustices that may accompany these privileges.

These and other such strategies will amount to little, however, if they are not integrated into whole-school strategies for inclusion and learning.

ENGENDERING WHOLE-SCHOOL APPROACHES

Effective approaches to diversity require whole-school approaches (Neito, 1992; May, 1994; Gillborn, 1995). To increase their prospects for success in their efforts to entrench inclusive practices in schools, administrators need to involve whole school communities in these enterprises. This entails making inclusion an essential and routine part of educational practice in ways that ensure its longevity and protect it against wider changes in educational policy. While the administrators in this study recognized the importance of working against exclusionary practices like racism, their attitudes and the practices they put into place did not always favour whole-school practices. This was particularly evident in the responses on the survey. Respondents believed that antiracism programs were the second least effective means of combating racism. Also, many of the administrators we interviewed directed their efforts at eliminating individual indiscretions and not at systemic or institutional racism. They tended, moreover, to focus on only one segment of their school community – the students. However, this did not apply to all study participants; some favored aspects of comprehensive approaches. The best chances for success rest with initiatives that involve all segments of the school community in programs like antiracism that target both personal and systemic racism, and acknowledge that everyone – and not just students – can be implicated in racism.

One key element in this whole-school approach is education. If administrators, teachers, students and parents are to have the opportunity to reflect on, and learn about the often invisible patterns of advantage and disadvantage that obstruct inclusion, then they must have opportunities to routinely do so with others. Well-meaning but individual attempts to learn about diversity and inclusion, and to follow up on this learning, will most often amount to very little if they don't extend beyond the well-intentioned individuals who are the prime movers. If those committed to change do not receive support from those they work and interact with, change initiatives of this sort will probably not succeed (Sleeter, 1992). Teachers, students, parents and particularly administrators, all have to be involved in the learning enterprise. This learning enterprise also has to become a routine part of school life, that is, part of the culture of the school. Administrators in this study spoke of influencing this kind of school atmosphere. Besides the measures they took to overtly influence others and put processes in place, they also spoke about some of the more subtle means of establishing a learning culture. These included modeling the behaviour that they wished to see in others and constantly talking about the things in which they believed.

There is no shortage of advice for administrators wishing to nurture or develop particular cultures or climates in their schools. Much of this advice has come from management literature (e.g., Peters & Waterman, 1982) and been adapted for educational institutions. The basic premise of this line of thinking is that managers will get the most out of their employees if they can find ways to engender in them a type of motivating collective ethos or spirit. The idea is that employees – teachers in this case – will be more committed to the organization if this commitment appears to originate naturally with them rather than being imposed by management. One of the many ways in which administrators can supposedly nurture this type of shared culture is to manipulate the symbols with which members of their organizations identify. Reitzug and Reeves (1992), for example, describe the ways in which a principal used symbolic language, time and resources to develop shared meanings with staff. In this vein, Deal and Peterson (1994), on the other hand, emphasize the symbol-related roles that leaders can play in managing and engendering shared cultures. These roles include (1) a *historian* who reads current events and reinterprets them for the rest of the staff, (2) an *anthropological detective* who searches for meaning in the behaviour of others, (3) a *visionary* who projects hopes and dreams for the entire staff, and (4) a *symbol* in him or herself, by making sure important routines and ceremonies in the school's life are reliable and communicate caring.

Administrators, however, need to be cautious about jumping onto the culture bandwagon. There are a number of problems with approaching whole-school enterprises in this manner, as critics (Bates, 1987; Angus, 1996) have pointed out. These difficulties revolve around the interpretations that proponents have of culture and the ends to which culture-shaping efforts are directed. Neither are consistent with inclusive schooling. The more bald-faced versions are explicitly manipulative. (Mis)construing culture as a variable, proponents encourage administrators to use elements of culture in order to move members of the organization to think and behave in ways that promote organizational interests. Unfortunately, these interests do not generally coincide with the interests of all members of the organization. Instead, the interests are most often those of management, represented in such things as management-generated vision statements. The version of culture that these academics and management consultants employ is also trivial and static (Bates, 1987). It fails to account for the complexities of culture in organizations like schools that display more than one culture. These cultures are dynamic, contested and rich, and they extend far beyond the boundaries of the school.

If administrators are interested in promoting whole-school initiatives, that is, school cultures that foster education for inclusion, then they will need to acknowledge the complexities of culture and be sensitive to the ends to which their efforts are directed. An inclusive approach to leadership demands that the efforts of members of the school community should promote everyone's interests – not just those of management. So vision statements, for example, need to emanate not just from management, but equitably from all segments of the school community. Whatever shared values emerge around whole-school efforts to educate the community for inclusion must represent all groups and all groups must benefit equally from these diverse values. This means taking a more realistic view of culture. Administrators need to find ways to make space for traditionally marginalized cultures to be part of this process. Their values and lifestyles need to be honored and thus incorporated into the content and process of these educative efforts.

Inevitably, however, for administrators to enshrine whole-school educative practices consistent with inclusion they will have to ensure that more than a few members of the school community understand them in similar ways. In other words, they need to work at building meanings in their schools that favour these values. Principals need to attend to the process of meaning-making because meanings are the glue that hold socially-constructed institutions like schools together (Greenfield, & Ribbins, 1993). No educational enterprise or program will succeed if students, teachers, parents and administrators do not share some common understandings about them. This is not to say that it will always be possible for everyone to come to similar understandings in these diverse contexts, but that there will need to be at least some level of agreement – however fleeting and fluid – for dynamics to work out for the best. Principals are often in a better position to influence these meanings than others (Riehl, 2000). Among other things, they can influence meaning-making through the day-to-day management of meaning, the mediation of conflict, and the resolution of contradictions in their own ideological perspectives (Anderson, 1990). They should, however, be careful not to unilaterally impose their own meanings on others, as would proponents of the corporate culture view. Rather, they need to engage all others in their school communities in democratic discourse processes (Corson, 1995). Such processes represent the best option for all groups to fairly negotiate the construction of meanings that work in everyone's interests. Because meanings are not permanent, however, everyone has to continually work at these processes.

This sort of approach to developing meanings associated with a learning culture in schools can be used in conjunction with comparatively recent ideas that feature the concept of a learning organization (see for example, Senge, 1990; Senge et. al., 2000; Leithwood & Louis, 1999; Leithwood, 2000). This is not to say that these learning organization ideas can be used for ends other than inclusion. They can be, and no doubt have been, used for such purposes. But Senge's so-called disciplines of personal mastery, shared vision, mental models, team learning and systems thinking, if employed in becoming ways, can allow for school communities to pursue collective, persistent and critical learning. Learning organizations of the sort that Senge envisions emphasize personal development, mutual purpose, critical reflection, collective learning, dialogue and interaction, and systems thinking – practices consistent with inclusion. Such practices allow all members of school communities to have their respective cultures honored and incorporated into the learning experience, to have a say in the nature of that learning experience, and to have the opportunity to critically examine and eventually challenge systemic forms of exclusion. These practices also make it possible for school communities to adjust to the perpetually changing conditions that characterize diverse postmodern communities (Pajak & Evans, 2000).

Many examples of professional learning opportunities emerge in the literature. All but absent are examples from diverse school settings. The administrators in this study spoke of both formal and informal efforts to engender learning on the part of themselves and their teaching staffs. However, few spoke of whole-school enterprises. And if they did, it was not on the scale that organizational learning advocates would recommend. Such efforts also fall short of the practices of

Richmond Road, a multiethnic school in Auckland, New Zealand. Richmond Road provided its teaching staff with many opportunities to learn about themselves, their craft and the world by building forms of staff development into their weekly routines. So at least once a week teachers would meet for three to four hours to critically discuss ideas from articles that dealt with diversity and education. In doing so, the school looked to provide these individuals with a critical and reflective knowledge base for teaching and learning from which to contest unjust forces at work in the school and community, and as a consequence, make it a more inclusive place (May, 1994).

EMPHASIZING STUDENT LEARNING

Promoting whole-school approaches to learning is an important component of inclusion. But this in itself is not sufficient. Schools and educators also need to prioritize student learning. Changes in the ways schools are organized to favour inclusion will mean little if student learning is not affected and achievement does not improve. Unfortunately, there is no necessary connection between structural reforms designed to increase inclusion and student learning, as recent evidence from urban centers in the United States indicates (Hess, 1999; Shipps et. al., 1999). This research shows that structural changes designed to provide parents with power may not have an impact on student achievement if these reforms do not specifically target teaching and learning. Despite comparatively substantive changes that give parents positions in decision-making bodies, changes in student achievement in these urban areas have to date been inconsistent at best (Hess, 1999; Shipps et. al., 1999). So, for reforms to have an impact on student achievement, they must also target teaching and learning. Long-term improvement in student achievement will require the development of the capacity of professional educators. This is because constraints on the exercise of these capacities will inevitably limit the improvement in student learning opportunities. Those wishing to promote inclusion then must ensure that management or organizational changes and administrative practices are geared toward improving the professional expertise and commitment of educators.

Over the years, many administrators have directed efforts at improving teaching and learning in their schools. These efforts have been recorded by researchers who have subsequently referred to them as forms of instructional leadership. These researchers claim that instructional leadership has a marked impact on teaching and learning. Not only does it affect the way teachers approach their work (Shepphard, 1996; Blase & Blase, 1999; Louis, Kruse et al. 1995), it also improves student commitment and achievement (Hess et al. 1990; Krug, 1992; Louis, Kruse et al. 1995). This also applies to diverse contexts. In fact, some of the first studies in the effective schools tradition that pointed to the importance of instructional leadership were done in diverse urban contexts (Riehl, 2000). While some of those in this line of research mistakenly attempted to export their findings to (all) other contexts (Ryan, 1995), there is little question that the results are relevant to at least some schools in similar contexts. This research found that in higher achieving (diverse) schools principals exerted strong instructional leadership. They had high expectations for student achievement, maintained high visibility, visited classrooms frequently, provided high support for staff and advocated strong goal and task orientations (Edmonds, 1979; Purkey & Smith, 1983; Rosenholtz, 1985).

Much of the research in this area has attempted to establish relationships between instructional leadership behaviour and the work and attitudes of teachers and students. In the process, it has identified those behaviors associated with both leadership activity and the various effects that it has on teachers and students. However, there has been little agreement on the meaning of the term instructional leadership and the behaviors associated with it, beyond a general notion of action taken to promote student learning (Leithwood & Duke, 1996). Even so, a number of researchers have attempted to categorize these behaviors (Hess et al. 1990; Krug, 1992; Kleine-Kracht 1993; Louis, Kruse et al. 1995; Shepphard, 1996; Blase & Blase, 1999). Perhaps the division that makes the most sense is a two dimensional one. Kleine-Kracht (1993), for example, separates instructional leadership behaviors into "direct" and "indirect." Along these same lines, Shepphard (1996) speaks of "narrow" and "broad", while Blase and Blase (1999) categorize instructional leadership behaviors into either talking with teachers or promoting professional growth. The first, or direct kind, includes the immediate interactions of principals with teachers and others about classroom, teaching, student performance and the curriculum. It includes curriculum planning, teacher observation, informal feedback, selection of instructional materials, staff development, and teacher supervision. It has a "hands on" and "face to face" quality (Kleine-Kracht, 1993).

Although direct involvement in teaching and learning has been shown to have a positive impact on the latter, not all principals engage in this type of activity. If what Martin and Willower (1981) told us over two decades ago still holds today, then it would seem that principals do not spend much time with direct instructional activities. Today, their overwhelming workloads would make it difficult for them to spend substantial amounts of time directly supervising their teachers. Most school principals have seen their workloads increase over the past several years (Waite & Fernandez, 2000). They now have more bureaucratic forms to fill out and file, more regulations to abide by, and fewer people to help them with their rapidly expanding administrative and supervisory tasks and responsibilities. Other changes in the organization of the education system may also boost workloads. The principals in this study, for example, found that their designation by the provincial government as managers and their expulsion from the teacher unions meant that they could no longer rely on teachers to do administration-related tasks that the latter had performed as a matter of course in the past. Secondary school principals may have even more difficulty than elementary principals conducting direct instructional supervision. Both Martin and Willower (1981) and Blank (1987) note that these individuals spend less time in these activities than their elementary counterparts. There are at least two reasons for this. The first is that they are responsible for more teachers. Some secondary principals in this study, for example, worked with well over 100 teachers. The other reason is that principals may not have experience or expertise with various subjects. They may not feel comfortable speaking with someone who has more experience teaching in a particular area and who is perceived to have much more knowledge of the subject matter. On the other hand, research indicates that teachers do not always readily accept principals as instructional leaders (Pellicer, 1982; Rallis & Highsmith, 1987).

It seems more realistic for principals to concentrate more on indirect or broad forms of instructional leadership. Principals' time would be put to better use if they devoted more of their efforts to indirect forms of instructional leadership, and left the direct activities to others. Hence, principals would clear the way for other administrators, department heads or experienced teachers to carry out these tasks by providing structures that make it possible for them to do so. As part of their indirect contributions to teaching and learning, principals would organize resources and time to free up these people for these "hands on" tasks. In areas where principals are required to conduct formal evaluations of teachers, principals might devise ways to work with these people, without necessarily shirking their duties. Such arrangements would help both teachers and principals, who when they do conduct evaluations, often do so as a one-time-only observation and feedback session. While it may be in a principal's best interest to leave the more direct instructional work to others, particularly in high schools, this does not mean that they should not do any of it. To reflect these priorities, they should make an effort to engage in direct instructional supervision when they can.

Direct instructional leadership activities often go by names like clinical supervision. There is no shortage of studies on this type of work. Many of these studies are quantitative in nature and generally seek to establish relationships between supervisory activities and their effects. One notable exception is a study conducted by Blase and Blase (1999). Their work provides more detail on both direct and indirect sides of the instructional enterprise than the many quantitative studies in the area. Blase and Blase's (1999) study illustrates first and foremost that talking with teachers in and outside of instructional conferences is the cornerstone of effective instructional leadership. Particularly effective are dialogues that encourage teachers to become aware of, and critically reflect on, their learning and professional practice. Blase and Blase (1999) are not the only ones who value critical dialogue in these sorts of interactions. Waite (1995) and Waite and Fernandez (2000) also advocate a dialogical approach for the instructional supervision of teachers. They believe that the face-to-face communication that is part of this process should be based on mutual respect, be reflective and open to critique. But it is not just the teacher's talk, action and beliefs that are the subject of critique. The supervisor's beliefs, perceptions and favored practices are also open to interrogation. In these sessions supervisors need to be prepared to give, invite and receive critique, and encourage and instruct others how to do so as well. In doing so, they empower teachers in this process and make it possible for both parties to work toward shaping curriculum, pedagogy and evaluation in the interests of improving the life chances of all students (Smyth, 1997).

These critical conversations revolve around teaching practices and learning. In an inclusive spirit, teachers and supervisors need to interrogate ways of delivering the curriculum in diverse contexts that will include and empower all students. They will have to consider evidence of what has been shown to be successful in these settings. This includes honoring different ways of knowing and sources of knowledge, allowing students to speak and write in their own vernacular and using culturally-compatible communication styles themselves. Teachers can also promote learning in diverse contexts when they express cultural solidarity with their students, empower and demonstrate that they care about them, and adhere to high expectations for all (Riehl, 2000). Teacher and supervisor need to work together to interrogate these and other such ideas, figure out how they might apply them to the areas of the curriculum for which they are responsible, think about how they might work out in their own unique contexts, and consider alternatives to them.

How might these critical conversations proceed? In Blase and Blase's (1999) study principals used five talking strategies with teachers to promote critical reflection. These included making suggestions, giving feedback, modeling, using inquiry and soliciting advice and opinions and giving praise. Suggestions focused on listening, sharing experiences, using examples and demonstrations, giving teachers a choice, challenging outdated policies, encouraging risk taking, offering professional literature, recognizing teacher strengths, and maintaining a focus on improving instruction. Blase and Blase (1999) reasoned that these suggestions strongly enhanced teachers' reflective behaviors. The feedback that they observed focused primarily on observed classroom behaviour. It was also detailed and specific, expressed caring, interest and support in a nonjudgmental way, provided praise, established a problem-solving orientation based on trust and respect, responded to concerns about student behaviour, discussed teacher-student interaction, and indicated the principal's availability.

Indirect instructional leadership activities provide the conditions under which these kinds of conversations can take place. Instead of directly targeting teaching and learning, they shape an atmosphere that facilitates, catalyzes and supports the efforts of teachers and students. Administrators concern themselves with activities that deal with schools' internal and external environments, the physical and cultural context that surrounds the classroom, teaching and the curriculum, and the meanings that principals' actions have for teachers (Kleine-Kracht, 1993). This includes clarifying and communicating school goals, supporting collaborative and coaching efforts, providing structural arrangements conducive to teaching and learning, and monitoring student progress.

Clarifying and communicating school goals are particularly important in diverse contexts (Rosenholtz, 1985). This is because members of various groups may not know or understand what many in other more homogeneous contexts may take for granted about schools and their purposes. It is also important to increase teachers' certainty about their goals for student achievement, their ability to meet them and their awareness of when they meet these goals. Administrators also need to emphasize the importance of student learning and of teacher professional development. The principal in Kleine-Kracht's (1993) study, for example, spent much time and effort making sure that everyone knew that student welfare was a priority at the school. The value that he placed on it shaped both his actions and the actions of his teachers. He only hired new teachers and appointed those to positions of responsibility who shared these same values and he endorsed changes in programs only when it could be demonstrated that they benefited student learning.

Supporting collaborative and coaching efforts also enhances teaching practices and student learning. Administrators can encourage collaboration among teachers by modeling a philosophy of teamwork, providing time for collaboration and advocating for sharing and peer observation. Clearing the way for peers to coach can also enhance teaching and learning. Given the right conditions, fellow teachers can devote more time to coaching than most principals. Moreover, teachers tend to respect colleagues that they know posses the expertise and experience to help them. In this regard Joyce and Showers (1995) maintain that classroom implementation of a training design is effective only when training includes coaching from peers. The principal in Kleine-Kracht's (1993) study exemplifies the delegation of direct supervision of teachers to the division chairs. He had confidence in these people as coaches because they were what he believed to be curriculum and teaching experts. On the other hand, teachers accepted the division chairs' instructional leadership because they also recognized this expertise. The principal supported these individuals in their tasks. He allocated them the time and resources necessary to improve instruction, develop curriculum and grow professionally.

Another important indirect instructional leadership task is encouraging and supporting program changes. Administrators can accomplish this by providing teachers with time to collaborate on new programs and by providing conditions that encourage teachers to experiment. Teachers need to have the confidence to try new things without fearing the consequences of failure. Principals can instill this confidence by expressing their support for experimentation and by protecting teachers from any fall-out that may result. They also need to protect teachers from pressures that may originate from outside influences. While involving parents and community advisory groups in the development of new programs is desirable, unorganized and haphazard intrusions can sometimes be unproductive. Effective principals are able to channel various community influences into more coordinated efforts that help rather than hinder such processes (Hess et al., 1990).

Principals need to have a comprehensive and fair system of monitoring student progress. Most schools in the Western world these days have comprehensive evaluation systems; students are assessed regularly and these results are sent home, and sometimes advertised in the local paper. The problem for principals of diverse schools then is not one of developing monitoring systems from nothing, but of either tempering or supplementing current systems. In doing this, they need to understand the strengths and weaknesses of various approaches. They will have to know, for example, that the kind of standardized testing currently in vogue can have deleterious effects on diverse student populations (McNeil, 2000). It will be up to them to modify the effects of this form of testing and to promote alternative forms of evaluation that are fair to all students and help them learn things important to them. They need to help to teach teachers to use the results of assessment to improve teacher and student learning and to help parents understand where and why improvement is needed (Krug, 1992). In all of this, they need to advocate for those groups that are not always served well by current systems of evaluation and by the school system generally (Cummins, 1986).

If possible, these approaches to instructional supervision and school strategies for learning should be entrenched in policy.

ADVOCATING FOR COLLECTIVE POLICY PROCEDURES

Administrators need to assume roles as advocates if they wish to help their school communities become inclusive places (Bates, 1987). They need to advocate for groups that are traditionally not well served by the school system and for those practices that will engender their inclusion. Administrators are in a unique position to do this because their formal positions in the educational hierarchy confer on them a certain amount of power. As individuals who are responsible for what goes on in their respective buildings, they have comparatively more discretion at their disposal than others who work in the same settings. Administrators therefore have a duty to advocate for arrangements that work in the interests of all segments of their respective school communities. Doing so, however, may require that they relinquish some of their power in order to see that others are genuinely empowered.

One of the fundamental areas that requires such advocacy is policy and decision-making. Not only should the outcome of school policies and decision-making favour inclusion, but the processes associated with them also need to be inclusive. This means that all interests in the school community ought to be represented in these processes and that all groups have an equal chance at influencing the outcome of the processes. This is a tall order, particularly in diverse contexts where efforts to include school communities in policy making have not always been successful. In this (see Chapter 6) and other studies (Hatcher et al., 1996; Fine, 1993; Lewis & Nakagawa, 1995), it is obvious that some communities prefer not to participate in school activities, let alone ones that involve decision-making. Some groups believe that the school and not parents should be engaged in these activities, while others either don't have the time or lack confidence to participate. But even when non-Anglo groups come to the table, they find that they don't always have the specialized knowledge to make their cases or that they lack sufficient grasp of the preferred language or meeting rules to successfully insert themselves meaningfully into conversations to have an impact on the outcome.

The principal's role in the policy process is crucial if it is to be an inclusive one. First and foremost, administrators must be prepared to initiate or facilitate policy deliberations. In order to accomplish this, they will need to know their respective communities. As we have seen in this study, administrators can acquire this knowledge in various ways. They can circulate surveys and they can get to know individuals from the connections they make with these individuals and with community organizations. The knowledge that they gain from these strategies can boost their understandings of community situations and point to areas that need attention or, simultaneously, whether they can sort out the degree to which policies from Ministries of Education or from central office will need to be tailored. One administrator in this study, for example, recognized a need for a policy process on the basis of his acquired knowledge of the community some time after he assumed his position (see Chapter 5). This sort of knowledge will also help administrators to respond in appropriate ways to requests from members of their communities for action. Such requests may originate with staff or with the community, often in response to one or more situations. This occurred in Gillborn's (1995) study when a number of teachers registered their wish for antiracism policies to help deal with the problems and crises that were associated with increasing incidents of name-calling and other such problems.

Administrators will also have to ensure that all community interests are fairly represented among the people engaged in policy deliberations. This means that the circle of policy makers needs to include people who are in touch with the values, interests and wishes of the people that the policy affects (Corson, 1996). So bringing in outsiders – that is, those who don't normally associate themselves with school activities – can have a positive impact on the policy process. Besides representing various interests, their special and local expertise can broaden interpretations of problem situations and yield fresh insights into decision-making possibilities. Unfortunately, as we have seen, it is not always easy to get such individuals to engage in these sorts of activities. So principals may have to take the initiative and approach individuals for these tasks, as some principals in this study did. Once again, their knowledge of the community and relationships with individuals should help them out here. The best way to ensure that everyone is represented in such processes, however, is to already have good school-community relationships in place. This was the case at Richmond Road School in New Zealand where parents felt comfortable approaching the school at any time and for any reason. They felt at ease deliberating policy matters as they did offering their expertise in the classroom (May, 1994).

Once the policy makers have been identified, then an appropriate context for the deliberations needs to be established. This includes the setting and tone for the meetings. Administrators need to find a place for meetings where everyone is comfortable. This may require holding meetings away from the school. Administrators also need to find ways to give everyone a voice in policy deliberations. Some scholars, like Corson (1996), recommend that administrators withdraw from centre stage in the process, as they may be tempted to use their power to dictate the outcome, as has been the case in a number of situations (Leithwood et al. 1999; Dehli, 1994; Malen & Ogawa, 1990). Corson recommends that if administrators are to participate, then they should limit themselves to consultative contributions, offer their opinions last and be clear that they will accept any decision arrived at by democratic consensus. Withdrawing in this manner, however, leaves policy makers to their own devices in settings where not all have equal power. While in some situations it may be appropriate, in others it is not. Where it is not appropriate, principals can use their own power to ensure that those with fewer resources can participate in the conversations and have fair opportunities to influence the outcome. They can ensure that the language used is not so specialized or exclusive that all can understand and use it (translation services may be needed), all members have sufficient background information on the various issues, everyone has an opportunity to speak their mind, and no one unfairly dominates deliberations. This may require that administrators work with members to set rules for these meetings that all are comfortable with, that they sometimes act as "interpreters," clarifying the positions of some members for others, and intervene in deliberations to make sure that they are fair. Administrators, however, must be mindful that they can never be neutral in their stances and that they might unwittingly dominate deliberations.

The next step in the policy process will be identifying the problems associated with the issues at hand (Corson, 1996). This is not necessarily a straightforward matter, particularly in diverse contexts. People will inevitably see different problems in similar situations. So, for example, persistent conflicts between teachers and students may be seen either as attempts to take advantage of teachers or as racism. In these cases, efforts should be made to reach consensus on a problem. This means being able to frame it in language that everyone can agree on. Agreement, however, will not always be forthcoming. If policy makers cannot agree on language to frame a problem, then it should be treated as more than one problem, as Corson (1996) recommends. Such disagreements should not be discouraged. But in instances where there is a lack of agreement, policy makers should be encouraged to adopt other people's problems as their own. They should try to see the world from the different points of view of others. Once the problems have been identified, a range of proposed solutions needs to be discussed and tentatively adopted.

After policy makers complete the first draft of a policy, they need to consult with the people who will be affected by this policy. Gillborn (1995) provides an example of how this might be done in his description of the policy making-process in one of the schools that he studied. In this particular school, the policy makers made every effort to consult with teachers, students and the community as they crafted an antiracism policy. They kept teachers informed during the process to the point that everyone knew of the policy's development and recognized the main features of it. The policy group also sought student input. With the support of the school's administration, and with the encouragement of the student council, they posted a draft of the policy in every classroom, and each teacher discussed the document during class time. Moreover, students were invited to send in written comments. Policy makers also made attempts to consult with the community. Students told their parents and quizzed community workers. Drafts of the policy document were also sent to community organizations. Policy makers also consulted on an individual basis with members of the community. They received mostly constructive comments on their draft, recruited a few people to help them refine their document, and incorporated many of these suggestions into it.

This drafting of the policy should not be seen as the final step in the process. Corson (1996) recommends that policy makers not be too hasty. Policies need to be tested and monitored. So all policies ought to be considered as tentative. They need to go through trial periods where information is collected on the policy in action. Richmond Road School in New Zealand was one school that conducted such trials when they introduced new policies. For example, over a number of years several senior teachers conducted trials of a new student grouping structure. Information from the teachers and others in the school community played an important part in the adjustments that were eventually made to the policy. Schools should also continue to monitor policies after these trials. This is because changing circumstances may produce new demands and problems. One of the schools that Gillborn (1995) studied implemented a policy that required continual monitoring of the circumstances associated with its antiracism policy. This policy required that course selection and student achievement be monitored annually. It specified that causes for concern were to be discussed by staff and if needed, given attention the following year.

Not all school problems require more-or-less formal policy making processes. Instituting policy proceedings for every problem that comes along will take time away from the more important issues that demand more intense deliberations. So it is up to the principal to determine what problems are best addressed by policy and what problems require decisions from them. Generally speaking, more routine issues should be handled by the principals. With respect to issues that are not quite as routine and associated with circumstances that are in some ways unique, but not quite as important as others, administrators may want to take a middle road. Of the various options available, they may want to convene a committee or simply informally consult interested parties and those who the decision will affect. In this vein, one of the principals in the study struck up a committee to make decisions on school activities in December, while many spoke of consulting others, either in person or by survey (See Chapter 7). Whatever path they take, however, it needs to be consistent with an inclusive philosophy.

PRINCIPAL CONTRIBUTIONS TO INCLUSIVE LEADERSHIP

Principals have much to contribute to the implementation and maintenance of inclusive practices in diverse schools. Their knowledge, experience and position in educational organizations enable them to influence inclusion in ways that few others can. As illustrated above, they can help introduce and maintain processes that are integral to inclusion. Principals can promote inclusion by nurturing and sustaining dialogue between and among themselves and the various constituencies in the school community, developing a critical consciousness in themselves and others, institutionalizing whole-school approaches to inclusion and learning, emphasizing student learning, and advocating for communal and equitable policy making.

These tasks are part of a process of inclusive leadership. I emphasize the term *process* here. Inclusive leadership is best seen as a process and not a set of skills, traits or activities that are associated with a single individual (Pajak & Evans, 2000). It is a communal process in which all groups participate equitably to work for socially just, democratic and inclusive schools and communities. This process displays a number of characteristics. Inclusive educational leadership is critical, educative, reflective, transformative, advocacy-oriented, collective, equitable and dialogical.

The first characteristic of inclusive leadership is that it is critical. This means that those who take part in inclusive leadership practices will look critically at themselves and the world about them. In doing so, they take a step back and examine critically taken-for-granted aspects of life. This process allows people to understand how personal and systemic forms of life, like racism, provide unfair advantages for some and penalize others. It is not always easy to be critical, however, particularly for some administrators. So sometimes people need to find ways to help them understand the diverse forms of life that shape what they and others do in schools and out. This help comes in the form of education; inclusive leadership is also necessarily educative. Inclusive leadership processes generate the means for people to learn things about which they had previously known little. They also help people to reflect on the situations of which they are a part. Deliberately inquiring into one's thoughts and actions can open people's eyes to things that they had either taken-for-granted or not understood or considered. Reflection and education are important strategies for acquiring a critical understanding of social conditions that are not always fair.

But inclusive leadership involves more than just understanding life. It also involves practice. So in this sense it is transformative. Inclusive leadership is geared towards making changes not only in people's consciousness, but also in actual social conditions that give rise to these ways of thinking. It looks to resist and change both local and more global social practices that are exclusive. Doing this requires a degree of advocacy. As a consequence, those involved in the process must advocate for inclusion and for those groups who have not always fared well in school and in society. Inclusive leadership is also communal, participatory and non-hierarchical. It seeks to involve or represent everyone in the process of leadership in a fair and equitable way. This sort of involvement becomes possible when dialogue across differences is initiated and sustained in enduring and equitable relationships. Only in this way can leadership be truly inclusive.

REFERENCES

Alladin, I. (Ed.). (1996). *Racism in Canadian Schools.* Toronto: Harcourt Brace.

Anderson, A. & Frideres, J. (1981). *Ethnicity in Canada: Theoretical perspectives.* Toronto: Butterworths.

Anderson, G. (1990). Toward a Critical Constructivist Approach to School Administration: Invisibility, Legitimation, and the Study of Non-Events. *Educational Administration Quarterly* 26 (1), 38-59.

Anderson, G. (1996). The Cultural Politics of Schools: Implications for Leadership. In K. Leithwood, J. Chapman, D. Corson, P. Hallinger & A. Hart (Eds.) *International Handbook of Educational Leadership and Administration* (pp. 947-966). Boston: Kluwer.

Angus, L (1996). Cultural dynamics and organizational analysis: Leadership, administration and the management of meaning in school. In K. Leithwood, J. Chapman, D. Corson, P. Hallinger & A Hart (Eds.). *International handbook of educational leadership and administration.* (pp. 967-998). Boston: Kluwer.

Anson, A.R., Cook, T.D., Habib, F., Grady, M.K., Haynes, N. & Comer, J.P. (1991). The Comer school development program: a theoretical analysis. *Urban Education,* 26, 56-82.

Apple, M. (2000). Racing Toward Educational Reform. In R. Mahalingam & C. McCarthy (Eds.) *Multicultural Curriculum* (pp. 84-107). New York: Routledge.

Appleton, N. (1983). *Cultural pluralism in education.* New York: Longman.

Arnold, G.C. (1995). Teacher dialogues: A Constructivist Model of Staff Development. *Journal of Staff Development* 16 (4), 34-38.

Au, K. (1978). Participant Structures in a Reading Lesson with Hawaiian Children: Analysis of a Culturally Appropriate Instructional Event. *Anthropology and Education Quarterly* 9 (2), 91-115.

Australian Bureau of Statistics. (1995). *1995 Year Book Australia.* No. 77. Canberra: Australian Bureau of Statistics.

Australian Bureau of Statistics. (2001). Population: Country of birth. (http://www.abs.gov.au/). Accessed 12/11/01.

Avolio, B. & Bass, B. (1998). Transformational Leadership, Charisma and Beyond. In J. Hunt, B. Baliga, H Dachler & C. Schriesheim (Eds.), *Emerging Leadership Vistas* (pp. 29-49). Lexington: Lexington Books.

Ball, S. (1987). *The Micropolitics of the School: Toward a Theory of School Organization.* New York: Methuen.

Ball, S., Bowe, R. & Gerwitz, S. (1994). Market Forces and Parental Choice. In S. Tomlinson (Ed.), *Educational Reform and Its Consequences* (pp. 13-25). London: IPPR/Rivers Oram Press.

Barman, J., Hébert, Y. & McCaskill (Eds.) (1987). *Indian Education in Canada, Volume 2: The Challenge.* Vancouver: University of British Columbia Press.

Barnard, C. (1938). *The Functions of the Executive.* Cambridge: Harvard University Press.

Bass, B. (1985). *Leadership and Performance Beyond Expectations.* New York: The Free Press.

Bass, B. & Aviolo, B. (1993). Transformational Leadership: A Response to Critics. In M. Chemers & R. Ayman (Eds.). *Leadership Theory and Research: Perspectives and Directions* (pp. 49-80). San Diego: Academic Press.

Bass, B. & Aviolo, B. (1994). *Improving Organizational Effectiveness through Transformational Leadership.* Thousand Oaks, CA: Sage.

Bates, R. (1987). Corporate culture, schooling and educational administration. *Educational Administration Quarterly* 23 (4), 79-115.

Bauman, Z. (1992). *Intimations of Postmodernity.* New York: Routledge.

Beck, L. (1994). *Reclaiming Educational Administration as a Caring Profession.* New York: Teachers College Press.

Bell, C. & Chase, S. (1993). The underrepresentation of Women in School Leadership. In C. Marshall (Ed.), *The New Politics of Race and Gender* (pp. 141-154). Bristol, PA: Falmer.

Bennett, C. (2001). Genres of Research in Multicultural Education. *Review of Educational Research* 71 (2), 171-218.

Berry, J. (1976). *Human Ecology and Cognitive Style.* New York: Sage.

Bissoondath, N. (1994). *Selling Illusions: The cult of multiculturalism in Canada.* Toronto: Penguin.

191

Blackmore, J. (1989). Educational Leadership: A Feminist Critique. In J. Smyth (Ed.) Critical Perspectives on Educational Leadership. London: Falmer.

Blackmore, J. (1995). Policy as Dialogue: Feminist Administrators Working for Educational Change. *Gender and Education* 7 (3), 293-313.

Blackmore, J. (1996). "Breaking the Silence": Feminist Contributions to Educational Administration and Policy. In K. Leithwood et. al. *International Handbook of Educational Leadership and Administration* (pp. 997-1042). The Netherlends: Kluwer.

Blank, R. (1987). The role of principal as leader: Analysis of variation in leadership in urban high schools. *Journal of Educational Research* 82 (2), 69-80.

Blase, J. (1993). The Micropolitics of Effective School-Based Leadership: Teacher Perspectives. *Educational Administration Quarterly*, 29 (2), 142-163.

Blase, J. & Blase, J. (1999). Implementation of Shared Governance for Instructional Improvement: Principals' Perspectives. *Journal of Educational Administration* 37 (5), 476-500.

Blase, J. & Blase, J. (1999). Principals' Instructional Leadership and Teacher Development: Teachers' Perspectives. *Educational Administration Quarterly* 35 (3), 349-378.

Bolin, F. (1989). Empowering Leadership. *Teachers College Record* 91 (1), 81-96.

Bogotch, I.. & Roy, C. (1997). The Contexts of Partial Truths: An Analysis of Principal's Discourse. *Journal of Educational Administration* 35 (3), 234-252.

Bonnett, A. (2000). *Anti-racism*. New York: Routledge.

Boscardin, M. & Jacobson, S. (1997). The Inclusive School: Integrating Diversity and Solidarity through Community -Based Management. *Journal of Educational Administration* 35 (5), 466 - 476.

Bowen, E. (1988). Getting Tough. *Time*. February 1. 100–106.

Boyd, D. (1996). Dominance Concealed Through Diversity: Implications of Indequate Perspectives on Cultural Pluralism. *Harvard Educational Review* 66 (3), 609-630.

Brah, A. & Minhas, R. (1985). Structural racism or cultural difference: Schooling for Asian girls. In G. Weiner (Ed.), *Just a bunch of girls: Feminist Approaches to Schooling*. Milton Keys: Open University Press.

Bullivant, B. (1981) *The Pluralist Dilemma in Education: Six Case Studies*. Sydney: Allen & Unwin.

Burbules, N. (1993). *Dialogue in Teaching: Theory and Practice*. New York: Teachers College Press.

Burns, J. (1978). *Leadership*. New York: Harper & Row.

Callahan, R. (1962). *Education and the Cult of Efficiency*. Chicago: University of Chicago Press.

Canadian Council on Social Development (2001). *Unequal Access: A Canadian Profile of Racial Differences in Education, Employment and Income*. Toronto: Canadian Race Relations Foundation.

Capper, C. (1993). Administrator Practice and Preparation for Social Reconstructionist Schooling. In C. Capper (Ed.) *Educational Administration in a Pluralist Society* (pp. 288-315). Albany: SUNY Press.

Carmichael, S. & Hamilton, C. (1967). *Black Power: The Politics of Liberation in America*. New York: Random House.

Carr, P. & Klassen, T. (1997). Different Perceptions of Race in Education: Racial Minority and White Teachers. *Canadian Journal of Education* 22 (1), 46-68.

Carrim, N. & Soudien, C. (1999). Critical antiracism in South Africa. In S. May (Ed.) *Critical multiculturalism: Rethinking multicultural and antiracist education* (pp. 153-171). Philadelphia: Falmer.

Cazden, C. & Leggett, E. (1981). Culturally responsive education: Recommendations for achieving Lau remedies II. In H. Trueba, G. Guthrie & K. Au (Eds.), *The Cultural and Bilingual Classroom* (pp. 69-86). London: Newbury.

Chambers, P. (2001). Ontario School Councils: Engaging Diversity. Masters Research Project. University of Toronto.

Clifton, R. (1975). Self-concept and attitudes: A comparison of Canadian Indians and non-Indian students. *Canadian Review of Sociology and Anthropology*, 12 (4), 577-584.

Clifton, R. (1977). Factors which Affect the Education of Canadian Indian Students. In R. Carlton, L. Colley, and N. MacKinnon (Eds.). *Education, Change and Society: A Sociology of Canadian Education*. Toronto: Gage.

Codd, J. (1989). Educational Leadership as Reflective Action. In J. Smyth (Ed.) *Critical Perspectives on Educational Leadership* (pp.157-178). London: Falmer.

Cole, M. & Scribner, S. (1974). *Culture and Thought: A Psychological Introduction*. Toronto: John Wiley & Sons.

Coleman et. al. (1966). *Equality of Educational Opportunity*. Washington, D.C.: United States Government Printing Office.

College Board (1985). *Equality and excellence: The educational status of Black Americans*. New York: College Board.

Comer, J.P. (1981). New Haven's School Community Connection. *Educational Leadership* (March) 42-8.

Comer, J. (1986). Parent Participation in the Schools. *Phi Delta Kappan* 67 (6) 442-446.

Coombs, C. (2002). *Reflective Practice: Developing Habits of Mind*. Doctoral Thesis. University of Toronto.

Corson, D. (1992). Minority Cultural Values and Discourse Norms in Majority Cultural Classrooms. *The Canadian Modern Language Review* 48 (3), 472-496.

Corson, D. (1993). *Language, Minority Education and Gender: Linking Social Justice and Power*. Clevedon: Multilingual Matters.

Corson, D. (1995). Ideology and Distortion in the Administration of Outgroup Interests. In D. Corson (Ed.) *Discourse and Power in Educational Organizations* (pp. 133-148). Cresskill, N.J.: Hampton Press.

Corson, D. (1996) Critical Policy Making: Emancipatory School-Site Leadership in Multi-Ethnic Schools. *Forum of Education* 52 (2)

Corson, D. (1998). *Changing Education for Diversity*. Philadelphia: The Open University Press.

Cummins, J. (1986). Empowering Minority students: A Framework for Intervention. *Harvard Educational Review* 56 (1), 18-36.

Darling-Hammond, L. (1995). Inequality and Access to Knowledge. In J. Banks & C. McGee Banks (Eds.) *Handbook of Research on Multicultural Education*, pp. 465-483. Toronto: MacMillan.

Das, J., Kirby, J. & Jarman, R. (1979). *Simultaneous and Successive Cognitive Processes*. New York: Academic Press.

Davis, B. (1995) *How to iInvolve Parents in a Multicultural School*. Alexandria, VA: Association for Supervision and Curriculum Development, 14.

Deal, T. & Peterson, K. (1994). *The Leadership Paradox: Balancing Logic and Artistry in Schools*. San Francisco: Jossey-Bass.

Department of Education and Science (1985). Education for All. London: HMSO.

Delhi, K. (1994). *Parent Activism and School Reform in Toronto: A Report*. Toronto: Department of Sociology in Education, Ontario Institute for Studies in Education.

Dei, G. (1996). *Anti-racism Education: Theory and Practice*. Halifax: Fernwood.

Dei, G. (1998). "Why Write Back?": The Role of Afrocentric Discourse in Social Change. *Canadian Journal of Education* 23 (2), 200-208.

Dei, G., Mazzuco, J, McIsaac, E., & Zine, J. (1997). *Reconstructing "Dropout": A Critical Ethnography of the Dymanics of Black Students' Disengagement from School*. Toronto: University of Toronto Press.

Delgado-Gaitan, C. (1991). Involving Parents in Schools: A Process of Empowerment. *American Journal of Education* 100 (1) 20-46.

Delpit, L. (1988). The Silenced Dialogue: Power and Pedagogy in Educating Other People's Children. *Harvard Educational Review* 58, 280-298.

Derkatz, M. (1996). "It's Not the School, It's the Principal of the Thing:" School Administrators Talk About Administrative Behavior in Culturally Diverse Settings. *The Canadian Administrator* 36 (1), 1-11.

Deutsh, M. (1976). *The Disadvantaged Child*. New York: Basic Books.

Derrida, J. (1978). *Writing and Difference*. Chicago: University of Chicago Press.

Deyhle, D. (1983). Between Games and Failure: A Micro-ethnographic Study of Navajo and Testing. *Curriculum Inquiry* 13 (4), 347-376.

Deyhle, D. (1986). Success and Failure: A Micro-ethnographic comparison of Navajo and Anglo Students' Perceptions of Testing. *Curriculum Inquiry*, 16 (4), 365-389.

Dickinson, G. M., & Dolmage, W. R. (1996). Education, Religion, and the Courts in Ontario. *Canadian Journal of Education* 21(4), 363-383.

Divoky, D. (1988). The Model Minority Goes to School. *Phi Delta Kappan*, 70 (3), 219-222.

Drake, S. & Ryan, J. (1994). Narrative and Knowledge: Inclusive Pedagogy for Comtemporary Times. *Curriculum and Teaching* 9 (1), 45-56.

Duke, D. (1987). *School Leadership and Instructional Improvement*. New York: Random House.

Edmonds, R. (1979). Effective Schools for the Urban Poor. *Educational Leadership* 37 (1), 15-18, 20-24.

Ellsworth, E. (1989). Why Doesn't this Feel Empowering? Working Through the Repressive Myths of Critical Pedagogy. *Harvard Educational Review* 59 (3), 297-324.

English, F. (1996). *Theory in Educational Administration*. New York: Harper Collins.

Epstein, J.L. (1993). A Response (to Ap parent Involvement). *Teachers College Record*, 94 (4), 710-17.

Epstein, J. (1997). *School, Family and Community Partnerships: Your Handbook for Action*. Thousand Oaks, Ca: Corwin Press.

Erickson, F. & Mohatt, G. (1982). Cultural Organization of Participant Structures in Two Classrooms of Indian Students. In G. Spindler (Ed.), *Doing the Ethnography of Schooling*. Toronto: Holt Rinehart & Winston.

Erickson, F. (1987). Transformation and School Success: The Politics of Culture and Educational Achievement. *Anthropology and Education Quarterly* 18 (1), 335-356.

Evan, W. (1973). Hierarchy, Alienation, Commitment and Organization Effectiveness. *Human Relations* 30, 77-94.

Evans, R. (1999). *The Pedagogic Principal*. Edmonton: Qual Institute Press.

Fay, B. (1987). *Critical Social Science*. Ithica: N.Y.: Cornell University Press.

Fiedler, F. (1967). *A Theory of Leadership Effectiveness*. New York: McGraw-Hill.

Fine, M. (1993) [Ap]parent Involvement: Reflections on Parents, Power, and Urban Public Schools. *Teachers College Record* 94 (4), 682-710.

Finkel, J. & and Bolin, G. (1996). Linking Racial Identity Theory to Integrating the Curriculum. *College Teaching* 44 (1), 34-36.

Fisk, J. (1996). *Media matters: Race and gender in US politics*. Minneapolis: University of Minneapolis Press.

Foucault, M. (1970). *The Order of Things: An Archeology of the Human Sciences*. New York: Vintage.

Foucault, M. (1973). *The Birth of the Clinic: An Archeology of Medical Perception*. New York: Vintage.

Foucault, M. (1979). *Discipline and Punish: The Birth of the Prison*. New York: Vintage.

Foucault, M. (1980). *Power/knowledge: Selected Interviews and Other Writings 1972-1977*. New York: Pantheon Books.

Foster, W. (1989). Toward a Critical Practice of Leadership. In Smyth, J. (Ed.). *Critical Perspectives on Educational Leadership*. (pp. 39-62). London: The Falmer Press.

Friere, P. (1970). *Pedagogy of the Oppressed*. New York: Herder and Herder.

Fuller, S. (2000). Social Epistemology as a Critical Philosophy of Multiculturalism. In R. Mahalingam & C. McCarthy (Eds.) *Multicultural Curriculum. New directions for Social Theory, Practice and Policy* (pp. 15-36). New York: Routledge.

Furman, G. & Merz, C. (1996). Schools and Community Connections: Applying a Sociological Framework. In J. Cibulka & W. Kritek (Eds.) *Coordination among Schools, Families, and Communities: Prospects for Educational Reform* (pp. 323-348). Albany: SUNY Press.

Gay, J. & Cole, M. (1967). *The New Mathematics of an Old Culture: A Study of Learning among the Kpelle of Liberia*. New York: Holt, Rinehart and Winston.

Gibson, M. (1976). Approaches to Multicultural Education in the United States: A Comparative Review. *Anthropology and Education Quarterly* 7 (4), 7-18.

Gibson, M. (1987). The School Performance of Immigrant Minorities: A Comparative View. *Anthropology and Education Quarterly* 18 (1), 262-275.

Gillborn, D. (1995). *Racism and Antiracism in Real Schools*. Philadelphia: Open University Press.

Gillborn, D. & Youdel, D. (1998). School league tables and selection in multiethnic secondary schools. Paper presented at the annual conference of the American Educational Research Association, SanDiego.

Goldman, S. & McDermott, R. (1987). The Culture of Competition in American Schools. In G. Spindler (Ed.), *Education and cultural process: Anthropological approaches* (2nd Ed.). Prospect Heights, IL.: Waveland Press.

Gould, S. (1994). The Barometer of Race. *Discovery*, November, 65-69.

Gould, S. (1981). *The Mismeasure of Man*. New York: W.W. Norton.

Greenfield, T. (1975). Theory about Organization: A New Perspective and its Implications for Schools. In M. Hughes (Ed.) *Administering Education: International Challenge* (pp. 71-99). London: Athlone Press.

Greenfield, T. (1981). Understanding Educational Organizations as Cultural Entities: Some Ideas Methods and Metaphors. Paper Prepared for Administrative Leadership: New Perspectives on Theory and Practice, a Conference Sponsored by the Department of Administration, Higher and Continuing Education, University of Illinois at Urbana-Champaign, June.

Greenfield, T. (1986). The Decline and Fall of Science in Educational Administration. *Interchange* 17 (2), 57-80.

Greenfield, T. & Ribbins, P. (1993). *Greenfield on Educational Administration: Towards a Humane Science*. London: Routledge.

Griffin, G. (1987). The School in Society and The Social Organization of the School: Social Implications for Staff Development. In M. Wideen & I. Andrews (Eds.) *Staff Development for School Improvement* (pp. 19-37). Toronto: Lorimer.

Gronn, P. (1983). Talk as the Work: The Accomplishment of School Administration. *Administrative Science Quarterly* 28, 1-21.

Gronn, P. (1983). *Rethinking Educational Administration: T.B. Greenfield and his Critics*. Victoria: Deakin University.

Gronn, P. (1995). Greatness Re-visited: The Current Obsession with Transformational Leadership. *Leading and Managing* 1 (1), 14-27.

Gronn, P. (1996). From Transactions to Transformations: A New World Order in the Study of Leadership. *Educational Management and Administration* 24 (1), 7-30.

Gronn, P. (1999). Leadership from a Distance: Institutionalizing Values and Forming Character at Timbertop, 1951-61. In P. Begley & P. Leonard (Eds.) *The Values of Educational Administration*. (pp. 140-167). London: Falmer.

Gronn, P. & Ribbins, P. (1996). Leaders in Context: Postpositivist Approaches to Understanding Educational Leadership. *Educational Administration Quarterly* 32 (3), 452-473.

Grygier, T. (1977). The bottom of a titled mosaic: The Italian community in urban Canada. In R. Carlton, L. Colley & N. MacKinnon (Eds.), *Education, change and society: A sociology of Canadian education*. Toronto: Gage.

Gue, L. (1975). Patterns in Native Education. *CSSE Yearbook*, 1, 7-20.

Gue, L. (1977). Ethnocentrism in Educational Administration. *The Canadian Administrator* 16 (4), 1-6.

Guzman, N. (1997). Leadership for Successful Inclusive Schools: A Study of Principal Behaviours. *Journal of Educational Administration* 35 (5), 439-450.

Habermas, J. (1971). *Knowledge and Human Interests*. Boston: Beacon Press.

Habermas, J. (1987). *The Theory of Communicative Action*. Boston: Beacon Press.

Hallinger, P. & Murphy, J. (1985). Assessing the Intructional Management Behaviour of Principals. *Elementary School Journal* 86 (2), 217-247.

Hallinger, P. & Heck, R. (1998). Exploring the Principal's Contribution to School Effectiveness: 1980-1995. *School Effectiveness and School Improvement*. 9 (2), 157-191.

Handscombe, J. (1989). Mainstreaming: Who Needs It? In J. Esling (Ed.). *Multicultural Education and Policy: ESL in the 1990s* (pp. 18-35). Toronto: OISE Press.

Hatcher, R. Troyna, B. & Gewirtz, D. (1996). *Racial Equality and the Local Management of Schools*. Stattfordshire: Trentham Books.

Haw, K. (1998). *Educating Muslim girls: Shifting discourses*. Philadelphia: Open University Press.

Haynes, N. & Comer, J. (1993). The Yale School Development Program: Process, Outcomes and Policy Implications. *Urban Education* 28 (2), 166-199.

Heck, R., Larsen, T. & Marcoulides, G. (1990). Instructional Leadership and School Achievement: Validation of a Causal Model. *Educational Administration Quarterly* 26 (2), 94-125.

Heck, R. & Hallinger, P. (1996). Next Generation Methods for the Study of Leadership and School Improvement. . In In K. Leithwood et. al. *International Handbook of Educational Leadership and Administration* (pp. 141-162). The Netherlands: Kluwer.

Henriques, J. (1984). Social Psychology and the Politics of Racism. In J. Henriques, W. Holloway, C. Urwin, C. Venn and V. Walkerdine. *Changing the Subject: Psychology, Social Regulation and Subjectivity* (pp. 60-89). London: Methuen.

Henze, R., Katz, A. & Norte, E. (2000). Rethinking the Concept of Racial or Ethnic Conflict in Schools: A Leadership Perspective. *Race, Ethnicity and Education* 3 (2), 195 – 206.

Herrnstein, R. & Murray, C. (1994). *The Bell Curve: Intelligence and Class Structure in American Life*. New York: The Free Press.

Herrity, V. A. and Glasman, N. S. (1999). Training administrators for culturally and linguistically diverse school populations: Opinions of expert practitioners. Journal of School Leadership, 9, 235-253.

Hess, G. (1995). *Restructuring Urban Schools: A Chicago Perspective*. New York: Teachers College Press.

Hess, G. (1999). Expectations, Opportunity, Capacity and Will: The Four Essential Components of Chicago School Reform. *Educational Policy* 13 (4), 494-517.

Hess, R. & Shipman, V. (1965). Early Experience and The Socialization of Cognitive Modes in Children. *Child Development* 34, 869-886.

Hess, R.D. & Azuma, H. (1991) Cultural Support for Schooling: Contrasts Between Japan and the United States. *Educational Research* 20 (9), 2-8.

Hodgkinson, C. (1978). *Towards a Philosophy of Administration*. Oxford: Basil Blackwell.

Hodgkinson, C. (1991). *Educational Leadership: The Moral Art*. Albany: SUNY Press.

Holland, P. & Obermiller, M. (2000). Possibilities of Postmodern Supervision. In J. Glantz & L. Behar-Horenstein (Eds.) *Paradigm Debates in Curriculum and Supervision: Modern and Postmodern Perspectives*. (pp. 212-228). Wesport: Bergin & Garvey.

Holloway, D. (1988). Concepts of Ability and Effort in Japan and the United States. *Review of Educational Research* 58 (3), 327-345.

House, R. (1977). A 1976 Theory of Leadership. In J. Hunt & L. Larson (Eds.) *Leadership: The Cutting Edge* (pp. 189-207). Carbondale: Southern Illinois University Press.

Ibrahim, A. (1997). Becoming Black: Race, Language, Culture and the Politics of Identity. Unpublished Ph.D. Thesis. University of Toronto.

Ingram, P. (1997). Leadership Behaviours of Principals of Inclusive Educational Settings. *Journal of Educational Administration* 35 (5), 411-417.

Johnston, I. (1996). Point of View in Literary Texts: A Perspective on Unexamined Racist Ideologies in the High School English Curriculum. In I. Alladin, (Ed.). *Racism in Canadian Schools* (pp. 107-119). Toronto: Harcourt Brace.

Joyce, B. & Showers, B. (1995) *Student Achievement through Staff Development*. New York: Longman.

Kalantiz, M. & and Cope, B. (1999). Multicultural Education: Transforming the Mainstream. In S. May (Ed.) *Critical Multiculturalism: Rethinking Multicultural and Antiracist Education* (pp. 245-276). Philadelphia: Falmer.

Katz, D. & Kahn, R. (1978). *The Social Psychology of Organizations* (2nd Ed.). New York: Wiley.

Keys, M., Hanley-Maxwell, C. & Capper, C. (1999). "Spirituality? It's the Core of My Leadership": Empowering Leadership in an Inclusive Elementary School. *Educational Administration Quarterly* 35 (2), 203-237.

Kysel, F. (1988). Ethnic Background and Examination Results. *Educational Research* 30 (2), 83-89.

Kincheloe, J. & Steinberg, S. (1997). *Changing Multiculturalism*. Philadelphia: Open University Press.

Kleine-Kracht, P. (1993). Indirect Instructional Leadership: An Administrator's Choice. *Educational Administrative Quarterly* 29 (2), 187-211.

Kozol, J. (1991). *Savage Inequalities: Children in America's Schools*. New York: Crown Publishers.

Krug, S. (1992). Instructional Leadership: A Constructivist Perspective. *Educational Administration Quarterly* 28 (3), 430-443.

Kurty, K. (1995). Women Principals -- Leading with Power. In D. Dunlap & P. Schmuck (Eds.). *Women Leading Education*. (pp. 380-406) Albany: SUNY Press.

Lakomski, G. (1999). Against Leadership: A Concept Without a Cause. . In P. Begley & P. Leonard (Eds.) *The Values of Educational Administration*. (pp. 36-50). London: Falmer.

Lee, S. (1996). *Unravelling the "Model Minority" Stereotype*. New York: Teachers' College Press.

Lees, K. A. (1995). Advancing Democratic Leadership through Critical Theory. *Journal of School Leadership* 5 (3), 220-230.

Leithwood, K. (1994). Leadership for School Restructuring. *Educational Administration Quarterly* 30, 498-518.

Leithwood, K. (1998). Accountability: Its Meaning and Consequences in Secondary Schools. Research Proposal. Toronto.

Leithwood, K. (1999). An Organizational Perspective on Values for Leaders of Future Schools. In P. Begley (Ed.) *Values and Educational Leadership* (pp. 25-50). Albany: SUNY Press.

Leithwood, K. (Ed.) (2000). *Understanding Schools as Intelligent Systems*. Stamford, CT: JAI Press.

Leithwood, K. (2001). Personal Communication.

Leithwood, K. & Duke, D. (1996). A Century's Quest to Understand School Leadership. In In K. Leithwood et. al. *International Handbook of Educational Leadership and Administration* (pp. 45-72). The Netherlands: Kluwer.

Leithwood, K. & Jantzi, D. (1999a). Transformational School Leadership Effects: A Replication. *School Effectiveness and School Improvement* 10 (4), 451-479.

Leithwood, K. & Jantzi, D. (1999b). The Relative Effects of Principal and Teacher Sources of Leadership on Student Engagement with School. *Educational Administration Quarterly* 35, 679-706.

Leithwood, K. & Jantzi, D. (2000). The Effects of Transformational Leadership on Organizational Conditions and Student Engagement with School. *Journal of Educational Administration* 38 (2), 112-129.

Leithwood, K., Jantzi, D. & Steinbach, R. (1999a). *Changing Leadership for Changing Times*. London: Open University Press.

Leithwood, K., Jantzi, D. & Steinbach, R. (1999b). Do School Councils Matter? *Educational Policy* 13 (4), 467-493.

Leithwood, K. & Louis, K. (Eds.). (1998). *Organizational Learning in Schools*. Exton: Swetz & Zeitlinger.

Leithwood, K. & Stager, M. (1989). Expertise in Principal's Problem Solving. *Educational Administration Quarterly* 25 (2), 126-161.

Levin, H. (Ed.) (1970). *Community Control of Schools*. New York: Clarion.

Levine-Rasky, C. (1993). Listening as an Appropriate Response by Members of Privileged Groups. Paper presented at the CSAA Meeting. Carleton University, Ottawa.

Levinson, B. (1992). Ogbu's Anthropology and the Critical Ethnography of Education: A Reciprocal Interrogation. *Qualitative Studies in Education* 5 (3), 205-225.

Lewis, D. & Nakagawa, K. (1995). *Race and Educational Reform in the American Metropolis: A Study of School Decentralization*. Albany: SUNY Press.

Lightfoot, S.L. (1978). *Worlds Apart: Relationships between Families and Schools*. New York: Basic Books.

Lipman, P. (1998). *Race, Class, and Power in School Restructuring*. Albany: SUNY Press.

Loeb, M. (1994). Where Leaders Come From. *Fortune* (September), 41-42.

Louis, K., Kruse, S. & Associates (1995). Professionalism and Community; Perspectives on Reforming Urban Schools. Thousand Oaks, CA: Corwin Press.

MacKinnon, D. & Brown, M. (1994). Inclusion in Secondary Schools: An Analysis of School Structure Based on Teachers' Images of Change. *Educational Administration Quarterly* 30 (2), 126-152.

Macias, J. (1993). Forgotten History: Educational and Social Antecedents of High Achievement among Asian Immigrants in the United States. *Curriculum Inquiry* 23 (4), 409-423.

Malen, B. & Ogawa, R. (1992). Community Involvement: Parents, Teachers and Administrators Working Together. In S. Bacharach (Ed.) *Education Reform: Making Sense of it All* (pp. 103-119). Toronto: Allyn and Bacon.

Marshall, C. (1993). Politics of Denial: Gender and Race Issues in Administration. In C. Marshall (Ed.) *The New Politics of Race and Gender* (pp. 168-174). Bristol, PA.: Falmer.

Martin, W. & Willower, D. (1981). The Managerial Behaviour of High School Principals. *Educational Administration Quarterly* 17 (1), 69-90.

Maughan, B. & Rutter, M. (1986). "Black pupils" progress in secondary schools: ll. Examination Achievements. *British Journal of Developmental Psychology* 4(1), 19-29.

Maxcy, S. (1998). Preparing School Principals for Ethno-Democratic Leadership. *The International Journal for Leadership in Education*. 1 (3), 217-235.

May, S. (1994). *Making Multicultural Education Work*. Clevedon, UK: Multilingual Matters.

May, S. (1999). Critical Multiculturalism and Cultural difference: Avoiding Essentialism. In S. May (Ed.) *Critical Multiculturalism: Rethinking Multicultural and Antiracist Education* (pp. 11-43). Philadelphia: Falmer.

Mayrowetz, D. & Weinstein, C. (1999). Sources of Leadership for Inclusive Education: Creating Schools for all Children. *Educational Administration Quarterly* 35 (3), 423-449.

McAndrew, M. (1987). Ethnicity, Multiculturalism and Multicultural Education in Canada. In R. Ghosh & D. Ray (Eds.) *Social Change and Education in Canada* (pp. 143-155). Toronto: Harcourt Brace Jovanovich.

McCarthy, C. (1990). *Race and Curriculum: Social Inequality and the Theories and Politics of Difference in Contemporary Research on Schooling*. New York: Falmer.

McCarthy, C. (1993). After the Canon: Knowledge and Ideological Representation in the Multicultural Discourse on Curriculum Reform. In C. McCarthy & W. Crichlow. (Eds.) *Race, Identity and Representation in Education* (pp. 289-305). London: Routledge.

McCarthy, C. & Crichlow, W. (Eds.) (1993). Race, Identity and Representation in Education. London: Routledge.

McCarthy, C. & Dimitriadis, G. (2000). Globalizing pedagogies: Power, Resentment and the Renarration of Difference. In R. Mahalingam & C. McCarthy (Eds.) *Multicultural Curriculum. New Directions for Social Theory, Practice and Policy* (pp. 70-83). New York: Routledge.

McCarty, T., Lynch, R., Wallace, S. & Benally, A. (1991). Classroom Inquiry and Navajo Learning Styles: A Call for Reassessment. *Anthropology and Education Quarterly* 22 (1), 42-59.

McKeown, H. (1989). Race and Ethnocultural Equity: The Principal is the Key. *OPSF News*. April, 24-25.

McLaren, P. & Torres, R. (1999). Racism and Multicultural Education: Rethinking "Race" and "Whiteness" in Late Capitalism. In S. May (Ed.) *Critical Multiculturalism: Rethinking Multicultural and Antiracist Education*, pp. 42-76. London: Falmer.

McNeil, L. (2000). *Contradictions of School Reform: Educational Costs of Standardized Testing*. New York: Routledge.

Merchant, B. (2000). Education and Changing Demographics. In B.A. Jones (Ed.) *Educational Leadership: Policy Dimensions in the 21ˢᵗ Century* (pp. 83-90). Stanford, CT: Ablex.

Merleman, R. (1995). *Representing Black Culture: Racial Conflict and Cultural Politics in the United States*. New York: Routledge.

Miller, P. (1987). *Domination and Power*. London: Routledge and Kegan Paul.

Moodley, K. (1995) Multicultural education in Canada: Historical development and current status. In J. Banks & C. McGee Banks (Eds.) *Handbook of Research on Multicultural Education* (pp. 801-820). Toronto: MacMillan.

Morely, D. & Robbins, K. (1995). *Spaces of identity: Global, Electronic Landscapes and Cultural Boundaries*. London: Routledge.

National Board for Professional Teaching Standards (1998). What Teachers Should Know and Be Able to do. Published on Website.

Nieto, S. (1992). *Affirming Diversity: The Sociopolitical Context of Multicultural Education*. New York: Longman.

Nieto, S. (1999). Critical Multicultural Education and Students' Perspectives. In S. May (Ed.) *Critical Multiculturalism: Rethinking Multicultural and Antiracist Education* (pp. 191-215). Philadelphia: Falmer Press.

Noel, J. (1995). Preparing Teachers for Diversity Through Critical Conversation. *Journal of Professional Studies* 3 (1), 69-73.

Oakes, J. (1985). *Keeping track: How schools structure inequality*. New Haven: Yale University Press.

Odden, E. & Wohlsletter, P. (1995). Making School-Based Management Work. *Educational Leadership*, 52 (5), 32-36.

Odden, A. (1995). *Decentralized School Management in Victoria, Australia*. Washington, D.C.: World Bank.

Ogbu, J. (1982). Cultural Discontinuities and Schooling. *Anthropology and Education Quarterly* 8 (3), 290-307.

Ogbu, J. (1987). Variability in Minority School Performance: A Problem in Search of an Explanation. *Anthropology and Education Quarterly* 18 (1), 312-334.

Ogbu, J. (1992). Understanding Cultural Diversity and Learning. *Educational Researcher* 21 (8), 5-14.

Ogbu, J. (1994). Racial Stratification and Education in the United States: Why Inequality Persists. *Teachers College Record* 96 264-271.

Olneck, M. (1990). The Recurring Dream: Symbolism and Ideology in Intercultural and Multicultural Education. *American Journal of Education*, 98 (2), 147-174.

Olson, L. (1988). Crossing the schoolhouse Border: Immigrant Children in California. *Phi Delta Kappan*, 70 (3), 211-218.

Ontario Ministry of Education and Training. (1992). *Changing Perspectives: A Resource Guide for Antiracist and Ethnocultural-Equity Education*. Toronto: Ontario Ministry of Education and Training.

Ontario Ministry of Education and Training. (1993). *Antiracism and Ethnocutural Equity in School Boards: Guidelines for Policy Development and Implementation*. Toronto: Ontario Ministry of Education and Training.

Orfield, G. (1988). Exclusion of the Majority: Shrinking College Access and Public Policy in Metropolitan Los Angeles. *Urban Review* 20 (3), 147-163.

Orfield, G. (1999). Politics Matters: Educational Policy and Chicano Students. In J. Moreno (Ed.) The Elusive Quest for Equality [Special Issue] *Harvard Educational Review*, 111-119.

Owen, D. (1994). *Population Trends*. no. 78 Winter. Office of Population Censuses and Surveys (OPCS) London: HMSO p. 23-33.

Paquette, J. (1990). Minority Participation in Secondary Education: A Fine-Grained Descriptive Methodology. *Educational Evaluation and Policy Analysis* 13 (2), 139-158.

Pajak, E. & Evans, K. (2000). Communicative Action: A Postmodern Bridge for Supervision in Schools. In J. Glantz & L. Behar-Horenstein (Eds.) Paradigm Debates in Curriculum and Supervision: Modern and Postmodern Perspectives. (pp. 229-244). Wesport: Bergin & Garvey.

Pellicer, L. (1982). Providing Instructional Leadership: A Principal Challenge. *NASSP Bulletin* 66 (456), 27-31.

Perrow, C. (1986). *Complex Organizations.* New York: Random House.

Peters, T. & Waterman, R. (1982). *In Search of Excellence.* New York: Harper.

Philips, S. (1972). Participant Structures and Communicative Competence: Warm Springs Children in Community and Classroom. In C. Cazden, V. John & D. Hymes (Eds.) *Functions of Language in the Classroom.* New York: Teachers College Press.

Philips. S. (1983). *The Invisible Culture: Communication in Classroom, Community on the Warm Springs Indian Reservation.* New York: Longman.

Prentice, A. (1977). *The School Promoters: Education and Social Class in Mid-Nineteenth Century Upper Canada.* Toronto: McClelland and Stewart.

Purkey, C. & Smith, M. (1983). Effective Schools: A Review. *Elementary School Journal* 83 (4), 427-452.

Rallis, S. & Highsmith, M. (1987). The Myth of the Great Principal. *American Educator* 11 (1), 18-22.

Ramirez, M. (1989) A Bicognitive-Multicultural Model for Pluralistic Education. *Early Childhood Development and Care* 51, 129-136.

Rattansi, A. (1992). Changing the Subject? Racism, Culture and Education. In J. Donald & A. Rattansi (Eds.) *Race, Culture and Difference* (pp. 11-48). London: Sage.

Rattansi, A. (1999). Racism, "Postmodernism" and Reflexive Multiculturalism. In S. May (Ed.) *Critical Multiculturalism: Rethinking Multicultural and Antiracist Education* (pp. 77-112). Philadelphia: Falmer.

Reagan, T. (2000). *Non-Western Educational Traditions: Alternative Approaches to Educational Thought and Practice.* London: Lawrence Erlbaum Associates.

Real, T. (1998). *I Don't Want to Talk About It: Overcoming the Secret Legacy of Male Depression.* New York: Fireside.

Reitzug, U. & Reeves, J. (1992). Miss Lincoln Doesn't Teach Here Anymore: A Descriptive Narrative and Conceptual Analysis of a Principal's Symbolic Leadership Behavior. *Educational Administration Quarterly* 28 (2), 185-219.

Reyes, P. & Capper, C. (1991). Urban Principals: A Critical Perspective on the Context of Minority Student Dropout. *Educational Administration Quarterly* 27 (4), 530–557.

Rhodes, R. (1990). Measurements of Navajo and Hopi Brain Dominance and Learning Styles. *Journal of American Indian Education* 29 (3), 29-40.

Richmon, M. J. & Allison, D. J. (2003). Toward a Conceptual Framework for Leadership Inquiry. *Educational Management and Administration* 31 (1), 31-50.

Riddington, R. (1988). Knowledge and Power in the Subarctic. *American Anthropologist* 90 (1), 98-110.

Riehl, C. (2000). The Principal's Role in Creating Inclusive Schools for Diverse Students: A Review of Normative, Empirical, and Critical Literature on the Practice of Educational Administration. *Review of Educational Research* 70 (1), 55-82.

Rist, R. (1978). *The Invisible Children: School Integration in American Society.* Cambridge, M.A.: Harvard University Press.

Rizvi, F. (1992). Educative Leadership in a Multicultural Society. In P. Duignan & R. Macpherson (Eds.) *Educative Leadership: A Practical Theory for New Administrators and Managers* (pp. 134-169). London: Falmer.

Rizvi, F. (1993a). Critical Introduction: Researching Racism and Education. In Troyna, B. *Racism and Education* (pp. 1-17). Buckingham: Open University Press.

Rizvi, F. (1993b). Race, Gender and the Cultural Assumptions of Schooling. In C. Marshall (Ed.) *The New Politics of Race and Gender* (pp. 203-217). Bristol, PA.: Falmer Press.

Robertson, L. (1998) Educators' Responses to Equity In-service. Doctoral Thesis. University of Toronto.

Robinson, G. (1999). Administrator Views of, and Strategies for, Dealing with Conflicts Involving New Canadians. Unpublished Doctoral Thesis. The University of Toronto.

Robinson, V. (1996). Critical Theory and the Social Psychology of Change. In K. Leithwood et. al. (Eds.). *International Handbook of Educational Leadership and Administration* (pp. 1069-1096). The Netherlands: Kluwer.

Rosenholtz, S. (1985). Effective Schools: Interpreting the Evidence. *American Journal of Education* 93 (3), 352-388.

Ross, A. (1989). Brain Hemispheric Functions and the Native American. *Journal of American Indian Education* (Special Issue) 72-76.

Rushames, L. (1962). *Racial Thought in America: A Documentary History*. Amherst: University of Massachusetts Press.

Ryan, J. (1988). Disciplining the Inuit: Social Form and Control in Bush, Community and School. Doctoral Thesis. University of Toronto.

Ryan, J. (1989). Disciplining the Inuit: Normalization, Characterization and Schooling. *Curriculum Inquiry*. 19 (4), 379-403.

Ryan, J. (1991). Finding Time: The Impact of Space and Time Constraints on Post-Secondary Native Students. Paper presented at the Annual Conference of the Canadian Society for the Study of Education. Kingston, Ontario.

Ryan, J. (1992a) Formal Schooling and Deculturation: Nursing Practice and the Erosion of Native Communication Styles. *The Alberta Journal of Educational Research*, 38 (2), 91-103.

Ryan, J. (1992b).Eroding Innu Cultural Tradition: Individualization and Communality. *Journal of Canadian Studies*, 26 (4), 94-111.

Ryan, J. (1993a). Aboriginal Learning Styles: A Critical Review. *Language, Culture and Curriculum*. 5 (3), 161-183.

Ryan, J. (1993b). Studying Effective Schools and Districts: The Problem with Universals and Uniformity. *Canadian Journal of Education* 18 (1), 79-85.

Ryan, J. (1997). Understanding Greenfield. *International Studies in Educational* Administration. 25 (2), 95-105.

Ryan, J. (1998a). Critical Leadership for Education in a Postmodern World: Emancipation, Resistance and Communal Action. *International Journal of Leadership In Education*..3 (1), 257-278.

Ryan, J. (1998b). Understanding Racial/Ethnic Stereotyping in Schools: From Image to Discourse. *Alberta Journal of Educational Research* 44 (3), 284-301.

Ryan, J. (1999a). *Race and Ethnicity in Multiethnic Schools*. Clevedon: Multilingual Matters.

Ryan, J. (1999b). Inclusive Leadership for Culturally Diverse Schools: Initiating and Sustaining Dialogue. Paper Prepared for the Annual Conference of the American Educational Research Association. Montreal.

Ryan, J. & Tucker, J. (1997). Principal Perceptions of Diversity and Diversity-Related Strategies. Paper Prepared for the Annual Conference of the Canadian Society for the Study of Education. St. John's.

Ryan, J. & Wignall, R. (1996). Administering for Differences: Dilemmas in Multiethnic Schools. In S. Jacobson, E. Hickcox & B. Stephenson (Eds.) *School Administration: Persistent Dilemmas in Preparation and Practice* (pp. 47-62). Westport, CT: Praeger.

Said, E. (1978). *Orientalism*. Harmondsworth: Penguin.

Samuels, F. (2000). Samuels, F. E. (2001). The Peer Mediation Process in Secondary Schools. Unpublished doctoral thesis. University of Toronto. Toronto.

Sarwar, G. (1989). *Islam: Beliefs and Teaching*. London: Muslim Educational Trust.

Scarman, Lord. (1981). *The Brixton Disorders*. London: HMSO.

Schaffner, C. & Bushwell, B. (1996). Ten Critical Elements for Creating Inclusive and Effective School Communities. In S. Stainback & W. Stainback (Eds.), *Inclusion: A Guide for Educators* (pp. 49-65). Baltimore, MD.: Brookes.

Schlesinger, A. (1991). *The Disuniting of America*. Knoxville, TN: Whittle Direct Books.

Schon, D. (1983). *The Reflective Practitioner: How Professionals Think in Action*. New York: Basic Books.

Schutz, A. (1967). *The Phenomenology of the Social World* (Trans. G. Walsh & F. Lehnert). Evanston, IL: Northwestern University Press.

Scott, A., Pearce, D & Goldblast, P. (2001). The Sizes and Characteristics of the Minority Ethnic Populations of Great Britain – Latest Estimates. (http://www.statistics.gov.uk/). Accessed 12/11/01.

Senge, P. (1990). *The Fifth Discipline: The Art and Practice of the Learning Organization*. Toronto: Doubleday.

Senge, P, Cambron-McCabe, N, Lucas, T., Smith, B, Dutton, J. & Kleiner, A. (2000). *Schools That Learn*. Toronto: Doubleday.

Sergiovanni, T. (1992). *Moral Leadership: Getting to the Heart of School Reform*. San Francisco: Jossey Bass.

Sergiovanni, T. (1984). *Value-Added Leadership: How to Get Extraordinary Performance In Schools*. Toronto: Harcourt Brace Jovanovich.

Shanker, A. (1994). Full Inclusion is Neither Free nor Appropriate. *Educational Leadership* 52 (4), 18-21.

Sheppard, B. (1996). Exploring the Transformational Nature of Instructional Leadership. *The Alberta Journal of Educational Research* 42 (4), 325-344.

Shields, C. (2002). Towards a Dialogic Approach to Understanding Values. Paper Presented at the 7th Annual Conference of the Centre for Values and Leadership. Toronto.

Shipps, D., Kahne, J. & Smylie, M. (1999). The Politics of Urban School Reform: Legitimacy, City Growth and School Improvement in Chicago. *Educational Policy* 13 (4), 518-545.

Shohat, E. & Stam, R. (1994). *Unthinking Eurocentrism: Multiculturalism and the Media.* New York: Routledge.

Shor, I. (1992). *Empowering Education: Critical Teaching for Social Change.* Chicago: University of Chicago Press.

Shor, I. & Friere, P. (1987). What is the "Dialogical Method" of Teaching? *Journal of Education* 169 (3), 11-31.

Short, G. & Carrington, B. (1999). Children's Constructions of Their National Identity: Implications for Critical Multiculturalism, pp. 172-190. In S. May (Ed.) *Critical Multiculturalism: Rethinking Multicultural and Antiracist Education* (pp. 172-190). London: Falmer.

Short, P. & Greer, J. (1997). *Leadership in Empowered Schools: Themes from Innovative Efforts.* Columbus, Ohio: Merrill.

Shreeve, J. (1994). Terms of Estrangement. *Discover* November, 57-63.

Simon, H.A. (1947). *Administrative Behavior.* New York: Free Press.

Sklair, L. (2001). *The Transnational Capitalist Class.* Oxford: Blackwell.

Sleeter, C. (1989). Multicultural Education as a Form of Resistance. *Journal of Education* 171 (3), 51-71.

Sleeter, C. (1992) Restructuring Schools for Multicultural Education. *Journal of Teacher Education* 4 (2), 141-148.

Sleeter, C. (1993). How White Teachers Construct Race. In McCarthy, C. & Crichlow, W. (Eds.) *Race, Identity and Representation in Education* (pp. 157-171). New York: Routledge.

Smrekar, C. & Mawhinney, H. (1999). Integrated Services: Challenges in Linking Schools, Families and Communities. In J. Murphy and K.S. Louis (Eds.), *Handbook of Research on Educational Administration* (2nd Edition) (pp. 443-461). San Francisco: Jossey-Bass.

Smith, D. & Tomlinson, S. (1989). *The School Effect: A Study of Multi-Racial Comprehensives.* London: Policy Studies Institute.

Smith, W. & Andrews, R. (1989). *Instructional Leadership: How Principals Make a Difference.* Alexandria: Association for Supervision and Curriculum Development.

Smyth, J. (1989). A "Pedagogical" and "Educative" View of Leadership. In Smyth, J. (Ed.). *Critical Perspectives on Educational Leadership.* (pp. 179-204). London: The Falmer Press.

Smyth, J. (1997). Is Supervision More Than the Surveillance of Instruction? In J. Glanz & R. Neville (Eds.) *Educational Supervision: Perspectives, Issues and Controversies* (pp. 285-298). Norwood, MA: Christopher-Gordon.

Solomon, P. (1997). Educating African Americans. *Canadian Journal of Education*, 22 (1) 117-119.

Solomon, P. (2001). School Leaders and Anti-Racism: Overcoming Pedagogical and Political Obstacles. *Journal of School Leadership*, 12, 174-197.

Solomon, P. & Levine-Rasky, C. (1996). When Principle Meets Practice: Teachers' Contradictory Responses to Antiracist Education. *The Alberta Journal of Educational Research*, 42 (1) 19-33.

Sparks, D. (1994). A Paradigm Shift in Staff Development. *Journal of Staff Development*, 15 (4) 26-29.

Spring, J. (2001). *Globalization and Educational Rights: An Intercivilizational Analysis.* Mahwah, New Jersey: Lawrence Erlbaum.

Statistics Canada (1990). *Canada Year Book.* Ottawa: Ministry of Supply and Services.

Statistics Canada. (1993). *Ethnic Origin.* Ottawa: Ministry of Industry, Science and Technology.

Statistics Canada (2001). *Immigrant Population by Place of Birth, 1996 Census.* (http://www.statcan.ca/). Accessed 12/11/01.

Stevenson, H. & Lee, S. (1990). Contexts of Achievement: A Study of American, Chinese and Japanese Children. *Monographs of the Society for Research in Child Development.* Serial No. 221. Vol. 55 Nos. 1-2.

Taylor, C. (1991). *The malaise of modernity.* Concorde, ON: Anasi.

Taylor, E. (1998). Toward a Coherent Theory of Race in the Education of School Leaders: Fly Fishing Across the Racial Divide. *Race Ethnicity and Education* 1 (2), 225-239.

Tharp, R. (1989). Psychocultural Variables and Constants: Effects on Teaching and Learning in Schools. *American Psychologist*, 44 (2), 349-359.

Thomas, R., with Macanawai, S. & MacLaurin, C. (1997) Editorial. *Journal of Educational Administration* 35 (5), 385-396.

Thompson, A. (2002). Immigration Rule Changes Put on Hold: Public Outcry Sparks Six-Month Postponement. *Toronto Star.* February 26.

Tierney, W. (1993). *Building Communities of Difference: Higher Education in the Twenty-First Century.* Toronto: OISE Press.

Toronto Star. (2002). *GTA Population Jumps 9.8% Since '96.* March 12.

Trnavcevic, A. (2000). The Marketization Process in Slovenia: The Development of Public, Quasi Markets in Primary Schools. Ph.D. Thesis. University of Toronto.

Troyna, B. (1984). Multicultural Education: Emancipation or Containment? In L. Barton & S. Walker (Eds.). *Social Crisis and Educational Research* (pp. 75-92). Beckenham: Croom Helm.

Troyna, B. (1987). Beyond Multiculturalism: Towards the Enactment of Anti-Racist Education in Policy, Provision and Pedagogy. *Oxford Review of Education* 13 (3), 307-320.

Troyna, B. (1993). *Racism and Education.* Philadelphia: Open University Press.

Troyna, B. & Hatcher, R. (1992). *Racism in Children's Lives.* London: Routledge.

Trueba, H. (1988). Culturally Based Explanations of Minority Students' Academic Achievement. *Anthropology and Education Quarterly,* 19 (2), 270-287.

Tyler, J. & Holsinger, D. (1975). Locus of Control Differences Between Rural American Indian and White Children. *Journal of Social Psychology,* 95, 149-155.

United States Census Bureau. (1995). *Statistical Abstract of the United States:1995.* (115th ed) Washington, D.C.: US. Bureau of the Census.

United States Census Bureau. (2001). *Projections of the Resident Population by Age, Sex, Race and Hispanic Origin: 1999 to 2000.* (http://www.census.gov/). Accessed 12/11/01.

Valverde, L. (1988). Principals Creating Better Schools in Minority Communities. *Education and Urban Society* 20 (4) 319–326.

Vanderslice, V.J. (1988). Separating Leadership from Leaders: An Assessment of the Effect of Leader and Follower Roles. *Human Relations* 41 (9), 677-696.

Verma, G., et. al. (1994). *The Ethnic Crucible: Harmony and Hostility in Multi-Ethnic Schools.* London: Falmer.

Wagner, R. (1989). *Accountability in Education: A Philosophical Inquiry.* New York: Routledge.

Waite, D. (1995). *Rethinking Instructional Supervision: Notes on Language and Culture.* London: Falmer Press.

Waite, D. & Fernandes, M. R. (2000). Complicity in supervision: Another postmodern moment. In J. Glantz & L. Behar-Horenstein (Eds.) *Paradigm Debates in Curriculum and Supervision: Modern and Postmodern Perspectives.* (pp. 190-211). Wesport: Bergin & Garvey.

Wang, S. (1995). Chinese Parents' Views on Parent Choice and Parent Voice in an Ontario Community. Doctoral Thesis. University of Toronto.

Weber, M. (1947). *The Theory of Social and Economic Development.* New York: Oxford University Press.

West. C. (1994). *Race Matters.* New York: Vintage.

Whitty, G., Power, S. & Halpin, D. (1998). *Devolution and Choice in Education.* Buckingham: Open University Press.

Winfield, L., Johnson, R. & Manning, J. (1993). Managing Instructional Diversity. In P. Forsyth & M. Tallerico (Eds.) *City Schools: Leading the Way* (pp. 97-130). Newbury Park, CA: Corwin Press.

Wodak, R. (1996) Power, Discourse, and Styles of Female Leadership in School Committee Meetings. In Corson, D. (Ed.). *Discourse and Power in Educational Organizations* (pp. 31-54) Toronto: OISE Press.

Wolcott, H. (1973). *The Man in the Principal's Office: An Ethnography.* New York: Holt, Rinehart and Winston.

Young, A. (1989). Television Viewing. *Canadian Social Trends.* Autumn, 14-15.

Young, B., Stasenski, D., McIntyre & Joly, L. (1993). Care and Justice in Educational Leadership. *The Canadian Administrator* 33 (2), 1-8.

Young, M. & Laible, J. (2000). White Racism, Antiracism and School Leadership Preparation. *Journal of School Leadership* 10, 374-415.

Young, R. (1995). *Colonial Desire: Hybridity in Theory, Culture and Race.* New York: Routledge.

Yukl, G. (1994). *Leadership in Organizations.* Englewood Cliffs, New Jersey: Prentice Hall.

Zenter, H. (1971). The Impending Identity Crisis among Native People. In D. Davis & K. Herman (Eds.), *Social Space: Canadian Perspectives.* Toronto: New Press.

INDEX

STUDIES IN EDUCATIONAL LEADERSHIP

1. P.T. Begley and O. Johansson (eds.): *The Ethical Dimensions of School Leadership.*
    2003   ISBN Hb 1-4020-1159-8; Pb 1-4020-1160-1
2. J. Ryan: *Leading Diverse Schools.* 2003
                                          ISBN Hb 1-4020-1243-8; Pb 1-4020-1253-5

KLUWER ACADEMIC PUBLISHERS – DORDRECHT / BOSTON / LONDON